A THEOLOGY OF ENGAGEMENT

Challenges in Contemporary Theology

Series Editors: Gareth Jones and Lewis Ayres
Canterbury Christ Church University College, UK and Emory University, US

Challenges in Contemporary Theology is a series aimed at producing clear orientations in, and research on, areas of "challenge" in contemporary theology. These carefully coordinated books engage traditional theological concerns with mainstreams in modern thought and culture that challenge those concerns. The "challenges" implied are to be understood in two senses: those presented by society to contemporary theology, and those posed by theology to society.

Published

These Three are One
David S. Cunningham

After Writing
Catherine Pickstock

Mystical Theology
Mark A. McIntosh

Engaging Scripture
Stephen E. Fowl

Torture and Eucharist
William T. Cavanaugh

Sexuality and the Christian Body
Eugene F. Rogers, Jr

On Christian Theology
Rowan Williams

The Promised End
Paul S. Fiddes

Powers and Submissions: Spirituality, Philosophy, and Gender
Sarah Coakley

A Theology of Engagement
Ian S. Markham

Forthcoming

Alien Sex: The Body and Desire in Cinema and Theology
Gerard Loughlin

A THEOLOGY OF ENGAGEMENT

Ian S. Markham

350 Main Street, Malden, MA 02148-5020, USA
108 Cowley Road, Oxford OX4 1JF, UK
550 Swanston Street, Carlton, Victoria 3053, Australia

First published 2003 by Blackwell Publishing Ltd

Library of Congress Cataloging-in-Publication Data

Markham, Ian S.
  A theology of engagement / by Ian S. Markham.
      p.   cm. – (Challenges in contemporary theology)
Includes bibliographical references and index.
  ISBN 0-631-23601-5 (hardcover : alk. paper) – ISBN 0-631-23602-3
(pbk. : alk. paper)
  1. Christianity and other religions.   2. Religious pluralism – Christianity.   I. Title.
II. Series.

BR127.M29   2003
261.2 – dc21   2002155055

A catalogue record for this title is available from the British Library.

Set in 10.5 on 12.5pt Bembo
by SNP Best-set Typesetter Ltd., Hong Kong
Printed and bound in the United Kingdom
by MPG Books Ltd, Bodmin, Cornwall

For further information on
Blackwell Publishing, visit our website:
http://www.blackwellpublishing.com

I dedicate this book to my three sisters:
Rosemary Sowden
Jacqueline Draycott
Debbie Markham

CONTENTS

ACKNOWLEDGMENTS

This book has had a long gestation period. Various important communities have shaped it. My academic home, Hartford Seminary in Connecticut, has provided a setting with rich conversation partners. For the energetic exchanges and willingness to read parts of the manuscript, I am extremely grateful. In particular my thanks go the President, Heidi Hadsell, for providing a generous atmosphere in which to work, and Ibrahim Abu-Rabi', and Kelton Cobb, who both read parts of the manuscript. Different parts of the book were written at different times in different places. Chapters 1 and 2 were written while I was a Claggett Fellow attached to the Washington National Cathedral. For the marvelous time of friendship and stimulation, I thank Dean Baxter, Fred Schmidt, Larry Keller, Mark Bean, and Meinrado F. Samala. The chapters on the concept of toleration and secularism in India were written originally as Teape Seminars at the University of Cambridge. For the kindness of Julius Lipner, Brian Hebblethwaite, and Douglas Headley, I am grateful. The chapter on Nursi and Globalization was delivered at the Nursi Conference in Istanbul, Turkey. I am grateful for the kindness of my hosts. Parts of the book were written while I was Dean and Professor of Theology and Public Life at Liverpool Hope University College. As I reflect on my five years at Hope, I do so with considerable pleasure. I learnt much from Professor Lee (the Rector and Chief Executive); I appreciated the many conversations with Professor Newport, Dr. John Elford, Dr. Tinu Ruparell, and Dr. J'annine Jobling. Dr. Jobling proved invaluable in providing completely candid advice about the quality of the chapter on feminist theology and helping me to improve it. It is so precious having friends who are good at being ruthless.

Earlier versions of two chapters appear in two journals. Chapter 12 took an earlier form as an Inaugural Lecture at Liverpool Hope University College entitled "Shades of Grey: The Pope, Christian Ethics, and the Ambiguity of Human Situations" and appeared in *Briefing* vol. 27, issue 7, July 1997 and a version of the Teape Seminars appeared in *Humanitas*, The Journal of the George Bell Institute, vol. 2, no. 2, April 2001. I am grateful for permission to reproduce aspects of these articles in this book. In addition I acknowledge with gratitude "SHADES OF GRAY" Words and Music by Cynthia Weil and Barry Mann [c] 1967, Screen Gems-EMI Music Inc, USA. Reproduced by permission of Screen Gems-EMI Music Ltd, London WC2H 0EA.

An engaged theology ends up engaging with many minds. I am especially grateful to the following: Robin Gill, Shaun Coates, Giles Legood, Melanie Phillips, William Markham, Elaine Croft, Karen Rollins, Nick Rengger, Meg Wichser Krajcik, Marilyn Garcia, George Newlands, Nicola Sowden, Oliver Markham, Bill Eakins, Keith Ward, and Gavin D'Costa. Martyn Percy served as an adjunct Professor at Hartford Seminary as I was finishing the book: my debt to his willingness to discuss the issues and help me clarify the argument is considerable. The manuscript was much improved by Shannon Ledbetter's willingness to read, discuss, and challenge me on the ideas and arguments. Amy Gullickson persuaded me of the legitimacy of the personal story, which proved important for aspects of this book. And for Leslie Houlden's insights and wisdom, I continue to remain deeply grateful. Daily I am thankful for the order that Yvonne Bowen-Mack brings to my life; she is an excellent Executive Assistant.

I owe a particular debt to the publisher. The series editors are both outstanding scholars and marvelous friends. Gareth Jones and Lewis Ayres understand the importance of the theological task and in their separate ways have given me so much. Rebecca Harkin was the commissioning editor. For her engagement and commitment to the issues explored in this book, I am extremely grateful. The team at Blackwell Publishing, especially Laura Barry, has, as ever, been outstanding.

I am now at the end of my first year at Hartford Seminary. My wife Lesley has been kind and fun as she adapted to her US lifestyle; and my six-year-old son Luke has made me smile a thousand times. May I retain the capacity to enjoy the moment as much as he does.

Brothers and sisters are one of the great delights in life. No one can completely understand the extraordinary set of factors that shape one's character save for those who have lived many of them with you. In this book I would like to honor my sisters. They have provided the candid advice (often unasked for), the support in the difficult moments, and many a smile and a laugh thanks to shared recollections. It is to my three sisters that I dedicate this book.

Ian Markham, Hartford Seminary

INTRODUCTION

It must not be forgotten that reason too needs to be sustained in all its searching by trusting dialogue and sincere friendship. A climate of suspicion and distrust, which can beset speculative research ignores the teaching of the ancient philosophers who proposed friendship as one of the most appropriate contexts for sound philosophical inquiry.[1]

Faith needs reason and reason needs friendship explains Pope John Paul II in *Fides et Ratio*. Theology needs both faith and reason because it is in the truth business. Our task as theologians is to build on the experience of God's people and arrive at better understandings of God and God's relations with the world. And this needs the friendship of our fellow truth seekers. Given our subject matter (and God is about as big as you can get), it is madness to believe that we can "go it alone." And the best theologians in the Christian tradition have recognized this. Their theology was an engaged theology. It was a theology ready and willing to learn from non-Christian sources.

This seems so obvious yet it is today so contentious. For some, the problems are philosophical: different traditions, explain Milbank, have incommensurable rationalities that make engagement very difficult.[2] For others, it is a matter of fidelity to the tradition: Karl Barth talks of secular philosophy as the "classical point for the invasion of alien powers."[3] This book does not simply want to oppose these positions, it wants to claim that these positions are a betrayal of the tradition we have inherited and then demonstrate the alternative through a set of case studies that sees how engagement can shape positively our understanding of God and God's relations with the world.

We start our work in the opening chapter where engagement is defined and its implications explored. It will show that a theology of engagement is an encounter that subsequently shapes the theology itself. It distinguishes itself from the approach of Stanley Hauerwas, where engagement is simply "location." In the second chapter, the claim that this approach to theology is an act of fidelity to the dominant theological method of the tradition is defended through an examination of St. Augustine's approach. Augustine has been an important battleground for theological method in recent years: and in this chapter, an attempt is made to demonstrate that he can be read as sympathetic to an "open" and "engaging" mode of theology. In so doing, those Christians who want to identify with such a disposition should not feel uncomfortable or awkward in so doing. In the third chapter, three ways of engaging are identified. These are "assimilation," "resistance" and "overhearing." Sometimes engagement requires the assimilation of an insight from a non-Christian source; at other times we must resist an idea; and sometimes we find our theology being shaped as a result of "overhearing" the argument between two or more non-Christian traditions.

In chapters 4 to 10, we have six case studies, each illustrating a different internal dynamic of engagement. We start with the ostensibly secular discourse of human rights; this is a language that we should not simply assimilate, but the case can be made that human rights language needs a theistic underpinning. In short it needs religion. We look at the different ways in which different branches of the Christian family have assimilated this discourse, from the Roman Catholic to the Orthodox. However, this exercise in assimilation generates an engagement dynamic of its own: it forces us to resist the equally modern discourse of "state sovereignty." From Kosovo to Pinochet, human rights language undermines talk of state sovereignty, which is too easily a vehicle for oppression, and this the church should welcome.

In chapter 6, assimilation this time requires repentance and modification. We start a conversation with Feminist and Black theology. It is vitally important that Christian theology engages with the fact that for many it is an oppressive discourse. For feminists, it provided a justification for patriarchy; for African-Americans, it underpinned racism. If one is going to claim to be a methodological heir to Augustine, then the dark side of his theology needs to be confronted. The task, I argue, in this chapter involves repentance and modification.

In chapters 7 and 8, we embark on two exercises of "overhearing." The first is the clash between conservative Hindus and the secular Indian state. The clash between a religious worldview and a secular state has been felt in many parts of the world. The second is the Hinduism of the Bharatiya

Janata Party (BJP) and its arguments for toleration that take a form of strong inclusivism. I suggest as we embark on this task of overhearing, Christians might want to modify their enthusiasm for an inclusivist attitude to other religions.

In chapters 9 and 10, we mix modes. The focus is the twin issues of economics and globalization. On the former, I argue that the Christian tradition needs to "assimilate" the discovery of the 1989 Eastern European revolution that some form of "market economy" is an important part of any effective economic life. On the latter, we both assimilate and overhear (overhear the Marxists and the Muslims) on globalization and argue that the church must work to make globalization work for the poor in the world.

At the end of these case studies, we have a sense of the dynamic of engagement. We then have three concluding chapters that link this project with the projects of fellow travelers. In chapter 11, we look at the theological methodology of Keith Ward. This chapter is making clear that much of the methodology underpinning this book is learnt from his remarkable comparative theology. In chapter 12, we engage with Pope John Paul II. There are two reasons why he needs engagement: first, he is the single most influential religious leader in the world; and second, while he is in some respect an engaged theologian, his method does not acknowledge sufficiently the complexity and ambiguity of the world. In short, his theology is too rigid: it does not celebrate the grace that can be granted through the paradoxes of human life. An engaged theology must handle these complexities, which will inevitably arise.

This leads to the last substantial chapter: it makes explicit the theological assumptions underpinning the project. A theology of engagement is a perpetually relocating theology. We are not allowed to stand still or imagine that we have arrived. As we work within this framework, we need to see ourselves differently. This book is commending a theology of generosity;[4] it is celebrating the value of friendship and dialogue with those friends. We need to learn of God and we need to do so through engagement with each other.

All in all, this book is commending a certain vision of church. For many theologians today, the church is a self-referring, self-contained agent of God hope in a hostile world. I want to commend an alternative vision: the church should see God's hope everywhere; we need to be connected and engaged with God's grace wherever it is found. And perhaps it may help the reader to have a sense of my personal story underpinning my own commitment to this alternative vision of church. It was Graham

Greene who reportedly said "Childhood is the bank balance of the writer."
And my childhood is distinctive.

I was born into, what others call, "The Exclusive Brethren." This movement has its roots in the nineteenth-century sect known as the Plymouth
Brethren who in the 1840s had a schism over the issue of the autonomy
of the local assembly. Two different groups were formed. The "Open
Brethren" wanted each assembly to have its own jurisdiction over local
membership. While J.N. Darby (1800–82 – best known for his views on
dispensationalism) insisted that the all assemblies should "be of one heart,
one mind, and one spirit." And therefore the so-called "Darbyites" insisted
all assemblies should recognize a national "leadership" (i.e., J.N. Darby),
which became the seeds of the Exclusive Brethren.

By 1962, when I was born, the Exclusives were a small fundamentalist
group, committed to separation from the world, and expecting its immi-
nent demise. And over time the restrictions had gradually increased. They
attempted to keep contact with the world to a complete minimum: so
naturally television, and radio were all forbidden. No one outside the
assembly was permitted to enter the home nor could we go to their houses
(2 John 10). Therefore I never attended a birthday party of a school friend;
we did not observe Christmas (it was an inherited pagan festival); and I
had to eat apart from the rest of the children at school. Education was
limited simply to that required by the law of the land: so it stopped with
compulsory schooling. Therefore higher education was forbidden. As a
result women married young, for example, my sister married at 17. And
the men tended to work for other people in the assembly in small self-
employed businesses.

The religious duties were intense. We would go to worship at 6am on
Sunday morning (after all Mary was "up early" to seek her resurrected
Lord). And then would be followed by a further four meetings on Sunday
(9am, 12 noon, 3pm, and 5pm).

The assembly took the view that one could not belong to anything
other than the "body of Christ." Therefore all forms of association or
organization were forbidden from Boy Scouts to trade unions. In the case
of my father, legislation was introduced in the UK that meant that his
profession as a pharmacist now required membership of the Pharmaceu-
tical Society. (My father was trained prior to the restrictions on graduate
education.) He stopped practicing as a pharmacist and attempted to
become a supplier of chemist sundries to pharmacy shops. With a family
that was growing (I was one of six children), he realized that he was not
earning enough to support his family. After much agonizing with my

mother, he decided to leave the Exclusive Brethren in order to return to his profession and earn a proper living. I was eight when he made that decision. As a family, it meant that everyone we knew in our universe would never speak to us again. We all knew, that for the Exclusive Brethren, because we had "seen the light and then rejected it," we became the most wicked of people and no one would have any contact with us. My father knew he would never see his father or siblings again; my mother made a comparable decision. So all the friends and relatives within the Brethren, I have not seen since.

Naturally one doesn't leave the Exclusive Brethren and simply move to a regular denomination. For my father, after 40 years in the Exclusives, he was still persuaded of the dangers of the world, the apostasy of the main-line churches, and of the fact that we living in the last days. So we entered a twilight world of ex-members of the Exclusives with whom we would meet in a brother's home for the breaking of the bread on a Sunday morning. We lived in that world for several years, before joining a small assembly, that was technically "Open Brethren," in Bodmin, Cornwall (the southwest tip of England). Even amongst "Open Brethren" Assemblies this was a conservative group. They viewed with suspicion those Assemblies that were sympathetic to ecumenical evangelical crusades and the like. In many respects, they were similar to the Exclusives, save for the fact that my Father could work as pharmacist and we celebrated Christmas. In other words, they shared much of the theology, albeit not taking to such an extreme the injunction to be separate from the world. In this setting I became a boy preacher (it started when I was 12). My parents were wise enough to see the similarities with the damaging aspects of the Exclusive Brethren and moved to a Baptist Church, where evangelical religion coalesced in a healthy way with an affirmation of life. However, sadly, I was too involved with the Assembly in Bodmin and spent many of my teenage years at the heart of a deeply intolerant community. It took a sensitive Religious Education teacher – John Keast – and the superb faculty in Theology at King's College, London to show me how it is possibly to see the Gospel as a life-enhancing message.

The Exclusive Brethren accepted that there are different ways of reasoning and thinking and that the Scriptural mode of rationality is at odds with secular or worldly reasoning; they accepted that they must simply be church and provide a pacifist witness. They were completely persuaded of the cultural war: we are living in times comparable with those before Noah; there was no grace in the world or in modernity. Now it would be completely wrong to imply that the vision of church

advocated by contemporary postliberal, radical orthodox theologians corresponds to the Exclusive Brethren. However, I do invoke my story as a
warning. I have lived with a vision of church that is strongly "against
culture," and sees engagement as betrayal of the gospel. It is both ugly and
deeply destructive. For me, one aspect of the theological task is to make
it methodologically impossible for our celebration of the Gospel to lead
to such a damaging vision of church. The safeguard against an Exclusive
Brethren tendency needs to be theological: a pragmatic sociologically
dynamic is insufficient. The fact that, sociologically, many Christian
denominations are much larger than the Exclusive Brethren and therefore
are less likely to be so effective in seeking to be separate from the world
just means that the damage will be reduced. It takes a theological shift to
remove the damaging potential and ensure that our theology serves the
goal of enabling human life to be lived in all fullness.

    We need to have more confidence in the God we worship. The grace
of God is at work everywhere. We need to live in a community of church
that is connected, ready and willing to learn from those who disagree,
deeply committed to pluralism, and persuaded that our capacity to do this
is a vitally important witness to the gospel values of constructive peace
making.

1

ENGAGEMENT: WHAT IT IS AND WHY IT MATTERS

Most of the world is not Christian. Despite two centuries of intensive evangelization, backed with all the resources that the first world has to offer, we find that the percentage of Christians is stubbornly fixed at 33 percent.[1] And, of course, this percentage includes plenty of Christians that other Christians would not recognize as such. Some conservative evangelicals, for example, are deeply suspicious of Roman Catholics and suspect that they will not be keeping their company at the eschaton. So for many Christians this percentage is smaller. Beyond the Christian "family," we find other forms of organized religious affiliation. We still have significant numbers of Hindus, Buddhists, Muslims, and Jews, as well as a robust proliferation of new religious movements. Other more secular ideologies some with a "spiritual" dimension, others wanting to challenge the power of religion, such as certain versions of feminism and the lingering effects of Marxism in some nationalist movements, have arisen. And there are localized "primitive" religions of numerous kinds. It is an obvious key theological question how Christians relate themselves to such diversity.

One misguided answer that continues to dominate much theological analysis insists that such diversity of perspectives should have no impact on Christianity, save perhaps to stress the imperative of even greater evangelization. Christianity is committed to the revelation of God in Christ documented in the Bible and shaped by the tradition of the church. The task of theology is to explicate the truth within the tradition, live out that truth within the church, and preach it to the world. Karl Barth, perhaps unfairly,[2] gets much of the credit for this understanding of the theological task. So Karl Barth explains that the position of theology thus:

> Behind it, theology has Holy Scripture as witness to revelation, and its attestation in the earlier confessions and knowledge of the church. Before it, it

has the church and the activity of proclamation. Thus placed, theology can reveal, unfold and shape itself in dogmatics as a characteristic branch of knowledge.[3]

For Barth, knowledge is possible in theology by focusing the task of theology on the Bible within the church. He resolutely sets himself against any engagement with "secular" philosophy (and for secular philosophy also read any non-Christian religions) by explaining that "this is the classical point for the invasion of alien powers, the injection of metaphysical systems which are secretly in conflict with the Bible and the church."[4]

This position is misguided (especially when grounded in a possible misunderstanding of Barth) for several reasons. First, it seems fairly clear that the cultural diversity of the creation is intended by God.[5] We believe in a God who is responsible for the vastness of space. A God who approximately 15 billion years ago, opted to created many potentially habitable planets, and allowed the diversity of life forms to emerge on earth. And as humanity emerged, a God who waited many thousands of years before revealing the truth of monotheism to Abraham. It seems an extraordinarily attenuated view of the cosmic God to insist that God's activity is simply confined to the faith that emerged amongst the Hebrews some four thousand years ago and the life and ministry of Jesus of Nazareth and the development of the church in Europe. The God who cares for every sparrow that falls to the ground certainly cares for the lives of people in India, Africa, and Latin America. God was, presumably, at work in the lives of those who wrote the Upanishads or in the developing Native American rituals. To think otherwise is a fundamental denial of the God we worship as, in the state of modern knowledge, we must see God. It is not surprising that some "solve" the problem by refusing to accept modern cosmology and the like, on biblical grounds.

This position is also misguided for a second reason. The Christian Scriptures and tradition are clearly shaped by numerous non-Christian sources. The Bible was not written in a vacuum. It clearly spoke to the people living at the time: and it was clearly shaped by the narratives and traditions of the cultures from which the text emerged. The Christian tradition, inevitably, made rich use of non-Christian philosophy. As we shall see in chapter 2, Augustine of Hippo used Neoplatonism. In the thirteenth century Aquinas accessed the Islamic rediscovery of Aristotle and put it into imaginative conversation with the Platonism of the Augustinian tradition. And modern "critical" Christianity, harder to turn into a satisfactory synthesis, is a fruit of the Enlightenment. It is a distortion of the Christian

Scriptures and tradition to imagine that they come to us untouched by any other cultural influence or mode of thought. It is indefensible to insist that a tradition that has come to us shaped by non-Christian sources should now be fossilized. We are part of a living tradition: what Augustine of Hippo did in the past we need to do for the present. This theme will be developed at much greater length in chapter 2.

The third reason this position is bizarre is that its consequences are damaging. The world needs a positive relationship with diversity: in this sense Hans Küng is right when he states that there will be no peace among the nations without peace among religions.[6] To confine the engagement with other faith traditions to evangelization simply is not sufficient to bring about a stronger and more constructive set of relationships with other religions. However, this attitude to non-Christian sources (i.e., religious and secular sources) has other problematic effects. John Macquarrie speaks accurately of the "fragmentation of modern culture." He writes:

> We often hear it said that ours is a split culture, and nobody claims that this is a healthy state of affairs. The split is very obvious when we consider theology in relation to other disciplines, for often it seems to have lost touch with secular studies altogether and to have become compartmentalized and esoteric. We have, so to speak, a Sunday mentality and an everyday mentality. We may succeed in keeping them apart and in this way we prevent latent conflicts between them from flaring up, and this is done at the expense of restricting religion to a special and somewhat rarefied sector of life. To explore the borders between theology and other disciplines with a view not only to removing conflicts but, more positively, in the hope of gaining reciprocal illumination, is a task that cannot be avoided if we are dissatisfied with the fragmentation of life and culture.[7]

Macquarrie's preoccupation, as was Barth's, is the relationship of theology and philosophy. In Macquarrie's case, it involved the attempt to restate the central themes of Christianity using the resources of existentialist philosophy. However, his point applies to the issue of cultural and religious diversity much more widely. The exploration of the borders between theology and other faiths also brings benefits: it removes conflicts; it might generate reciprocal illumination; and most important of all it helps us come to terms with the God-given diversity of creation, thereby healing that aspect of the fragmentation between our Sunday Christianity and our weekday awareness of enormous diversity.

This book is advocating an alternative vision of the theological enterprise. It is one that makes "engagement" the key term. Now at this point many suggest that this is a "liberal" alternative to the conservative vision of Karl Barth outlined above. But, as just hinted, it is wholly traditional for the Christian tradition constantly to seek to make itself intelligible by entering into dialogue with contemporary forms of thoughts. However, before developing this point further, it is necessary for me to clarify precisely what is meant here by the term engagement.

1   Engagement as a "Changing" Encounter

Post-Wittgenstein, we have an appropriate sense of the problems involved in offering definitions. The dynamic nature of language often means that usage provides a better guide to meaning than the dictionary's sometimes fossilized attempt to provide an all-embracing description applicable to every use of the word.[8] So, the word "engagement" is used in a variety of ways. Some we can exclude: the decision of a couple to get married, or an appointment, for example of a professional person with a client, are both irrelevant for our purposes. However, "an engagement in war" or a statement like "the children were engaged by the film" carries connotations that I am interested in developing.

"Engagement" has affinities with "involvement," "participation," "being engrossed," and "being committed." It may carry a sense of "opposition" (e.g., an engagement in war is hardly friendly) or "constructive change" (e.g., the children watching the film). So the attachments may carry a wide range of attitudes. It involves both positive participation and at the same time observation. A theology of engagement involves the following: **it is an encounter that subsequently shapes the theology itself**.

The word "shapes" is deliberately vague. The crucial point is that, as against Karl Barth, theology is not determined primarily and exclusively by the church and Bible. A "theology of engagement" sees theology as shaped, consciously and appropriately, perhaps inevitably, by non-Christian sources. However, the encounter may or may not be a positive one. A positive encounter, where Christian theology can appropriate an insight from another tradition, is good. But sometimes this will not be the case. In much the same way as a country engaged in war is shaped by the encounter, so theology might find itself shaped by the encounter with certain trends that are very antagonistic to theology and be modified by a kind of recoil, a negative reaction. The shape of such a theology might be in opposition to the previous trend. The encounter could also be "observational': the wary observation of a disagreement between two traditions might well shape subsequent Christian theology. So, for example, if certain forms of Islam were to engage with modern secular feminism, then the result might well provide illumination for the comparable engagement between conservative forms of Christianity and feminism.

Used in these senses, the term "engagement" overlaps with other terms such as "dialogue" or "conversation." David Tracy, primarily in the context of the interpretation of texts, describes "conversation" thus:

> It is a game where we learn to give in to the movement required by questions worth exploring. The movement in conversation is questioning itself. . . . A conversation is a rare phenomenon, even for Socrates. It is not a confrontation. It is not a debate. It is not an exam. It is questioning itself. It is a willingness to follow the question wherever it may go. It is dia-logue.[9]

For Tracy, conversation, which is understood as involving questioning, is supplemented by "argument." So Tracy explains:

> As any of us become more conscious of other interpretations, we become more aware of the occasional need to interrupt the conversation. Argument may be necessary. Argument is not synonymous with conversation. . . . Rather, argument is a vital moment within conversation that occasionally is needed if the conversation itself is to move forward.[10]

The advantage of the term "engagement" is that it embraces both these elements, conversation and argument. The term does not commit us in advance to the precise form of engagement involved, but leaves it to develop as appropriate.

The related term "dialogue" itself has a variety of meanings. For David Lochhead, it simply describes, in this context, one form of approach to religious diversity, while for Leonard Swidler it is more positive and includes an expectation that it will bring about changes in the participants. In Lochhead's thoughtful and engaging book, *The Dialogical Imperative*, he writes that "the concept of dialogue . . . is rich enough not only to support a theology of interfaith relations, but to support a theology of mission as well. The word 'dialogue' names the fundamental attitude with which the church is called to encounter the world. It follows that there is no need to move "beyond dialogue". In this sense, dialogue is an end in itself."[11] The focus for Lochhead is on the attitude prior to the dialogue itself, while for Swidler the dialogue has a potential to bring about change. Swidler makes the point thus:

> Dialogue is conversation between two or more persons with differing views, the primary purpose of which is for each participant to learn from the other so that he or she can change and grow – of course, both partners will also want to share their understanding with their partner. Minimally, the very fact that I learn that my dialogue partner believes "this" rather than "that" changes my attitude towards her; and a change in my attitude is a significant change, and growth, in me. We enter into dialogue, therefore, primarily so that we can learn, change and grow, not so that we can force change on the other.[12]

Although Swidler is primarily preoccupied with individual Christians encountering individual adherents of other faith traditions, the sense that dialogue brings about change is helpful in wider contexts. The concept of "engagement" operating in this book, then, is closer to Swidler than to Lochhead. It is transformative of the current theological understanding.

Having outlined the meaning of "engagement," it is now necessary to firmly distance this account from a usage found in the work of those sympathetic to a version of "postliberal" Christian Ethics. There are many possible examples, of whom I select two, Stanley Hauerwas and Michael Banner. Despite their having a theology that is manifestly preoccupied with the story of the church and largely confined to explicating its witness, they both resent the charge that they are not interested in "engagement." However, I suspect they would both be happy to acknowledge that they are not interested in "engagement" as defined in this chapter. And the difference between us is illuminating.

Hauerwas has an extended discussion of this question at the start of *Christian Existence Today*.[13] Gustafson had accused Hauerwas of "sectarianism," suggesting the following explanation for the latter's theology: in an increasingly secular and pluralist age, the temptation for the church is to resort to some form of sectarianism. In its quest for a clear identity and distinctive beliefs, this sectarianism protects the church from the secular attack. For Gustafson, the steps in Hauerwas's position are as follows: there is a move from philosophical fideism (Wittgenstein's influence on Lindbeck is given the blame here), to theological fideism (the corollary of such a philosophy that stresses the distinctiveness of theology apart from all other subjects), then to a sociological tribalism (the distinctive narrative of the church needs to be articulated), which culminates in an impoverished and narrowly focused ethic.

To the charge of philosophical fideism, Hauerwas responds by insisting that he holds that "Christian theology has a stake in a qualified epistemological realism,"[14] and that the church's "worship of God requires it to be open to continual 'reality checks'."[15] So Hauerwas is conceding that he is critical of "foundationalism'; however, he wants to insist that a form of realism survives and that it is self-critical. Later in Hauerwas's work, his philosophical framework is clarified. His enthusiasm for Radical Orthodoxy and the theological realism of John Milbank enables him to insist that the Christian tradition is both a metanarrative which is true although it is not to be evaluated by the rationality of liberal modernity.[16] (Just in passing, it is important to clarify the epistemological assumptions that makes engagement possible. This I will do later in this chapter. Suffice to note at this point the "engagement" advocated in this book depends upon a version of critical realism.)

Concentrating for now on Hauerwas, to the cluster of criticisms in relation to "tribalism" and the "lack of engagement': he insists that he is committed to "engaging critically other perspectives as well as remaining open to the challenge of other perspectives."[17] Hauerwas defines the core issue in the following way:

> The core issue is how the church can provide the interpretative categories to help Christians better understand the positive and negative aspects of their societies and guide their subsequent selective participation.[18]

For Hauerwas, this means that the "engagement" process starts with the church being clear about its interpretative categories for understanding society. This includes understanding the church as an alternative political community and recovering the sense of the integrity of the church. Thus equipped, the church can embark on engagement. From this perspective, Hauerwas believes he is very committed to engagement. He wonders how the term "sectarian" can be applied to him, when the following is taken seriously:

> [T]he fact that I have written about why and how Christians should support as well as serve the medical and legal professions, Christian relations with Judaism, how we might think about justice, as well as an analysis of the moral debate concerning nuclear war seems to have no effect on those who are convinced I am a "withdrawn" sectarian.[19]

The difference with the account of "engagement" being commended in this book and Hauerwas's account is that my model insists that engagement with non-Christian sources can and should actually shape the church's interpretative categories for understanding itself. It is not that our theology is determined and then we are in a position to engage, but that our understanding of God and God's relations with the world can itself be shaped by the engagement with non-Christian sources. For Hauerwas, the engagement is a form of "location." The church, having arrived at a clear self-understanding, is in a position to participate selectively: in other words, the church, secure in its own position, is able to affirm certain aspects of modern society and challenge others. It has the task of clarifying the appropriate relations with other movements within modernity. In other words it is an engagement that amounts to judgment. This I suggest is closer to "locating" rather than "engaging'.

This interpretation of Hauerwas is confirmed when we turn to the work of one of his disciples in the United Kingdom, Michael Banner. Banner in his book, *Christian Ethics and Contemporary Moral Problems*, uses an overtly Barthian framework to shape his theology. He complains, in response to reviewers who thought otherwise, that his theology is deeply interested in building connections with non-Christian sources. So he claims that his critics (in this case Bishop Richard Harries of Oxford and Dr. Alan Suggate) are wrong when they suppose that it is not:

> Contra the Bishop I do engage in dialogue with non-Christian traditions (and specifically enjoin it) and contra Dr. Suggate, nothing I say forbids the practice. In the book of essays to which they refer there are countless places where I acknowledge debts to thinkers of all sorts, some of whom consciously reject the Christian tradition, perhaps chief amongst them Marx, Nietzsche, and Freud. Indeed far from avoiding such dialogue I would contend that those amongst my colleagues (O'Donovan and Hauerwas) whose work I most admire as most thoroughly and consistently and properly theological, make a point, as I do, of dealing with a range of thinkers far more diverse and weighty than those who appear in the work of writers belonging to what Dr. Suggate stipulates to be "the mainstream Anglican tradition."[20]

What Banner actually offers in his book, however, is an "engagement" that really means location. Nietzsche is cited as a witness to a form of "Christianity which speaks from its unfounded giveness and not from supposed point of contact'[21]; and Marx and Engels provide an intellectual strand of thought partly responsible for "the transformation of children into 'simple articles of commerce' and a further step in the dissolution of the family.'[22] His theology is not changed or shaped by this encounter. Instead one takes a position and to advance that position one then searches for similarities with and argument strategies from non-Christian traditions. So to take his own illustration of the type of engagement that he commends he offers the following: "A theologian who is concerned to maintain the tradition of Christian teaching in relation to abortion may profitably compare the work of philosophers in addressing questions associated on the one hand with the beginning of human life, and on the other hand with the environment."[23] The result, explains Banner, is that we arrive "at an apologetic strategy to maintain traditional teaching on the subject of abortion in the face of contemporary dissent . . ."[24]

As with Hauerwas, the meaning of "engagement" operating here is, in practice, simply "location," as his work shows. The theology is not shaped by the encounter with secular thought: instead, Banner simply defines his version of the Christian tradition by locating himself in relation to these thinkers. The task of location, although a worthy and necessary enterprise, should not be referred to as engagement. Engagement entails a theology open to being shaped and changed by the encounter.

2 Assumptions of Engagement

Having explained what "engagement" is, it is now necessary to identify some of the assumptions that are underpinning this account. The first assumption is that "engagement" across traditions is possible and that this depends on a version of "critical realism." The second assumption, which is linked to the first, is that the category "theism" is a useful tool to facilitate engagement between religious traditions. The third is that engagement both with the past and across religious traditions can build usefully on certain discoveries of modernity, such as a critical study of Scripture. I shall now expound and, briefly, defend these three assumptions underpinning this account of engagement.

The first assumption is that engagement across traditions is possible. John Milbank, for example, thinks that engagement is very difficult. Different traditions have different ways of thinking; and it is the illusion of the modern liberal project to imagine that we can compare and decide between traditions. For Milbank, arguments that appeal across traditions are impossible. He explains that part of his project is:

> the detachment of virtue from dialectics. There is for me no method, no mode of argument that charts as smoothly past the Scylla of foundationalism and the Charybdis of difference. Nor do I find it possible to defend the notion of "traditioned reason" in general, outside my attachment to a

tradition which grounds this idea in the belief in the historical guidance of the Holy Spirit.[25]

Milbank insists that the only option is a reason grounded in a tradition, which for Christianity entails a commitment to the providential action of God's Holy Spirit in the church.

One of Milbank's targets in this section of his *Theology and Social Theory* is Alasdair MacIntyre. Contra Milbank, my view is that MacIntyre's proposal does succeed in holding together, on the one hand hand, a recognition that we are all grounded in traditions and, on the other, the possibility of engaging with contrasting traditions. And it is worth summarizing MacIntyre's argument for these two propositions.

In MacIntyre's *Whose Justice? Which Rationality?*, he suggests that one explanation for the emergence of traditions is the task of "making sense of the world." Within the histories of the pre-Enlightenment traditions, MacIntyre believes the principles of tradition-constituted inquiry are expressed. For example, Aquinas did not have a belief in neutral vantage points transcending the various conflicting traditions surrounding us, but he still managed to make certain "rational" judgments. In Aquinas, as we shall see in chapter 3, there are two conflicting traditions that are engaged in debate and ultimately synthesized. Aquinas harmonizes an Aristotelian structure with an Augustinian psychology. Using this as one example, MacIntyre's entire book is a study of the principles of engagement between traditions within a historical and cultural framework. The question is: how is this possible?

Initially, argues MacIntyre, traditions are founded within a community. A tradition can be said to begin when particular beliefs, institutions, and practices are articulated by certain people and/or in certain texts. In such a community authority will be conferred on these texts and voices. In discussing these texts, procedures for inquiry will be established. A rationality will develop. Problems for the community arise for any of the following reasons: one, when there are different and incompatible interpretations; two, when incoherences and inadequacies are identified; and three, when there is a confrontation with different systems.[26] When these problems arise, the community faces "an epistemological crisis".[27] The term "epistemological crisis" describes a state where the traditional modes of inquiry are generating problems which the tradition lacks the resources to solve. Such a crisis itself generates the need for an imaginative conceptual innovation,[28] which gives rise to new beliefs that can be compared and contrasted with the older and less adequate beliefs. Such a comparison obviously requires a standard. Here MacIntyre outlines a variation on the correspondence theory of truth.[29] Ultimately, such traditions are trying to explain reality in as comprehensive a way as possible. Truth is ultimately achieved when the beliefs correspond with reality.

A tradition is successfully maintained if it can be shown that any proposed modification in belief and outlook can be demonstrated to stand in continuity with the rest of the tradition. It is possible that during an epistemological crisis, arising as a result of a conflict with another tradition, the adherents may decide that the new tradition is more appropriate than the earlier one. This is crucial. MacIntyre believes that it is possible for one tradition when engaging another, to find that the other has better conceptual tools to understand human life and activity. A tradition can founder. Although there is no neutral rationality to appeal to, the adherents of an existing tradition can come to find a different tradition's rationality more plausible. A judgment has been made between the two traditions. MacIntyre suggests that the developments leading to the science of Newton and Galileo might be of this type.[30]

So, for MacIntyre, engagement is possible by living in one tradition, entering into the life and narrative of another tradition. And then once one sees the world from the vantage point of both traditions, one can decide which tradition has the better resources to make sense of the complexity of the world. Granted this can be difficult (translation is imprecise and concepts in one culture are not necessarily found in another), it is, nevertheless, possible. The assumption of the "engagement" model in this book is that all traditions (all narratives, if you prefer) are in the business of making sense of the complexity of the world. The tools of coherence (the degree to which a narrative is internally consistent) and explanatory power (the degree to which a narrative explains various positive and negative features of the world) do provide means to determine which narratives are better than others. This is not to deny the complexity of traditions (all traditions divide into numerous other traditions) and often strands within one religion may have more in common with strands within another religion than they do with some of their own coreligionists. But despite these complexities, the critical realist instinct that "it is possible to describe the world in better and worse ways," is the necessary precondition for the model of engagement advocated in this book.

The second assumption is that the category of "theism" is helpful when comparing different religious traditions. Although this is moving beyond MacIntyre, it is compatible with the MacIntyrian mode of engagement outlined above. As a Trinitarian Christian living within the Christian narrative, I am persuaded that it is of importance to think of God as triune. However, when I enter into the narrative of say a Muslim, although the concept of the Trinity is not available in that tradition, the concept of God is. And it is possible for the Christian to recognize the following similarities. First, both Christians and Muslims believe that a secular naturalist is wrong to believe that the order of the universe is explicable in terms that deny the transcendent. And the God language is used in by both traditions as the mechanism of opposing secularism. Second, both Christians and Muslims affirm the reality of one God, which in both cases is forced upon us by our sense that worship of a plurality of ultimate beings is incoherent. And, of course, the church worked extremely hard to affirm the oneness of God, even though we believe in the Trinity. Third, both Christians and Muslims share a history that recognizes the central revelatory role of Judaism. In, at least, these three ways, the category of "theism" is a way in which Christians can engage with Islam as well as other religious traditions.

Furthermore it is the fact that Christians are both theists as well as Trinitarians that makes natural theology possible. The conviction that knowledge of God's existence is possible, by virtue of the idea that all people are created in the image of God, outside the community of church depends upon the intelligibility of the category of theism. It would seem then the idea that Christians can think of themselves as theists and that the doctrine of the Trinity is a development of our core belief in God should not be contentious and can be an important way to progress engagement with other religious traditions.

Yet it is contentious. Bruce Marshall, building on George Lindbeck's *The Nature of Doctrine*, wants to argue that "a genuinely theological account of truth and epistemic justification needs to be robustly Trinitarian. It ought to subject whatever ideas it may find useful to the formative discipline of the Christian community's convictions about the triune God."[31] Marshall goes on to argue that the ritual practice of the church is the key to understanding the core commitments of the Christian community and that this practice is firmly Trinitarian. Given this, all engagement, even the concept of "truth" that we assume in our discourse, should be shaped by the Trinity.

The key difficulty with this, which I will develop further in my concluding chapter, is how the Christian then tells the story of our past. Judaism does not describe itself as Trinitarian, even allowing for the enthusiasm in parts of the Hebrew Bible for such ideas as "wisdom." If the Trinity becomes the control on the grammar of our theological discourse, then it is difficult to see how the Hebrew Bible contributes to the Christian self-understanding, without overt anachronism. The problem with this stress on Christian distinctness will result in a distortion of our history and a potential distortion with our contemporary relations with other traditions.

This is not to say that the Trinity is not vitally important. In chapter 3, a Trinitarian structure to engagement will be suggested. I am a Trinitarian Christian who believes that the doctrine illuminates much that is true about God, it is just that I do not see the Trinitarian discourse as excluding the theistic one.

The final assumption that I want to identify at this stage in the book is the commitment to the achievements of modernity. I am assuming that the engagement with the Christian past is helped with some of the tools of modernity. Discrimination is, of course, essential. We should be discriminating about which aspects of the past we want to continue to affirm in the present; and we should be discriminating about which aspects of the present that we want to shape our interpretations of the past. For example, what this might mean in practice is that we have to admit that the relatively modern feminist discovery of the evil of patriarchy should make us affirm feminism and revisit our past searching for the strands that affirm feminism and criticizing those strands that do not. Feminism, as we shall see in chapter 6, is an insight of modernity that should be used to shape our reading of the past.

In addition, amongst the tools that are used to make sense of the past are our modern historical sensitivity and the critical tools for the study of Scripture.[32] The task of attempting to determine "precisely what happened" is both modern and simultaneously very difficult. Yet we should affirm the project and inevitably it will change our understanding of the past. Unlike say the book of Chronicles in the Hebrew Scriptures, where the story of the past is told for the purposes of illuminating the moral dilemmas of the present, the task of the modern historian is to attempt to understand the past on its own terms.

Along with this distinctive historical sensitivity, we have a set of critical tools for the study of Scripture. The Bible is a text that invites critical study. The synoptic problem is not an invention of the modern era. Any careful reader of the text finds the first three gospels have considerable material in common, which is then treated in significantly different ways. The Sermon on the Mount (Matthew 5–7) and the Sermon on the Plain (Luke 6) are both similar and yet different. Now this has, of course, always been recognized. However, the explanations and debates in modern

New Testament scholarship, which recognize different interests at work in the organization and use of the material, are persuasive. Any plausible account of inspiration of Scripture needs to accommodate the picture of the nature of the text emerging from New Testament scholarship. We should still recognize the inspired nature of the experience underpinning the text and its authority in respect to the story of Jesus, but we must also recognize the human interests at work in shaping the text.

It is beyond the scope of this book to defend these three assumptions in detail. I shall, however, return to the second assumption at the end of the book. At this stage, I simply state these assumptions so that the following defense of engagement and the case studies that follow are intelligible to the reader.

3   Why it matters

Having explained what "engagement" is and named the assumptions underpinning this account, it is now necessary to outline why it matters. The key to the argument that follows is that "engagement" matters because it opens up a necessary option for the churches, as well as one thoroughly customary in the Christian tradition. Instead of insisting that "liberal" openness is at odds with the Christian tradition that we have inherited, I shall maintain that is not the case. Once that is recognized, it will be clear that a theology of engagement, entailing openness, should characterize the thought and practice of the church today. In practice, it may turn out to be an important way of redefining the somewhat sterile battle between "liberals" and "conservatives."

The great fault line running down the mainline churches is this "conservative" and "liberal" divide. It splits allegiances and determines the "tribes" that grapple for control of the senior appointments and the policies of the churches. Increasingly, the actual arguments of theologians are not examined, simply the consequences or outcomes of the arguments. No one is interested in the coherence or merits of the position taken by a writer, but only whether or not, he or she is pro or anti, for example, the ordination of women? Or, to take an even more contemporary question, is the theologian pro or anti the ordination of practicing gays and lesbians?

The precise issues that determine which tribe one belongs to at any one time depend very much on the moment. Tony Higton in the United

Kingdom suggested three issues that divide liberals and conservatives: the attitude to homosexuality, the attitude to interfaith worship, and the attitude to the credal faith. For Higton, this was the line in the sand: the point at which Biblical Christians must take a stand. What is interesting about Higton's list is that it doesn't include the ordination of women, although plenty of conservative Anglo-Catholics and indeed Evangelicals like Higton himself would insist that it is a "first order" issue. For my purposes, I shall define a "conservative," more widely, as a person who insists on fidelity to the Scriptures and tradition, which in practice involves accepting the historic creeds and continuing to believe them today. A "liberal" by contrast insists on adapting the tradition in the light of new insights, some of them derived from non-Christian sources, which in the case of Western Christianity must involve learning from the broad achievement of European thought, namely the Enlightenment and its numerous more recent effects.

The argument of the rest of this chapter is that both "liberals" and "conservatives" are mistaken. They share a key assumption: both assume that there is a "changeless" tradition that we must either affirm or modify/reject. As suggested earlier, this key assumption is mistaken. If Christians really are committed to the "tradition" then that commitment will involve a recognition that it is a dynamic entity that learnt from non-Christian sources and contemporary culture to modify the Christian understanding of the truth of God's relations with the world. In other words, the paradox is that to be a traditional Christian, one has to be open and liberal!

To develop this argument we shall start with two examples (one liberal, one conservative) which, mistakenly, interpret the tradition as an entity that one must accept or reject. To demonstrate that this is a problem for the mainline churches, both examples are Anglicans. The first is the famous American Bishop, John Selby Spong; the second is the prolific English theologian, Dr. Alister McGrath.[33]

Generally seen as an extreme case, Spong is, in one sense, an easy target. So let me start by distancing myself from some of the polemic he has attracted. He may be thought admirable for the courage and energy with which he has spoken out for a liberal agenda. In addition, he has managed to connect with those, to use his phrase, "living in exile" − those who, while willing and well disposed, find belief difficult in a modern scientific culture. One might say that, in the current situation, if Spong did not exist, it would be necessary to invent him. The church should always be big enough to welcome the Spong perspective, and one has been glad to give him public support.[34] Yet, all the same, I find Spong's view of the tradition deeply problematic.

It is worth reminding my readers that Spong is clearly deeply committed to faith. He describes himself thus, "I am what I would call a God-intoxicated human being."[35] Yet the way in which Christian experience has been documented in the Apostles' Creed and the Nicene Creed, argues Spong, is no longer an option. He writes, "The words . . . were fashioned inside a worldview that no longer exists. Indeed, it is quite alien to the world in which I live."[36] And later "credal language came out of another time. It reflects assumptions that this generation can no longer make."[37] Scattered throughout his work, one finds three reasons for the impossibility of affirming credal language. The first is the displacement of a pre-modern cosmology by our modern scientific worldview. Much like Bultmann before him, he makes much of the breakdown in the three-tier universe and the sheer vastness of space. Second, he finds much of the tradition morally suspect. This is not simply in terms of the traditional prohibitions (e.g., on sexual questions), but also in doctrine, especially aspects of the traditional doctrine of God. In *Why Christianity must Change or Die*, he explains that he finds the language of "Father Almighty" deeply offensive.[38] Third, he believes that it is wrong to privilege the "expertise" of the church Fathers. The triumph of orthodoxy, insists Spong, is simply the triumph of power. So he writes, "To be called an orthodox Christian does not mean that one's point of view is right. It only means that this point of view won out in the ancient debate."[39]

Most of the time, Spong rejects the past. So to explain his use of the image of "exile," he explains that "I live in a state of exile from the presuppositions of my own religious past. I am exiled from the literal understandings that shaped the creed at its creation."[40] Sometimes, however, he uses a different image: he wants to rework the tradition. So he writes, "I believe that we Christians must inevitably revisit Chalcedon and once again do the hard work of rethinking and redefining the Christian experience for our time and in words and concepts appropriate to our world."[41] What he means by this is that there is a core "Jesus experience" that he wants to recapture in new and modern terminology:

I enter this process because I can neither dismiss this Christ nor live comfortably with the way he has been traditionally interpreted. I am not prepared to conclude that the traditional ways of interpreting Jesus have exhausted the possibilities. I can with no great difficulty set aside those interpretations, but I cannot set aside the Christ experience, which created the necessity for those theistic interpretations of yesterday. I still find the power of Christ compelling.[42]

So for Spong our past is a big problem. It was shaped in a premodern world, making assumptions that are often false and even offensive. Yet at the heart of it all is a "Jesus/Christ experience" that he wants to recover. To do this he needs to discard the Bible and the tradition apart from their bearing on this "Jesus experience" as he perceives it.

Now this is very unfair to the tradition, at times it creates needless difficulties for Spong. For example, on the idea of God, he first explains how a three-tier universe gave birth to the picture of God as the highly anthropomorphic parent who constantly interferes with his creation, and then writes:

> These ideas of God were firmly set and universally believed, and they formed the essence of the faith of Christians for the first sixteen hundred years or so of their history. The language of the Christian creeds took form in this period of time. But when the modern age began to dawn, a new understanding of the shape of the universe began to grow and God's place as the heavenly director of human affairs began to totter.[43]

This "theistic" God, Spong wants us to reject. So in his discussion of Michael Goulder (the New Testament scholar turned nonaggressive atheist), he asks what sort of God Goulder has rejected. "The answer seems overwhelmingly obvious. He has rejected the idea of God defined as a supernatural person who invades life periodically to accomplish the divine will. This deity is an intensely human figure who does grandiose and expanded, but nonetheless, human things. This is a God clearly defined in what we might call the language of theism."[44]

Anyone vaguely acquainted with the work of, say, St. Augustine of Hippo and St. Thomas Aquinas knows that this is false. To anticipate a more sustained discussion, which will occur in chapters 2 and 3, we find in Aquinas an understanding of God that describes God as a necessary being. Now the concept of a necessary being is extremely complex and a matter of considerable scholarly debate but at the very least it involves a type of existence utterly unrelated to mere "contingent" human existence: God is nondependent and exists in all possible worlds. In addition, for Aquinas this God is changeless (mainly because any change, he argued, would bring about either improvement — which is impossible because God is already perfect – or a deterioration – which is equally impossible because God would then cease to be perfect). Moreover, if God is changeless, then God must be timeless. Link this in with the doctrine of divine "simplicity," and you have a God completely unlike any human. There are real difficulties with this account of God, but Spong's anxiety about anthropomorphism is not one of them.

Indeed when Spong arrives at his definition of God, he admits there are affinities with Thomism. This surprising disclosure occurs when he suggests an image of God beyond theism and uses Paul Tillich to do so. He writes, "Paul Tillich . . . suggested that we must abandon the external height images in which the theistic God has historically been perceived and replace them with internal depth images of a deity who is not apart from us but who is the very core and ground of all that is."[45] We then find the following footnote:

> Regius Professor of Divinity at Oxford Dr. Keith Ward has made the point (in conversation) that these Tillichian concepts can be found substantially in the writings of Thomas Aquinas. He emphasizes that in the world of academic theology, even the supposedly modern concepts have been around for quite a while.[46]

Quite so, Bishop Spong. This supposedly highly anthropomorphic tradition already has the account of God that Spong wants to commend. The problem that worried him so much is already solved by the tradition he has rejected. Spong's problem is that he rejects a Christian past that doesn't exist, at least at the level of major theological traditions. If it existed (and exists) at other levels, that is another matter and takes us into realms that are not here our immediate concern.

Let us now turn to the conservatives and see if they fair any better. McGrath, like Spong, is well known; unlike Spong, however, he sets out his position with much more care and precision. McGrath has only had one overt discussion of Spong: he has condemned the latter's tendency to offer a speculation, one view among others, as the assured result of New Testament scholarship.[47] It is a charge Spong probably ought to concede. For my purposes, however, McGrath is important for two reasons. First, he locates himself firmly in the tradition of contemporary Anglican conservative evangelicals. As author of James Packer's biography, he is proud of his association with this doyen of evangelicals. Second, he has an impressive corpus of writing in which he defends his evangelical credentials with care and sophistication.

He is careful in all his work to distinguish fundamentalism from evangelicalism. He is critical of opponents (e.g., James Barr and Michael Ramsey) who fail to do so. He insists that biblically, theologically, and sociologically they differ. Biblically, evangelicals accept the principle of biblical criticism, though they may apply it in a conservative way theologically, fundamentalists tend to have a narrower set of doctrinal commitments; and sociologically, evangelicals are much more sympathetic to social action and left-leaning politics generally whereas fundamentalists are often much less concerned with such matters.[48] He suggests that evangelical identity can be grouped around six (which later became four) fundamental convictions. These are:

1   the supreme authority of Scripture as a source of knowledge of God, and a guide to Christian living;
2   the majesty of Jesus Christ, both as Incarnate God and Lord, and as the saviour of sinful humanity;
3   the lordship of the Holy Spirit;
4   the need for personal conversion;
5   the priority of evangelism for both individual Christians and the church as a whole;
6   the importance of the Christian community for spiritual nourishment, fellowship and growth.[49]

It is noteworthy that this list excludes certain prominent features of American evangelicalism (for example, dispensationalism[50]) and admits that evangelicalism needs to be (in the jargon) a broad church. He provides the example of the Eucharist: "Thus, in the case of the 'real presence' question, three major views achieved wide influence within the Reformation by 1560: Luther's view, that the bread is literally to be identified with the body of Christ; Calvin's view, that the bread is an efficacious symbol of the presence of Christ, effecting what it signified: Zwingli's view, that the bread merely symbolizes Christ in his absence. All of these view can be justified on the basis of Scripture."[51] In a case like this, McGrath argues that it is important for evangelicals to permit diversity of viewpoint and to accept that where Scripture is not completely clear it is a case of a secondary issue on which Christian people can disagree.

Much of his work is preoccupied with the perception of evangelicalism in the academy. He is proud of its "counter-cultural" intuitions. Where liberalism is constantly wanting to make faith accessible to modern culture, evangelicalism is determined to challenge that culture. He cites with approval Karl Barth's involvement in the "Barmen Declaration" as an example of fidelity to the biblical interpretation of Christ which made any compromise with the Nazi Aryan Jesus impossible.[52] Unlike liberalism, insists McGrath, evangelicalism knows that secularism, the assumptions of "the world," is an enemy that needs fighting not a friend that needs accommodating.

Importantly for my purposes, McGrath insists that evangelicalism is mainstream. Partly no doubt this is a "political" device: he wants to define the norm of Christianity in terms of evangelicalism. (I suspect most Roman Catholics, especially, would find such a claim problematic!) It is at this point that we discover a monolithic past which we are required to affirm:

> Evangelicalism is historic Christianity. Its beliefs correspond to the central doctrines of the Christian churches down the ages, including the two most important doctrines of the patristic period: the doctrine of the "two natures," human and divine, of Jesus Christ, and the doctrine of the Trinity. In its vigorous defence of the biblical foundations, theological legitimacy and spiritual relevance of these doctrines, evangelicalism has shown itself to have every right to claim to be a standard-bearer of historic orthodox Christianity in the modern period.[53]

And elsewhere he co-writes with John Wenham, that the key to this historic Christianity is the commitment to Scripture:

> Scripture is, for evangelicals, the central legitimating resource of Christian faith and theology, the clearest window through which the face of Christ may be seen. In seeing Scripture as the inspired, authoritative and trustworthy word of God, evangelicals are reiterating the common faith of the Christian church, not inventing something new.[54]

In one sense this demonstrates my point. McGrath, as a representative of conservative Christianity, operates with one particular monolithic understanding of the Christian past that we are simply required to affirm. However, McGrath is too good an historian to make this mistake quite so crudely. He returns to the very simple question – what is it to affirm our doctrinal position?

In his impressive Bampton lectures *The Genesis of Doctrine*, he formulates an answer that is both sophisticated and interesting. Much of it is an attack on the Enlightenment problems with doctrine and authority. He identifies three arguments constructed by the Enlightenment against the traditional corpus of doctrine:

> 1   Doctrinal formulations are to be regarded as historically conditioned, perhaps appropriate to their own period, but of questionable modern relevance. While historical criticism is an appropriate tool for the evaluation and correction of doctrine formulations, history is incapable of disclosing rational truth.
> 2   The truths of reason are autonomous, and may be ascertained without any appeal to history in general, or any specified component in particular (such as the history of Jesus of Nazareth).
> 3   The past can only be known in a fragmentary, relative and corrigible manner; it is never anything more than, to anticipate Kierkegaard's luminous phrase, "approximation knowledge."[55]

He then provides the following response. First, the arguments used to justify these positions as held by Enlightenment thinkers are poor. McGrath makes a good case against any strong historical relativism. He demonstrates the ways in which "tradition" can legitimately be "handed over." Second, he proposes four theses that describe the role of doctrine:

1   doctrine functions as a social demarcation;
2   doctrine is generated by, and subsequently interprets the Christian narrative;
3   doctrine interprets experience;
4   doctrine makes truth claims.[56]

Third, McGrath insists that the "pre-event" of Jesus as conveyed in Scripture is a control on our understanding of legitimate development. This theme is important for him: he believes it is a distinctive emphasis of evangelicalism and therefore makes him suspicious of the community emphasis of much postliberalism. By this he means that the truth claim that Jesus the historical person was God is not simply an insight of the "community" of the church but the prior event creating the community of the church. To this point I shall return.

Despite McGrath's insistence that he is disinclined to get into any particular theory or justification of Scripture, this is what he now needs. He admits as much when elsewhere he chides the post-liberals for their lack of clarity on this point:

The specific criticism which evangelicalism directs against postliberalism at this point is the following: the prioritization of Scripture is not adequately grounded at the theological level. In effect, the priority of Scripture is defended on grounds which appear to be cultural, historical or contractual. The role of the Qur'an within Islam could be justified on similar grounds. The normative role of Scripture within the Christian community is unquestionably Christian (just as the normative role of the Qur'an within Islam is Islamic); but is it right? For the evangelical, truth claims cannot be eroded at this juncture. Scripture has authority, not because of what the Christian community has chosen to make of it, but because of what it is, and what it conveys.[57]

Scripture becomes a control on tradition, even though both tradition and the community are technically prior to the text (in that the earliest church was around before the earliest epistles were written and a long time before the New Testament canon was determined). For McGrath, the problem of history is ultimately solved by a high view of Scripture — a perfectly coherent position but one which is difficult to justify, which is probably why he is disinclined to do so. For McGrath, our situation is this: there is a Christ-experience in Scripture which the church has been forced to explain repeatedly in history. That continuity is the givenness that we all must live with. He is of course committed to holding that the great patristic doctrines (of the Trinity and the Person of Christ) are necessarily and correctly deduced from the New Testament where others find them less than wholly explicit.

We arrive then at a control and a sense of givenness that in fact replicates in its own way the error of Spong. He wants our Christian past to be primarily deductions from Scripture. This is our revelation that we then must explicate throughout the ages. When he talks about "tradition," he defines it as "the history of discipleship — of reading, interpreting and wrestling with Scripture. Tradition is a willingness to read Scripture, taking into account the ways in which it has been read in the past."[58] The creative achievement of the tradition and the imaginative use of non-Christian sources and philosophy have disappeared behind a text-driven picture of our past, which may not be easy to justify, and in any case is open to the judgment of historical inquiry: it can be verified or falsified.

It is at this point that it is necessary to construct an alternative way of understanding the past and therefore thinking about Christian identity. McGrath's picture of liberalism is a good place to begin. For McGrath, liberalism is the erosion of core beliefs intended to make Christianity more acceptable in the modern age. It operates with a post-Enlightenment view of rationality and secular assumptions about the nature of the world. It is true that English liberalism, which reached its nadir in *The Myth of God Incarnate* (1977), and perhaps the work of Bishop Spong, tend to operate with these assumptions. But the style of liberalism that I want to defend in this book is much more orthodox than either. It is willing to learn from a range of non-Christian sources, including of course the Enlightenment.

The Enlightenment and its' child, secularism, have taught the church much that is true about God's relations to the world. The new (or orthodox) liberalism that I am seeking to defend wants to supplement the Enlightenment with a whole range of additional sources from which we can learn about God. This liberalism is in this sense Catholic: it is committed to natural theology and to learning of God from creation. Liberalism in this sense is Anglican – leaning on Scripture, tradition, and reason, or, as developed by John Macquarrie, on the six factors that in his view shape the character of Christian thinking – Scripture, Tradition, Reason, Experience, Culture, and Revelation.

McGrath anticipates this view of liberalism when he writes:

> Indeed, academic integrity was widely seen as the exclusive prerogative of liberal writers, who encouraged the view that a concern for the intellectual climate in which Christianity finds itself at any moment is a unique, or even a defining, feature of liberalism. Yet Thomas Aquinas took seriously the Aristotelianism of the thirteenth-century University of Paris in writing both his *Summa contra Gentiles* and *Summa Theologiae*. I have yet to find Aquinas described as a liberal for that reason! . . . In short: there is nothing distinctively "liberal" about being academically serious and culturally informed.[59]

Naturally McGrath is right to insist that "intellectual" engagement is not in itself a liberal version (and he correctly cites Alvin Plantinga as modern example of a serious intellect), but he is wrong not to see that using non-Christian sources as a central part of your theological methodology is a feature of a liberal methodology that differs radically from his own biblicism.

A major hero of the new liberalism is Augustine, one of the greatest shapers of our tradition who used a methodology which was, on our present understanding, distinctively liberal. It is to this that we turn in the next chapter.

2

AUGUSTINE'S THEOLOGICAL METHODOLOGY

It was shown in the first chapter that underpinning much liberal and conservative theology is a fundamental misconception about the nature of the tradition. Both assume that the tradition tends to have a monolithic character that one must either affirm (if you are conservative) or reject (if you are a liberal). In this chapter, it will be shown that this is not the case.

St. Augustine of Hippo will be taken as a case study in orthodox theological method. He has been chosen because (a) he is a supreme example of the "orthodox" tradition for the western church, and (b) he is difficult – few would describe him as a liberal. In addition, Augustine has been chosen because he has become a central battleground in the debate about theological method. Most conservative theologians make Augustine central. John Milbank, for example, has made him central to his vision of theology.[1] The coherence of such conservative theologies would be undermined if we are able to show that they are making illegitimate use of Augustine.

So this chapter will start with a brief summary of the main highlights of Augustine's extraordinary life. Augustine was born at Thagaste in northern Africa on November 13, 354 C.E.. His mother, Monnica, was a Christian and his father was a pagan. Augustine describes his own background as poor, although in the small rural town where they lived they were probably relatively comfortable. After a good classical education, Augustine decided to become a Manichee in 372–3. This was a radical dualist movement, committed to two coeternal principles – one good (God) the other evil (Satan). His conversion to Christianity comes about as he reads various platonic texts in 386 C.E. and gets baptized by Bishop Ambrose in 387 (the same year that his mother dies). He is ordained a priest in Hippo in 391 and becomes bishop in 395. Much of his life is spent expounding his understanding of Christianity in the light of various controversies. His written output is prolific: his main work is the *City of God*; his longest work is his *Enarrations on the Psalms*; his most popular work is his own spiritual biography *Confessions*; and his most substantial theological work is his fifteen books *On the Trinity*. He died on August 28, 430 C.E.

For most liberals he is the great bête noire. He is undoubtedly responsible for the "orthodoxy" that endured for centuries. And for many it is an orthodoxy that is oppressive. The exercise of finding shocking passages in Augustine is a game that many like to play. For example, his doctrine of *massa peccatrix* as stated in *De Natura et Gratia* where Augustine writes:

> This grace of Christ, then, without which neither children nor adults can be saved, is given gratuitously and not for our merits, and for this reason it is called "grace." "[They are] justified," says the Apostle, "freely by his blood." Consequently, those who are not liberated through grace, either because they have not yet been able to hear, or because they have not wished to obey, or also because, when on account of their age they were not capable of hearing, they did not receive the bath of regeneration, which they could have received and by means of which they would have been saved, are justly condemned. For they are not without sin, either that which they contracted originally or that which they added through their own misconduct. "For all have sinned," either in Adam or in themselves, "and are deprived of the glory of God." Consequently, the whole human mass ought to be punished, and if the deserved punishment of damnation were rendered to all, beyond all doubt it would be justly rendered. This is why whose who are liberated from it by grace are not called vessels of their own merits but "vessels of mercy."[2]

Most Christians are unhappy with Augustine's views on predestination, which is linked with his conviction that only a minuscule number of people will be saved; and for his view that unbaptized infants are damned to hell, it is not surprising that limbo was invented by the medieval church. The package of original sin and eternal damnation is held to be responsible for a multitude of difficulties. Adherents in other faith traditions find his exclusivism problematic. Feminist theologians blame Augustine for a dualism (inherited from his Neoplatonism) that celebrates spirit and denigrates the body.[3] This, they argue, has directly underpinned patriarchy. The male was considered more spiritual and the female was less spiritual because of a link with sex and nature. The evidence for this analysis is built on Augustine's intricate analysis of the possibility of sexual intercourse found in his *City of God:* there, you will recall, Augustine arrives at the extraordinary view that prior to the Fall, passionless sex that leaves women in a virginal state would have been possible.

So to suggest that Augustine can also be a liberal hero seems manifestly problematic. Surely he is the great villain? My argument will be that methodologically Augustine is a liberal and therefore sympathetic to a theology of engagement. The argument is simple: Augustine's methodology involves three central components. First, reason clearly has a central role. Second, he draws heavily on non-Christian sources. Third, the experience of his life transformed by Christ and therefore the centrality of "experience." I shall show that in these three elements we have a surprisingly modern methodology operating: reason, the use of non-Christian wisdom, and experience. It is his willingness to learn from a range of sources that is Augustine's great strength. It is also this willingness that must make it both legitimate (in that it is true to Augustine's own method) and necessary to develop the tradition.

1   The Role of Reason

The issue of the role of "reason" in Augustine's thought is contentious. Significant difficulties confront us at the outset. Reason has a range of modern connotations that would make it anachronistic to impose on Augustine; in addition, it is not entirely clear whether Augustine held a consistent view on the nature of "reason," especially in relation to "faith" and "authority" across his vast corpus. The considerations highlighted at the outset, we turn to Augustine's work.

At the most basic level: if we start by considering a commitment to "reason" as involving the recognition of the importance of our human rational capacity and therefore the importance of reasons and good logical arguments, then no one can doubt Augustine's commitment to reason. Good arguments pervade his work: intellectual puzzles are stated and grappled with. There are numerous illustrations of this: for example, his reflections on the nature of time at the end of *The Confessions* or the problem of human knowledge and divine foreknowledge discussed in the *City of God.*[4]

His commitment to reason also arises out of his anthropology. So in *De animae quantitate* (On the greatness of the soul), Augustine writes, "If you wish a definition of what the soul is, I have a ready answer. It seems to be a certain kind of substance, sharing in reason, fitted to rule the body."[5] Later in *De trinitate*, Augustine writes:

> Desiring to train the Reader in the things that were made, in order that he might know Him by whom they were made, we have now at last arrived at His image which is man, in that whereby He is superior to other animals, namely, in reason and understanding, and whatever else can be said of the rational or intellectual soul that pertains to that thing which is called the mind or *animus*.[6]

The mind then, for Augustine, is the highest point of the soul. So it is not surprising that Augustine has a high regard for the rational capacity of the mind. Etienne Gilson brings out the significance of this for Augustine's view of the relationship between faith and reason when he points out that for Augustine:

> the very possibility of faith depends on reason. Of all the beings God created on earth, only man is capable of belief, because he alone is endowed with reason. Man exists, as do wood and stones; he lives, as the plants do; he moves and feels, as do animals; but in addition, he thinks. Moreover the mind, whereby man knows what is intelligible, is in his case the mark man left of His handiwork: it is in the mind that he is made to God's image. . . . In short, man is the image of God inasmuch as he is a mind which, by exercising its reason, acquires more and more understanding and grows progressively richer therein.[7]

Additional evidence that reasons and good arguments mattered to Augustine is demonstrated in his capacity to revisit older arguments and want to correct them. *The Retractationes* is a remarkable phenomenon that reflects well on his commitment to intellectual integrity. The opening of the *Retractationes* reflects both this commitment and a delightful self-deprecating irony. He writes:

> For a long time I have been thinking about and planning to do something which I, with God's assistance, am now undertaking because I do not think it should be postponed: with a kind of judicial severity, I am reviewing my works – books, letters, and sermons – and, as it were, with the pen of a censor, I am indicating what dissatisfies me. For, truly, only an ignorant man will have the hardihood to criticize me for criticizing my own errors. But if he maintains that I should not have said those things which, indeed,

dissatisfied me later, he speaks the truth and concurs with me. In fact, he and I are critics of the same thing, for I should not have criticized such things if it had been right to say them.[8]

It might be objected that too much is being made of the obvious intellectual depth of Augustine – this is after all why he is so widely read and why he was so influential. The point being stressed however is the important, but often overlooked fact that Augustine was rigorously self-critical and committed to formulating an account of faith that was both coherent and justified in terms of good arguments.

That said, the disagreement between Augustinian specialists over this issue arises when we confront the more modern question was "reason" in some sense a control on faith? This after all is part of the great liberal tradition emerging from the Enlightenment, where reason challenged authority in a whole range of areas from science to ethics. Or to state the question in a less provocative way and use the popular natural and revealed theology divide: does reason operate prior to faith?

To answer these questions, we can start with some of those explicit passages that give reason a significant role. In the last treatise written prior his ordination, Augustine states explicitly:

> There are two different methods, authority and reason. Authority demands belief and prepares man for reason. Reason leads to understanding and knowledge. But reason is not entirely absent from authority, for we have got to consider whom we have to believe, and the highest authority belongs to truth when it is clearly known.[9]

This does sound as if reason is important in every respect. Reason is important prior to accepting an authority and it is important afterwards because reason is the only mechanism that we have for deciding which authority is true.

We also find this refrain in an earlier work *Contra Academicos*. There he writes, "No one doubts but that we are helped in learning by a twofold force, that of authority and that of reason."[10] However, to introduce some of the complexity that pervades this question, this is also the text in which we find a marvelous exhortation to simply trust, which is worth quoting in full:

> To illustrate, let us picture two men traveling to one place. One of them has resolved not to believe anyone; the other believes everyone. They come

to a place where the road forks. The credulous traveler addresses a shepherd of some rustic standing on the spot: "Hello, my good man. Tell me,
please, which is the best way to that place?" The reply: "If you take this
road, you will not go wrong." He says to his companion: "What he says is
correct. Let us go this way." The careful traveler laughs and makes a fool of
the other for having given assent so quickly. While the other takes his way,
he remains at the junction of the roads. He is beginning to feel foolish
himself because of his hesitation, when from the road not taken by his
companion there appears and draws near an elegant and refined gentlemen
riding on horseback. The traveler rejoices. He salutes the man as he
approaches, and tells him what is on his mind. He asks him the way. Not
only that – he tells him why he has delayed so that by indicating his
preference for him rather than for the shepherd, he may make him the
better disposed to himself. He, however, happens to be an arrant knave, one
of those fellows now commonly called *samardoci*. The scoundrel indulges in
his usual practice, and that, too, without charging a penny: "Go this way,"
he says. "I have just come from there." So, he deceives him and passes on
his way. But our traveler would not be deceived! "Indeed," he says, "I shall
not assent to his information as true. But since it is probable, and since to
do nothing here is neither proper nor useful, I shall go the way he indicates." Meanwhile he who erred in assenting, too quickly judging that the
shepherd's words were true, is already resting in the place for which they
set out. But he who has not erred, since he follows the "probable," is lost
in some woods and has not yet found anybody who knows the place where
he proposed to go![11]

It is clear that Augustine was committed to the legitimacy of "trust." If
faith depends on complex arguments then what about the academically
less able? It was a pivotal moment in *The Confessions* when he conceded
the legitimacy of trust:

From this time on, however, I now gave my preference to the Catholic
faith. I thought it more modest and not in the least misleading to be told
by the Church to believe what could not be demonstrated – whether that
was because a demonstrated existed but could not be understood by all or
whether the matter was not one open to rational proof. . . . I considered
the innumerable things I believed which I had not seen, events which
occurred when I was not present, such as many incidents in the history of
nations, many facts concerning places and cities which I had never seen,
many things accepted on the word of friends, many from physicians, many
from other people. Unless we believed what we were told, we would do
nothing in this life.[12]

So, on the one hand, we have explicit recognition that reason is our God-given tool that should enable us to recognize which revelation (i.e., authority) to trust. On the other hand, we have a recognition that reasons are not available for everything the church teaches and therefore trust is essential. And trust is often essential in most aspects of life.

An extremely illuminating discussion of the role of reason occurs indirectly in Rowan Williams essay on book ten of *De trinitate*. This book has attracted considerable attention because of its striking parallels with Descartes *Second Meditation*. On first reading it looks as if Augustine is attempting to arrive at the certainty of self-knowledge as an example of innate knowledge.[13] Williams insists this is mistaken. He writes: "[T]he introspection of *De trinitate* . . . is not a search for epistemological buried treasure but something more like an invitation to observe what we can't but take for granted in speaking about mental life at all, as distinct from speaking about the process of registering external impressions."[14] Instead of reading this book in a foundationalist way and as a digression from the main argument of *De trinitate*, Williams insists it should be read as Augustine providing an exposition for knowledge claims in the moral and spiritual spheres. The details need not detain us here: however, Williams concludes that if one is going to embark on anachronistic comparisons then Wittgenstein's *On Certainty* is to be preferred:

> Wittgenstein's demonstration of the oddity of using "This is my hand" as a paradigm of a fact that I'm sure of has some striking points of contact with Augustine's *nosse-cogitare* distinction, in that it reminds us that what I cannot help assuming is not to be assimilated to what I *come to know*. The process of justification and explication involved in discussing the latter are inappropriate in respect of the former, not because "This is my hand" or whatever, is a supremely good example of something I know, but because we cannot begin to talk intelligibly about learning or giving reasons for holding it true.[15]

Wayne Hankey supplements Williams' argument by insisting that Augustine shares with Plotinus the conviction that knowledge does depend on illumination. Hankey writes, "For Augustine, also, illumination of the human mind by the divine intellectual light from above is essential. It can only discern its own structure and the ideas when they are seen and loved in the light of their principle."[16]

The following picture, then, is starting to emerge. No one disputes that arguments play an important role in Augustine's work. However, it runs parallel with a commitment to authority, a celebration of the legitimacy of trust, and an affirmation that ultimate knowledge of God is ultimately made possible by God.

What we seem to have here is a classic example of MacIntyre's "tradition-constituted rationality." A tradition-constituted rationality is one where there is no external or tradition transcendent justifications. Instead reason is located and operating in a distinct fashion according to the rules of that particular tradition. This is not incompatible with the commitment to "critical realism" outlined in the opening chapter. However, for now, we note the following: it seems that Augustine's "reason" is not a control on faith. His experience of a life transformed in Christ coupled with his confidence in Scripture means that he trusts his tradition even when he finds it rationally difficult. Perhaps one might want to argue, this is why he arrives at such unpalatable views on foreknowledge and predestination.

If this is where my treatment of Augustine's view of reason stops, then my "theology of engagement" would be in trouble. Engagement does require the God-given gift of reason to have space to challenge a traditional authority, whether the Bible or the tradition. But the treatment should not end here. It is important to recall that Augustine was "tradition-constituted" in a different tradition prior to his conversion to Christianity. He was a Manichee.

Undoubtedly Augustine was attracted to Manchaeism because of its rational plausibility. Peter Brown likens Manchaeism in Augustine's day to the attractiveness of communism in the 1930s. Augustine had tried the Bible but found that the text "seemed quite unworthy of comparison with the stately prose of Cicero."[17] The Manichees made much of the ethical difficulties of the patriarchs; it offered a complete explanation for the problem of evil; and so Augustine became a "Hearer" among them for nine years.[18]

Slowly Augustine changes his mind about the rational plausibility of Manchaeism. Granted one should not imagine that Augustine is simply, in a detached modern way, evaluating the options and deciding on the basis of reason which worldview is true. It is the case, as Peter Brown shows, that Manchaeism, for a "Hearer" as opposed the "Elect," was an ethically convenient worldview. The radical dualism of Manchaeism enabled Augustine to indulge the pleasures of his senses certain in the knowledge that there was an untouched goodness. It meant that he could enjoy his concubine aware that there was an innately good part of him undamaged. Brown claims, "For Augustine, the need to save an untarnished oasis of perfection within himself formed, perhaps, the deepest strain of his adherence to the Manichees."[19] Nevertheless it is a rational reevaluation of Manchaeism that leads to his departure. The revaluation does take into account the ethical dimension: he slowly decides that the strict and extreme dualism is implausible. He realizes that monotheism is not incoherent, he explains that when he was a Manichee:

> I thought it was outrageous to believe that you had the shape of a human body and were limited within the dimensions of limbs like our own. . . . I believed that evil, too, was some similar kind of substance, a shapeless, hideous mass, which might be solid, in which case the Manichees called it earth, or fine and rarefied like air. This they imagine as a kind of evil mind filtering through the substance they call earth. And because such little piety as I had compelled me to believe that God, who is good, could not have created an evil nature, I imagined that there were two antagonistic masses, both of which were infinite, yet the evil in a lesser and the good in a greater degree. All my other sacrilegious beliefs were the outcome of this first fatal mistake.[20]

Augustine has a set of conceptual difficulties with theism that made it difficult for him to embrace Christianity. It is as he sees the conceptual difficulties are greater when it comes to the dualism of Manchaeism that he decides that Christianity is an option. The difficulties with Manchaeism include the problem of a slightly stronger good – how can one be confident it will triumph – and the awareness that ethically we are integrated whole.[21]

This shows that "reason" did play a role in shifting Augustine from one tradition to another. The question is: could Augustine made a comparable shift in understanding Christianity? This does not necessarily have to be to a non-Christian tradition, but to a different, more liberal perhaps, understanding of Christianity. Could he have modified his views on say the inerrancy of Scripture?

There is, I suggest, some evidence that he could. Not least his reflection in *De bono perseverantiae*, when he wrote:

> I wish no one to accept all my views and to follow me except in those areas where he finds that I have not been mistaken. . . . Were I to claim that I am perfect at this stage of life and that my writings were free from error, I would be speaking with more arrogance than truth.[22]

Although Augustine's view of reason is complex – partly because truth is linked with God,[23] it is clear that he was always willing to offer good arguments and confront difficult opposing arguments. It is also true that when persuaded that a tradition was fundamentally misguided and incoherent, he searched for truth elsewhere. Although the Christian convictions of divine illumination coupled with his trust in the Christian scriptures enabled him to settle within the Christian tradition, he retained right to the end a willingness to let the "truth" alone be his ultimate judge. In this respect he was a good liberal. Liberals should recognize and appreciate the way that reason is used to expose conceptual confusions and difficulties. Augustine clearly has the expectation that the truth of worldview will in part be determined by the coherence and explanatory power of that worldview. Fideism is always the enemy of a liberal theology. Once one surrenders the need for reasons, then a faith becomes untouchable. Anything can be believed because there are no restrictions. Nonsense becomes an option. Both in his commitment to natural theology and in his use of reason to distinguish between alternative worldviews, Augustine has a rational control on his faith.

2 Use of Non-Christian Sources

Now we come to the heart of the argument: for a theology of engagement we need to look at how Augustine uses "non-Christian sources" in shaping his theology. Once again, in much the same way that "reason," interpreted as a commitment to good argument, is universally affirmed as true of Augustine's work so everyone agrees that Augustine was certainly shaped by his reading of Neoplatonism (the Platonism of Platonius and beyond). But as with the debate about the extent of reason's involvement with authority, so there is a comparable debate about Neoplatonism.

At one extreme we have Adolf von Harnack, who in 1888, argued that at the conversion, Augustine was no more than a Platonist influenced by Christianity rather than the other way round. At the other extreme we have G. Quispel who argued that there is no important doctrine in Augustine that is not grounded in the Bible.[24] The truth, like so many of these debates, is firmly in between.

There are two areas that require exploration. First, the influence of Neoplatonism on his conversion; and second, Augustine's explicit sympathies for Neoplatonism and his interpretation of their insights. It will be shown that Augustine affirms truth where ever it is found and allows non-Christian insights to shape his Christianity.

We start, then with the influence of Neoplatonism on his conversion. The primary source for this is *The Confessions*. Perhaps a comment is necessary on the attention I propose to give *The Confessions*. There are difficulties here: first it is not a traditional autobiography; it is more a chronicle of the journey of the heart. The traditional background to a biography is entirely neglected. So while we are fascinated by his concubine and find ourselves indignant about his decision to send her back to Africa because his career needs a socially advantageous marriage, this does not concern Augustine. What troubles us is not what troubles Augustine. Given the conventions of his age, this was not an issue. Second, some have questioned the historicity of *The Confessions*. For example, in *The Confessions* Augustine decides to leave his teaching post for religious reasons, elsewhere he suggests that he leaves on the grounds of ill-health. It is not my purpose to defend *The Confessions*, although I do take the view that most of the apparent discrepancies identified are more imagined than proven.[25] Anyway my interest in Augustine is methodological, given this the precise historicity is unimportant.

It is clear that Augustine's underlying principle is that all "truth belongs to God." So a love of wisdom wherever it is found drives Augustine on. He writes:

> In Greek the word "philosophy" means "love of wisdom," and it was with this love that the *Hortensius* inflamed me. There are people for whom philosophy is a means of misleading others, for they misuse its great name, its attractions, and its integrity to give color and gloss to their own errors. Most of these so-called philosophers who lived in Cicero's time and before are noted in the book. . . . (T)he only thing that pleased me in Cicero's book was his advice not simply to admire one or another of the schools of philosophy, but to love wisdom itself, whatever it might be, and to search for it, pursue it, hold it, and embrace it firmly.[26]

Cicero's *Hortensius* is Augustine's way into philosophy. From it, Augustine learns the importance of seeking wisdom. As Augustine became disillusioned with Manchaeism, so he discovered Neoplatonism (probably the writings of Plotinus). He finds in these writings good arguments for the existence of God and his eternal word. Augustine explains:

> So you [i.e., God] made use of a man, one who was bloated with the most outrageous pride, to procure me some of the books of the Platonists, translated from the Greek into Latin. In them I read – not, of course, word for word, though the sense was the same and it was supported by all kinds of

different arguments — that *at the beginning of time the Word already was; and God had the Word abiding with him, and the Word was God.* . . . In the same books I also read of the Word, God, that his *birth came not from human stock, not from nature's will or man's, but from God.* But I did not read in them that *the Word was made flesh and came to dwell among us.*[27]

Augustine's readings in Neoplatonism persuade him of God and the eternal word, although there is nothing about the Incarnation. He treats the illumination that these books provide him about God as intended by God. Although Cicero and Platonius are non-Christians, he has no difficulty in acknowledging the truth about God he finds within their writing.

The second area we need to explore is his explicit treatment of Neoplatonism in some of his writings. Although in the *Retractationes* he does express disquiet about the extent of his praise and admiration, the praise and admiration is still there and presumably reflects his view at the time. The discussions of Neoplatonism are extensive that selection is a major difficulty. Both in terms of content and method, the Neoplatonism is important. On the content front, we find in *Civitas Dei* that Augustine explicitly lists the connections between Neoplatonism and Christianity. John O'Meara, helpful summarizes thus, "They [i.e., the Neoplatonists] taught the existence of an incorporeal Creator, of Providence, the immortality of the soul, the honor of virtue, patriotism, true friendship, and good morals. Final happiness, moreover, they held to be attainable through participation of the soul in the Creator's unchangeable and incorporeal light."[28] On the method front, Etienne Gilson insists that Augustine's debt to Plotinus is considerable. He writes, "To Plotinus he is indebted for almost all the matter and for the whole technique of his philosophy. He is indebted to the Bible for the basic Christian notions which compelled him to make the inner transformation he performed on the Plotinian theses he borrowed and to construct in this way a new doctrine which represents one of the first, and one of the most original, contributions Christianity has made to enrich the history of philosophy."[29] Interestingly given the next chapter, Gilson goes on to draw an explicit parallel between Augustine and Aquinas, he writes, "[A]ll we can say is that he did for Plotinus what St. Thomas Aquinas was later to do for Aristotle, i.e., to make, in the light of faith, a rational revision of a great philosophical interpretation of the universe."[30]

Indeed such was his regard for the Neoplatonists, which he attributes directly to Plato he gives a very positive interpretation of Plato. He makes two striking claims:

1   if Plato was alive today, then he would be a Christian;
2   Plato has so much insight that it seems plausible to believe that he must of learned from Jeremiah the great Jewish prophet.

For the first this can be seen in *On True Religion*. Augustine writes:

> Suppose Plato were alive and would not spurn a question I would put to him; or rather suppose one of his own disciples, who lived at the same time as he did, had addressed him thus: "You have persuaded me that truth is seen not with the bodily eyes but by the pure mind, and that any soul that cleaves to truth is thereby made happy and perfect. . . . Therefore the mind has to be healed so that it may behold the immutable form of things which remains ever the same, preserving its beauty unchanged and unchangeable, knowing no spatial distance or temporal variation, abiding absolutely one and the same. . . . To the rational and intellectual soul is given to enjoy the contemplation of eternity, and by that contemplation it is armed and equipped so that it may obtain eternal life. . . . You, my master, have persuaded me to believe these things. Now, if some great and divine man should arise to persuade the peoples that such things were to be at least believed if they could not grasp them with mind, or that those who could grasp them should not allow themselves to be implicated in the depraved opinions of the multitude or to be overborne by vulgar errors, would you not judge that such a man is worthy of divine honors?" I believe Plato's answer would be: "That could not be done by man, unless the very virtue and wisdom of God delivered him from natural environment, illumined him from his cradle not by human teaching but by personal illumination, honored him with such grace, strengthened him with such firmness and exalted him with such majesty, that he should be able to despise all that wicked men desire, to suffer all that they dread, to do all that they marvel at, and so with the greatest love and authority to convert the human race to so sound a faith." . . . Now this very thing has come to pass.[31]

The argument here is interesting and subtle. Platonism discovered the problem facing human existence: knowledge of the good, the true, and the beautiful depends on transcending our human propensity to lust and preoccupation with matter. However, if Plato was asked don't we need a person who can demonstrate how this is possible. Plato would reply "yes, but it would be very difficult." And this, argues Augustine is precisely what has come to past.

We will return to the need of a life-transforming experience implied in this section later in this chapter. At this stage we simply note the way that Augustine can find in Plato a shared analysis of the human condition, that he is sure that Plato, if living after Christ, would have been a Christian. The other argument that Augustine expresses his sympathy for Plato occurs in *Civitas Dei*. Perhaps suggests Augustine we can explain Plato's knowledge because he must have had some contact with a Jewish prophet, for example Jeremiah. Augustine writes:

> Some of our fellow Christians are astonished to learn that Plato had such ideas about God and to realize how close they are to the truths of our faith. Some even have been led to suppose that he was influenced by the Prophet Jeremias during his travels in Egypt or at least, that he had access to the scriptural prophecies; and this opinion I followed in some of my writings. However, a careful calculation of dates according to historical chronology shows that Plato was born almost one hundred years after Jeremias prophesied.[32]

The greatest complement a Christian can pay a different tradition is that (a) if the founder were alive now then they would convert, and (b) the founder derived his or her insights from Christianity. This propensity to inclusiveness (i.e., attempting to demonstrate that insights in other traditions really belong to your tradition) is inevitable when you are handling truth questions. Augustine attempts both strategies and to his credit has the integrity to admit the latter is false. However, what it demonstrates overwhelmingly is his positive view of at least one non-Christian source.

It would be wrong to leave it there. Although the Neoplatonists attract most of Augustine's attention and praise, there are other non-Christian sources operating. Sabine MacCormack has shown the impact of the poet Vergil on Augustine; it is a creative conversation. She summarizes thus: "Augustine's engagement with Vergil was therefore sometimes in the nature of a dialogue and at other times in the nature of a confrontation."[33] She correctly warns against overemphasizing the significance of the illusions. The Bible is much more important. This, of course, is not surprising. It is after all the place where Augustine learns about Jesus.

3 Experience

The third element is "experience." He admits that he is driven to the doctrine of the Incarnation because he needs the strength to enjoy God. He writes, "I began to search for a means of gaining the strength I needed to enjoy you, but I could not find this means until I embraced the *mediator between God and men, Jesus Christ, who is a man, like them,* and also *rules as God over all things, blessed for ever.*"[34] John Rist captures Augustine's meaning extremely well when he writes, "Neoplatonism is incomplete; its underlying weakness is that it is theoretical, without the power to instigate right action."[35]

Augustine finds the "power" at the end of book eight. He is in a Milanese garden in August 386, tormented by sinfulness and asking God to explain why it was all so difficult. Then he writes:

> I was asking myself these questions, weeping all the while with most bitter sorrow in my heart, when all at once I heard the sing-song voice of a child in a nearby house. Whether it was the voice of a boy or a girl I cannot say, but again and again it repeated the refrain "Take it and read, take it and read." At this I looked up, thinking hard whether there was any kind of game in which children used to chant words like these, but I could not remember ever hearing them before. I stemmed my flood of tears and stood up, telling myself that this could only be a divine command to open my book of Scripture and read the first passage on which my eyes should fall.
> . . . So I hurried back to the place where Alypius was sitting, for when I stood up to move away I had put down the book containing Paul's Epistles. I seized it and opened it, and in silence I read the first passage on which my eyes fell: *Not in reveling and drunkenness, not in lust and wantonness, not in quarrels and rivalries. Rather, arm yourselves with the Lord Jesus Christ; spend no more thought on nature and nature's appetites.* I had no wish to read more and no need to do so. For in an instant, as I came to the end of the sentence, it was as though the light of confidence flooded into my heart and all the darkness of doubt was dispelled.[36]

This is an old-fashioned religious experience. As many others have, before and since, Augustine tormented by his moral failures finds in Jesus a confidence that he can triumph over sin.

Once again the term "experience" has a potentially anachronistic association. It is not the case that Augustine is the same as Schleiermacher. Instead it is more accurate to say that Augustine would not want to separate his experience from his philosophy. Armstong is helpful here when he insists that for Augustine and his contemporaries there is no distinction between philosophy and theology:

> It was an activity embracing the whole of human life, an attempt not merely to direct but to bring man to his goal through an understanding of the whole of reality. . . . If this is what philosophy meant, it is easy to see that

for Christians the only true philosophy could be nothing else but a lived and living theology, a reflection on the mysteries of faith, using all the resources of a Greek-trained intelligence, which determined the Christian way of life.[37]

Although Augustine would not appreciate my attempt to disentangle three sources of his theology, I want to suggest that the case can be made that Augustine arrives at faith using these three sources: reason, non-Christian sources of wisdom, and experience.

4 Objections

These three sources have become central to the liberal theological tradition. Augustine becomes problematic for the liberal because his experience of Jesus then became the prism through which everything else was seen. The third source (experience of the revelation of God) undermined the second (wisdom in other traditions) and the first (reason). In good traditional natural theology, the first two were useful in arriving at faith, the third made their usefulness redundant.

This illustrates an important danger. Experience freed from any critical reflection can become a tyranny. Experience linked with a conviction that the experience has discovered the absolute truth exclusively in a revelation is almost certainly going to be a tyranny. Experience should always recognize the other two sources of theology.

Yet to the question does Augustine provide a good reason why experience becomes primarily, one will search his writing in vain. The best one can find is a sense that experience is so transforming that it becomes everything. **Christology and soteriology become significant difficulties**. It transformed Augustine's sense of powerlessness of sin and selfishness into victory through Christ. However, for now, I simply note that this transformation is no reason, in itself, why the first two sources are so regulated.

Once this is conceded, then one is being true to the Augustinian tradition to continue to shape one's theological reflection by using one's reason, in conversation with the wisdom of non-Christian sources, and in attempting to make sense of one's continuing experience of God. One is being true to Augustine's method, when one disagrees with Augustine. For his method will challenge and unsettle; it will open up new and different theological futures.

One further objection, linked to the primacy given to Augustine's experience of Jesus, needs to be noted. Surely, a critic might point out Augustine's engagement with non-Christian sources is driven by his figural reading of Scripture and therefore to claim him as an heir to a liberal project, which assumes a historical-critical approach to Scripture, is misguided. The link between the past and the present in any tradition is always a mixture of continuity and change. I am claiming that the method of engagement being commended in this book is embedded in the pre-modern Christian tradition and therefore it is a faithful development of that tradition. There is a clear continuity with Augustine (in his commitment to reason, shaped by experience, in conversation with non-Christian sources) while, at the same time, there are clear changes from Augustine (not least in the way Scripture should be read). Therefore I am not claiming that Augustine would endorse every aspect of my program.

The problem of continuity and change is one that haunts all theological projects that want to take our tradition seriously. John Milbank's reading of Augustine makes the two cities central. He likes the way that Augustine has two contrasting cities, different in origin, different in role, and different in terms of ultimate outcome. Milbank then casts the secular against the church as two contrasting narratives that operate in entirely different ways. This is a postmodern reading of Augustine: there are clearly certain recognizable continuities with Augustine, but there is no way that Augustine recognize the postmodern underpinnings of Milbank's project.

Indeed I would go further. The argument of this chapter is that Milbank's reading of Augustine is less justified than my reading. The two cities were never supposed to represent contrasting or different rationalities. His method allows for the church to learn much from the secular city. A. Hilary Armstong makes this point well:

[C]hristians were always concerned with contemporary philosophy and contemporary culture, and at least from the great age of the Fathers onwards were the intellectual equals or superiors of the pagans and were just as well educated in the same way. . . . [I]t could never have occurred to them to try and create a little enclave of Christian culture and thought, remote and cut off from the contemporary world, and if it had we should have had no ancient Christian thought and culture to look back to, nostalgically or otherwise. The lesson for our time is obvious, though we cannot simply reproduce in our own very different culture and environment their attitude (incidentally a highly critical and selective one in some ways though not in others) to theirs. We must try to live in and cope with the present as they did, but as we can neither love the past in the way they loved it nor hate and repudiate it as some of our contemporaries do. We have new and very difficult problems, which the Fathers cannot help us to solve, in reconciling our ancient Faith with contemporary reason in a world which is so divorced from and so hostile to its past.[38]

3

ASSIMILATION, RESISTANCE, AND OVERHEARING

Having defined "engagement" in the opening chapter and looked at Augustine as a model "engaged" theologian, the task in this third chapter is to explore the types of engagement that we find in the Christian tradition. Martyn Percy in his impressive study, *The Salt of the Earth*, suggests that the interest of the church is in religious "resilience." And "resilience," explains Percy, is a term that:

> allows for the possibility of simultaneous critiques and affirmations, and yet is also capable of being read in two quite different ways. Substances or beliefs that are resilient can recoil from their environment; they bounce or spring back. In this sense, resilience can be understood as a form of resistance. However, resilience can also describe more malleable qualities. . . . Thus, resilience can also describe a process of recovery. . . . Or it can describe a transformation. . . . These are the two faces of religious resilience in modern times: resistance and accommodation.[1]

The role that resilience plays in Percy's theology is similar to the role that the word "engagement" is playing in this book. However, unlike Percy, the argument of this book is that all good theology has been and needs to be in the business of engagement. Therefore it is not simply an issue, as Percy seems to imply, that the two faces of religious resilience are only needed in "modern times." In addition, for Percy, this engagement has two modes: resistance and accommodation. Accommodation is a helpful category, although not the whole story. The problem with accommodation is that it can involve nothing more than "making room for," when there is a need for greater absorption. For this reason, the word "assimilation" is more helpful. Resistance is the correct word: engagement might well involve resisting a key idea because it would threaten the coherence and integrity of certain Christian insights. However, underpinning all this, we need the task of listening. One cannot assimilate or resist without first attending to the other. And in addition, listening may take the form of absorbing the implications of an argument outside the Christian tradition. In other words, a third form of engagement is "overhearing."

I shall now show that these three ways of "engagement" are grounded in the Christian tradition. The three ways, which will be the focus of this chapter, are not to be interpreted as a comprehensive of all the ways in which "engagement" occurs. Rather, they serve as broad categories that will assist with the organization of the case studies that follow in the rest of the book.

I have already explained that these three ways are i.e., assimilation, (b) resistance, and (c) overhearing. The act of assimilation is *the constructive use of a category or, more often, a set of categories, from a non-Christian source*. The illustration from the Christian tradition, which will be described briefly in this chapter, is the manner in which Augustine and Aquinas used Greek categories to absorb the language of scripture in formulating their concept of God. The act of resistance is *when a theologian decides that a certain approach, albeit tempting for various cultural reasons, should be rejected as incompatible with the heart of the Christian revelation*. For this, we shall examine the affirmation of the material (both in the definition of the Incarnation and the physicality of the resurrection). The way of overhearing comes into play *when a theologian finds significant illumination from the arguments and positions of theologians within another religious tradition*. For this, we shall look at Aquinas's engagement with the writings of Maimonides and Ibn Sina (Avicenna).[2]

In each case it is not my purpose to provide an extended discussion of the merits (or otherwise) of the assimilation, resistance or overhearing. The sole purpose of the brief description is to illustrate that these processes are at work in the tradition.[3] The distinction between the **process** in the development of tradition and the **content** of tradition is important. The process of tradition is the dynamic propensity for the engagement of non-Christian sources, which, I am suggesting can take three forms, assimilation, resistance, and overhearing. The content of the tradition is the decisions that those involved in the process decided upon. So, for example, these are the decisions in Augustine and Aquinas that when we think of God, we should think of a being that is timeless, immutable, and simple. The argument of this book is that the process is as important as the content. This means that to be committed to the tradition, we should continue to engage with non-Christian sources and as we do so it might

undermine the historic consensus about the content of the Christian tradition. In other words, as we engage, perhaps, with Hindu or Buddhist
thought this might undermine the Augustine and Aquinas view of God.

This is important to remember as we describe the processes of assimilation, resistance, and overhearing. In each case an illustration will be
given that demonstrates this process within the Christian tradition. My
purpose with each illustration is to establish the fact of the process: it is
not intended to affirm the decision of the particular theologian who was
involved in the process. So I do not intend to discuss in any detail
the considerable literature that has subsequently developed exploring the
problems with timelessness and divine action or impassibility and the
incarnation.

The final point that is worth establishing before developing these three
aspects to engagement is that this distinction between process and content
opens up an apologetic possibility for critics of the tradition. Most critics
find the decisions of say Augustine and Aquinas problematic; so feminists
are rightly critical of an account of God that implies a strong dualism
between God and the world. However, this process of engagement that
this chapter will now document means that feminists are entitled to draw
on non-Christian sources to shape an alternative understanding of God's
relationship with the world. These feminist critics are simply using the
process (or method) of the tradition against some of the decisions of the
tradition. Although they are challenging some of the decisions of the
tradition, this does not mean that they are betraying the tradition. In
drawing on non-Christian sources to shape an alternative account of God
and God's relationship with the world, they are heirs to a process that is
at the heart of development of doctrine within the tradition. And in so
doing these feminist critics are simply behaving in the same way that
Aquinas or Luther did before them. The act of using non-Christian sources
to question the previous decisions of the tradition is one that has happened many times before.

1   Assimilation

In chapter 1 we alluded briefly to a problem with Spong's understanding
of the classical account of God (namely, he believes mistakenly that it is
too anthropomorphic) and in chapter 2 we dwelt at some length on
Augustine's enthusiasm for Neoplatonism. These two areas will now be
developed a little more to illustrate the way of assimilation. I shall show

how the old Jewish scripture came to be read by Christians through Greek, often Platonist lenses. In so doing a very contrasting account of God emerged.

We start with the account of God in the Hebrew Bible. G.B. Caird in his *The Language and Imagery of the Bible* provides a defense of the anthropomorphism found in the Hebrew Bible. Caird writes, "[B]y far the greater proportion of the biblical language which refers to God is anthropomorphic. At the simplest level God is said to have head, face, eyes, eyelids, ears, nostrils, mouth, voice, arm, hand, palm, fingers, foot, heart, bosom, bowels."[4] And when it comes to divine action and attitudes, Caird lists the following:

> God sees and hears, speaks and answers, calls and whistles, punishes and rewards, wounds and heals, opposes and supports, fights, preserves and rescues, guides and guards, makes and unmakes, plans and fulfills, appoints and sends. He displays love, pity, patience, generosity, justice, mercy, jealousy, anger, regret, hatred, pleasure, and scorn. He is potter, builder, farmer, shepherd, hero, warrior, doctor, judge, king, husband and father.[5]

The impact of these anthropomorphic metaphors is to provide us with a very dynamic picture of God, or, to be accurate, a large number of such pictures. And as Caird noted much of the Hebrew Bible describes the relationship of God to the world in a variety of images. So God is a King, a Lord, a Master, a Father or Mother, and a Savior. A particular role, prevalent and significant in the society from which the text came, becomes a defining image for God.

Underpinning these rich metaphors are a certain set of assumptions about God. It is presumed, for example, that God is everlasting (literally, there was never a time when God was not and there will never be a time when God will cease to be). Human time seems to run parallel with divine time. Of course God has a better perspective on human events than humans themselves, but the message of, say, the prophet and God's words to them seem to be always in the present. So in the famous conversation between Abraham and God on the number of righteous souls in Sodom that would enable the city to be saved, the negotiations move from fifty down to five as a direct negotiation between God and Abraham in the time that the discussion takes. And as Jonah flees from the command of God that he should go and preach to the people of Nineveh, it is a conditional message that is laid upon him: if the people do not repent, then the city will be condemned.[6] Keith Ward is correct when he notes that the assumption in the writings of the prophets is that God is predicting a possible future rather than determining it. Ward writes, "For it is at the heart of the prophetic message that, though God threatens death and destruction, yet he stands ready to change his mind, if the people will only repent. What is the point of preaching, if they cannot? And what is the justification of punishing? The God of the prophets is one who responds to what his people do; and that means that he himself does not ordain everything."[7]

So we have a God who operates in time (perhaps a "divine" time because after all a day to the Lord is but a thousand years, but a time nevertheless), and who engages creatively in conversation and action with the nations of the world, especially the Jewish people. Yet by the time we get to the hero of chapter 2 – Augustine of Hippo – this concept of God has been absorbed into a radically different account. Amongst the key personnel in delivering this shift were the Apologists, of whom the most significant were Justin Martyr (c100–c165), Tatian (c160), Theophilus of Antioch (later second century) and Minucius Felix (second or third century). Where the Apologists were driven strategically to defend Christianity by way of engaging with Greek thought, the great theologians, such as Irenaeus (c120–202), Clement of Alexandria (c150–210), and Origen (c185–254), went further and interpreted their self-understanding as Christians in Hellenistic terminology. By the time we reach Augustine, the doctrines of God's timeless, divine simplicity, and immutability had been firmly established. God was incapable of change, immune to suffering and all kinds of "passive" behavior. God's glory was precisely that God was other than the creation. In this most fundamental of areas – our understanding of God, the Church had **assimilated** certain platonic categories for talking about perfection.

The assimilation of a Platonist view of perfection comes to dominate the Christian tradition. Aquinas in the thirteenth century does not deviate from Augustine in this respect. The reasoning here is worth making explicit. For Plato, it is important to appreciate that perfection is unsurpassable. For Christians, therefore, given that the God they worship is perfect, it follows that God must be unsurpassable, which seem to entail the Augustinian trilogy of three doctrines: timelessness, divine simplicity, and immutability. Although Aquinas, for example, often bases himself on a biblical text, his reasoning owes more to his Greek masters. So on the perfection of God, Aquinas starts with Matthew 5:48, "Be you perfect as also your heavenly Father is perfect," but then enters into conversation with Aristotle, to arrive at the following:

Now God is the first principle, not material, but in the order of efficient cause, which must be perfect. For just as matter, as such, is merely potential, an agent, as such, is in the state of actuality. Hence, the first active principle must needs be most actual, and therefore most perfect; for a thing is perfect in proportion to its state of actuality, because we call that perfect which lacks nothing of the mode of its perfection.[8]

Aquinas is here sharing the Aristotelian expectations of "perfection," taking issue with the view that the cause of everything must be "simply potential and thus most imperfect"[9], and explaining how God as an efficient cause must be perfect. On the doctrine of divine simplicity, Aquinas does not have a biblical text. Instead he cites Augustine who says that "God is truly and absolutely simple"[10] and shows this with a range of arguments about the impossibility of God having composition or parts. Aquinas concludes: "And so, since God is absolute form, or rather absolute being, He can be in no way composite."[11]

From divine perfection and divine simplicity, we arrive at its logical corollaries, namely the immutability of God and the eternity of God. On the immutability of God, Aquinas builds on Malachi 3:6 – "I am the Lord, and I change not" – and brings together his arguments on perfection and simplicity. He provides three arguments: first, he repeats his argument that, as the first cause that changes everything else, God must be beyond change (an argument alluded to under divine simplicity). Second, everything that changes involves composition and given there is no composition in God, then God must be changeless. Here Aquinas explicitly refers back to the doctrine of divine simplicity. And third, Aquinas brings us back to God's perfection. He writes:

But since God is infinite, comprehending in Himself all the plenitude of perfection of all being, He cannot acquire anything new, nor extend Himself to anything whereto He was not extended previously. Hence movement in no way belongs to Him. So, some of the ancients, constrained, as it were, by the truth, decided that the first principle was immovable.[12]

The perfection of God then entails, for Aquinas, the impossibility of all change. Change would entail either improvement or deterioration. Given that God is already the "plenitude of perfection of all being," it seems obvious that God cannot improve; and it would be impossible to conceive of God deteriorating; so Aquinas is driven to the doctrine of divine immutability. Immutability here is not simply a "consistency" of underlying character (the likely meaning of the Malachi verse that Aquinas cites "I am the Lord and I change not"), but a complete impossibility of any change whatsoever. God cannot have additional knowledge or change of movement as a result of a divine action. So from perfection to divine immutability and from divine immutability we are forced to timelessness. Time, at its simplest, is a measure of change. As God does not change at all, then there cannot be any time in God. Aquinas explains it thus:

> The idea of eternity follows immutability, as the idea of time follows move-ment. . . . Hence, as God is supremely immutable, it supremely belongs to Him to be eternal. Nor is He eternal only; but He is His own eternity; whereas, no other being is its own duration, as no other is its own being. Now God is His own uniform being; and hence, as He is His own essence, so He is His own eternity.[13]

There are a host of well-known and endlessly discussed difficulties with this account of God. The hardest is the relationship of God to action: how can a changeless, timeless God create if God has no time in which to do so. Returning to Augustine for a moment, he conceded that the question "what was God doing *before* the world was created?" seems a perfectly proper question, for all actions entail time. My action in making a cup of coffee entails a moment before, a moment during, and a moment after. And to imagine a cup of coffee being made without any moments is simply unintelligible.

The details of Augustine's famous solution need not detain us for long. Suffice to say, Augustine believed that time was the first entity that God created. And in the act of creation, God created all time – the beginning, middle, and end. And in that one timeless action of creating all time, God also did all actions within creation (parting the Red Sea, raising the dead, and bringing about the end of the world). For all the sophistication of this response, we are still left with the problem whether it is coherent to imagine a timeless action involving the creation of time. Let alone the implications for human agency and freedom, if God has timelessly deter-mined all divine actions in the act of creation. Judas, for example, did not have many options if the divine action of the resurrection was already timelessly determined. Nor need we spend any time on challenging the assumption that perfection entails immutability. Once again, let it suffice to say that A.N. Whitehead was surely right when he noted that perfec-tion and change should not been seen as opposites. Surely a perfect entity could be one that dynamically interacts with creation? And therefore the process theologians, at least in this respect, are correct to offer an alternative.

But here, our main point is that we have here an illustration of a non-Christian set of categories being assimilated into the Christian tradition. The timeless idea of God is not biblical. But God's timelessness became an assumption for much of the Christian tradition. At this point it is worth stressing again the distinction between process and content. The process of assimilation is much more important than the content as a result of that assimilation. As already hinted, along with Whitehead and many process and feminist theologians, I am sympathetic to the view that the biblical/platonic assimilation has been problematic. But the process/content distinction means that although we might find the content of the assimilation difficult, we should and can still affirm the process of the assimilation. Indeed we should allow our current understanding of the Christian drama to engage with other non-Christian sources that might lead to a different set of assumptions and ideas being assimilated. Feminists should force the Church to engage with the best of Enlightenment thought, especially in respect to the affirmation of equality. To do so is not a betrayal of the Christian tradition, it is simply an affirmation of the process of assimilation that is entirely grounded and justified by the Christian tradition.

2   Resistance

Having provided an illustration of assimilation, it is now necessary to provide an illustration of resistance. Here we note a significant irony: Hellenism was both assimilated and resisted in the same period. At the same time as the Church was assimilating a Platonic vision of perfection in response to the concept of God, it was resisting the same vision of perfection in respect to the concept of the Incarnation.

Celsus provides a good illustration. Henry Chadwick correctly observes that "there are perhaps few works of the early Christian Church which compare in interest or in importance"[14] with *contra Celsum*. He goes on to explain that the book "stands out as the culmination of the whole apologetic movement of the second and third centuries."[15] Celsus is a second-century opponent of Christianity, whose book *True Discourse* provoked Origen's reply *Contra Celsum* which appeared in the middle of the third century. Celsus' objections to Christianity ranged widely: he found the miraculous content of the Bible implausible and thought that Christianity was destructive of the State. However, Celsus' attack on the Incarnation is helpful for our present purposes. Origen quotes from Celsus' book thus:

> God is good and beautiful and happy, and exists in the most beautiful state. If then He comes down to men, He must undergo change, a change from good to bad, from beautiful to shameful, from happiness to misfortune, and from what is best to what is most wicked. Who would choose a change like this? It is the nature only of a mortal being to undergo change and remolding, whereas it is the nature of an immortal being to remain the same without alteration. Accordingly, God could not be capable of undergoing this change.[16]

The Incarnation therefore appears totally improper. How can the changeless nature of God accommodate a changing human body? It is not necessary to develop in any detail how the tradition responded to this objection. Suffice to say, Origen's response is to draw on the language of Philippians 2:6–11 and distinguished between the essence of Jesus and the human mortal form which he assumed. So he explains:

> He who came down to men was originally "in the form of God" and because of his love to men "emptied himself" that men might be able to receive him. But he underwent no change from good to bad; for "he did no sin"; nor from beautiful to shameful, for "he knew no sin." Nor did he pass from happiness to misfortune; although "he humbled himself," nevertheless he was happy, even when he humbled himself in the way expedient for our race. . . . If the immortal divine Word assume both a human body and a human soul, and by so doing appears to Celsus to be subject to change and remolding, let him learn that the Word remains Word in essence. He suffers nothing of the experience of the body or the soul.[17]

Once again it is not necessary to determine whether this response is adequate. The point is that the process involved here is one of resistance. The doctrine of the incarnation entailed strong resistance to the idea that it was conceptually impossible because of the changelessness of God.

It is worth noting how the doctrine of the Incarnation illustrates both the process of assimilation and the process of resistance. The roots of the expression of the doctrine and even of its very formation are probably grounded in Christian worship. Larry Hurtado writes, "There are basically two main identifying marks of early Christian worship, when considered in its religious context: (1) Christ is reverenced as divine along with God,

and (2) worship of all other gods is rejected."[18] Given that it is a fundamental theistic insight that all worship entails monotheism, it was
inevitable that, if Christ were an object of worship, the doctrine of the
Incarnation would emerge in some form. Put simply, the act of worship
involves the affirmation of ultimate value. Worship assumes that nothing
is greater, larger, or more appropriate as a focus of adoration. For the theist,
the picture of God as omnipotent, omniscient, and perfectly good is not,
as Feuerbach would have us believe, a projection of the finest human
qualities into the skies, but the logical ground of worship. For us to be
confident that our worship is not misplaced, we need to think of God as
not simply powerful, but infinitely powerful (such that God could never
be removed), and not simply as knowledgeable, but infinitely knowledgeable. Richard Swinburne makes this point well, when he starts to list some
of the properties necessary for God to be worthy of worship:

> First, in order to be supremely great and the ultimate source of our well-
> being, he must be perfectly free, for if he is in any way pushed into exer-
> cising his powers sovereignty is not fully his. . . . Fully to deserve worship,
> he must always have existed; he cannot have come into existence at some
> moment of past time. For if he came into existence at some moment of
> past time, his lordship over things would be limited.[19]

Given that it is clear that worship can only be offered to God, it follows
that any worship offered to Jesus must entail the claim that Jesus is God.
The alternative is that it is mistaken to offer worship to Jesus because he
was "just" a human person. However, if worship of Jesus is felt to be
appropriate or even inevitable, then the belief that he is truly divine as
well as truly human, as the Chalcedonian Definition of 451 lays down, is
needed.

Celsus provides a good illustration of the need to resist the view that
perfection cannot involve an incarnation, we find the act of assimilation
involved in the imaginative use of the terminology to formulate the
doctrine of the Incarnation. The terminology is taken, inevitably, from
non-Christian, Greek philosophical sources, and thereby the technical
framework of *hupostasis*, *prosōpon*, and *phusis* is developed. Commenting on
the particular problem of the relationship of the unchanging divine nature
to the human nature, Christopher Stead helpfully summarizes the
outcome:

> This raises two distinct problems: first the general problem, how can God
> act on the world at all without acquiring new, and therefore changed,

perceptions and relationships? Secondly, the specific problem, how can a divine being enter human life without himself suffering a change? The two problems were soon associated, and the Incarnation was commonly described in metaphors intended to suggest that the divine element in Christ suffered no change. Tertullian argued that the Word's becoming flesh did not mean that the Logos was converted into flesh, but rather clothed himself with flesh. . . . Again it was said that the Word assumed human nature as a man assumes an office, or lodged himself in a body as a house or temple; in which case the Platonic model of the soul entering the body is close at hand. All these analogies presuppose that God does something at a moment in time; they cannot secure God's immutability so long as this is interpreted in absolute metaphysical terms. *That* condition could only be met by interpreting all God's actions as new relationships which result from changes in other beings; to use Plato's illustration, . . . Socrates can remain unchanged and yet become smaller than Theaetetus because the young man outgrows him. The model is occasionally used by Christian writers; Origen sees the severity and the kindness of God as a single activity which pro-duces different effects on different recipients, just as the sun's heat both hardens mud and softens wax.[20]

It is not necessary for us to determine the adequacy of these responses. It is simply necessary for us to note the process. The point here is that aspects of contemporary culture needed to be "resisted" as Christians developed their conceptual understanding of the Incarnation. Assimilation and resistance are both found in the writings of the Fathers as Christian doctrine was formulated.

3 Overhearing

The two most important categories in this process are assimilation and resistance. These two, as we have just seen, are pivotal in the development of the doctrine of the Incarnation. Underpinning both is an obligation to listen. To assimilate and to resist we need to attend with care to the dynamic of the non-Christian source. Much of the time this will involve dealing with a text or an authoritative voice within a tradition. However, it is also important to attend to the unpublished source (the etymologi-cal derivation of the word anecdote).[21] In Luke's Gospel, Jesus is depicted as hearing the voices that others miss. So, for example, Jesus noticed Zacchaeus (Luke 19:5) and the women who touched the hem of his garment (Luke 9:45). We need to attend with some energy to the voices of the marginalized and neglected. This is not only an essential precondition of assimilation and resistance, it is also at the heart of a further category. Therefore we turn formally to this third category in the process of engagement, designated **overhearing**. The idea here is simple: overhearing involves the impact of a non-Christian viewpoint upon the Christian tradition. Unlike the first two categories, there are few examples of "overhearing." It is likely that debates in rival traditions have had a greater impact on the tradition than we usually appreciate, but explicit and conscious examples are harder to identify.

The traditional concept of God has been a central issue in the first three chapters of this book. And the example that we took from Aquinas is clearly a result of overhearing. David Burrell makes the case persuasively in his delightful book, *Knowing the Unknowable God*. Burrell explains that "the received doctrine of God in the West was already an intercultural, interfaith achievement."[22] Aquinas refines and clarifies the account of God after "overhearing" the debates surrounding Ibn Sina (Avicenna) (980–1037) and Maimonides (1135–1204). Burrell explains that:

> Aquinas respected Rabbi Moses and Avicenna as fellow travelers in an arduous intellectual attempt to reconcile the horizons of philosophers of ancient Greece, notably Aristotle, with those reflecting a revelation originating in ancient Israel, articulated initially in the divinely inspired writings of Moses. . . . We may wonder at Aquinas's welcoming assistance from Jewish and Muslim quarters, especially when we reflect on the character of his times: the popular response to the call of arms of the crusades as well as a nearly universal impression on the part of Christians that the new covenant had effectively eclipsed the old. Aquinas may have shared these sentiments, for all we know, yet his overriding concern in reaching out to other thinkers was always to learn from them in his search for the truth of the matters at hand. In this respect, he epitomized the medieval respect for learning, with its conviction that "truth was where one found it." So he was more inclined to examine the arguments of thinkers than their faith, trusting in the image of the creator in us all to search out traces of the divine handiwork, a theological premise that will prove useful in guiding our explorations into Aquinas' reliance on Jewish and Christian thinkers, and better than attributing to him an ecumenical or interfaith perspective *avant la lettre.*[23]

Burrell is correct to stress that Aquinas' use of Avicenna and Maimonides should not be interpreted as a modern interfaith meeting. Aquinas has much that was very critical to say about both Judaism and

Islam. Hence the suggestion here that we should use the word "overhears." The process is indirect — in this case the authors are accessed entirely through the texts — and then adapted into the Christian tradition.

The two key ideas that Burrell credits Avicenna and Maimonides with are as follows. From Ibn Sina, Aquinas derived help with his need to distinguish "existing" from "essence." Aquinas inherited a discourse where Aristotelian distinctions had been constrained within a Neoplatonic scheme of emanation. This blurs the distinction between the creation and the creator. Ibn Sina provides the notion of "essence in itself." It is not necessary to identify all the steps, but the net result, explains Burrell, is that "through a notion of creation, the difference of creator from creation will also mark what distinguishes the individual existent from its essential explanations."[24] It is a related difficulty with which Moses Maimonides helps Aquinas, namely, the relationship of God to time and the creation. This was also linked to the authority of the Aristotelian schema. Maimonides, in his *Guide of the Perplexed*, introduces three positions. The first is the position of those who believe in the Law of Moses. This is simply the view that God created *ex nihilo*. The second is the position of Plato that views matter as eternal sitting alongside a deity that is eternal and used by the deity as material for the creative work. And the third is the position of Aristotle from whom the changelessness of God must involve the eternity of the Universe. Burrell claims that locating Aristotle alongside Plato and Moses was the first achievement of this text for Aquinas. As Aquinas overhears the arguments of Maimonides, he finds a solution he needs for his own problem about the relationship of the eternity of God to the possible everlasting nature of the world.

Further examination of the ways in which Aquinas uses Ibn Sina and Maimonides are not necessary for my purpose. Once again I return to the point that it is helpful to distinguish between "content" of the tradition and the "process" of the tradition. In terms of content, we do have certain commitments (the Trinity and the Incarnation, although of course understood differently in different periods), but this should not be defining feature of orthodoxy. The "process" introduces the subject of the ways in which the tradition has interacted or engaged with non-Christian sources. This chapter has identified three: "assimilation," "resistance," and "overhearing."

The three-fold structure of engagement does have its parallel in the work of the persons within the Trinity. "Overhearing" is made possible by the Christian conviction that God's Holy Spirit is at work in the lives of all people and all cultures. As Gavin D'Costa, in a different context, noted:

[I]f we have good reasons to believe that the Spirit and Word are present and active in the religions of the world (in ways that cannot, a priori, be specified), then it is intrinsic to the vocation of the church to be attentive to the world religions. Otherwise, it willfully closes itself to the Spirit of truth, which it requires to remain faithful to the truth and be guided more deeply into it. The doctrine of the Spirit thereby provides the narrative space in which the testimonies of people from the world religions, in their own words and lives, can unmask the false ideologies and distorted narrative practices within Christian communities. At the same time, it allows Christians to be aware of God's self-disclosure within the world's religions, and through this process of learning, enrich its own self-understanding. Without listening to this testimony, Christians cease to be faithful to their own calling as Christians, in being inattentive to God.[25]

Engagement in the form of assimilation is clearly linked with the work of the second person of the Trinity. God becoming embodied and human is an act of assimilation. And engagement in the form of resistance is part of the work of the Father. Although the creation is totally dependent on God and, as shall become clearer in various parts of the book, I believe that the creation is part of God, God is not reducible to the creation. We should retain a sense that the creator is not simply the creation. In that sense there is a "resistance" between God and the creation (i.e., a proper and appropriate distance). The point is that the triune God that we worship makes these three aspects to engagement possible.[26]

Over the next seven chapters these three approaches will be illustrated in respect to a range of modern problems facing the church.

4

ASSIMILATION: ENGAGEMENT WITH HUMAN RIGHTS

Having defended in the first three chapters the need for engagement, the task now is to embark on this engagement and reflect on the shape of theology that emerges from the process. The first case study is human rights. The argument of this chapter is that human rights can and has been assimilated by the mainstream Christian traditions. It is assimilated, even though, it is a discourse firmly rooted in modernity. It is the contention of this chapter that assimilation is important not simply for the Christian tradition, but also for the discourse of human rights. It is my view that the claims embedded in human rights discourse are difficult to sustain unless there is a theistic worldview underpinning it. The chapter will proceed in the following way: first there will be a brief outline of the United Nations Declaration on Human Rights. Then we will look at Roman Catholic, Orthodox, and Protestant justifications of the discourse. This is, I shall suggest, a natural contender for assimilation by all these strands of Christianity.

The United Nations Declaration on Human Rights is a remarkable document. It is a clear and unequivocal statement of certain fundamental values: it sets a standard for national conduct which is demanding; and it places an appropriate value on human life. It is, therefore, ironic that the debates surrounding the Declaration in 1948 were not straightforward. The fact that it is a Declaration rather than part of the Charter was due to the lack of agreement between member states. Although there were no votes against the Declaration, there were eight abstentions.[1] Unlike the United Nations Charter, which was formulated at the same time, the Declaration was not a legally binding multilateral treaty. Today the Declaration is widely recognized as capturing certain fundamental truths about humanity, but fifty years ago, the Declaration was much more contentious.

Christians are accustomed to complicated historical events giving birth to real discoveries about the nature of God's world and God's expectations of humanity. Our history has numerous examples: the birth of our canon of Scripture was surrounded by disagreement; and the Creeds were formulated at meetings which were fraught with political pressures. For Christians, truths about the nature of humanity often emerge amidst controversy; it is only in retrospect that they become almost obvious.

The United Nations Declaration on Human Rights has clearly captured certain fundamental truths well. Almost all Christians today would want to endorse the declaration. Historically this is less obvious. Indeed the church in the past has been a prime violator of human rights. It is worth pausing and acknowledging both the extent of such violations and the reasons for them.

Although the historical details are extremely complex, broadly the following disposition characterized the church right up to the modern era. When the church has been in a position of power, the underlying assumption made by the church is that no person has "rights" against God. God is the creator and God is entitled to do whatever God wants to that that God has made. Given the will of God is expressed through the church, the church ought not tolerate different religious beliefs or lifestyles. So the church did not agree that people have an entitlement to say or write whatever they think.

Historically, then such an outlook meant that the record of Christian oppression of non-Christian groups is a poor one. Unlike the Qur'an which has an explicit celebration of diversity and an obligation to protect the "People of the Book," the church treated both Jews and Muslims badly. Now all of this is well known and Christians today should "repent" of their historical intolerance and cruelty, however, it is worth stressing that this is only one side of the story. The other side of the story involves a church that partly provided the metaphysics and some of the concepts that became important in the emergence of human rights. So although it is true that the language of rights is a relatively modern construct, the Christian tradition can take some of the credit for the emergence of such language.

The Roman Catholic tradition of natural law has clearly been important. Natural law provides a means to discover moral truths that are true for all people. It does not depend on revelation, instead, simply by using human reason, every person can in theory discover in nature what is right and wrong (though we may need guidance in order to do so). Natural law in due course generated the language of rights in two ways. First, it provided a potential methodology. The task was to spot God's purposes in creation. Observation of human nature enabled people to appreciate that we are intended to reproduce, acquire knowledge, and (if one believed) worship God. Thinking in these ways eventually generated the language of rights because it would be wrong to thwart these God intended ends of human life. Second, natural law stresses the way in which all authority ultimately resides in God. Even the royal authority of monarchs is granted by God. And therefore there is a higher authority that even the absolute ruler must recognize. The Monarch is not allowed to go against the Eternal law and the Eternal law recognizes a certain fundamental right for each person to live and thrive, which may, it is true, require careful interpretation if it is to be properly applied.

Secular versions of human rights language only emerged with Enlightenment philosophy. Three alternatives were suggested to replace the God of natural law. The first was nature. For example, each person is naturally created free and therefore protecting this freedom is an obligation on legitimate government, or natural law. The second was reason; that is, there are certain basic intuitions which are built into our minds. And the third was consensus; that is, the cultural convergence of many nations around certain ethical fundamentals. Difficulties with all these strategies were rapidly spotted. Jeremy Bentham, for example, insisted that "[T]here are no such things as natural rights – no such things as rights anterior to the establishment of government – no such things as natural rights opposed to, in contradistinction to, legal. . . . Natural rights is simple nonsense: natural and imprescriptable rights, rhetorical nonsense, – nonsense upon stilts."[2]

The major alternative to a version of natural law became positivism. Building on David Hume's dictum that one cannot derive "an ought from an is," thereby attacking the assumptions of natural law, John Austin suggested that valid laws are commands of the ruling political power backed up with appropriate sanctions. Rights on this view are purely empirical and, probably, local. They are the state laws that protect individuals and their property. But the weakness of this is obvious: the state determines what is right and if the state, for example, determines that slavery for a certain group is acceptable, then on this account there are no grounds to object. Nor does it help to insist that law ought to be linked with the moral codes of the community as a whole as H.L.A. Hart's suggests. After all, Nazi Germany did have significant support from its national community for the anti-Semitic policies of the regime.

So for a Christian it is clear: Christianity is not just committed to human rights; rather, human rights need a theistic framework to survive.

Human rights are making universal claims: all people everywhere are entitled to claim these rights, however hard it may be to define or apply them
precisely in varying societies. Human rights i.e., transcend all cultural differences: they assert boldly that no cultural difference is allowed to undermine these fundamentals.

It is helpful to divide rights into negative and positive rights. Raymond
Plant explains that "a negative right would be a right to be free from coer-
cion, interference, power, intimidation and so forth."[3] Negative rights are
all those which forbid interference by others, for example, a right to life
(i.e., not to have one's life taken away), a right to freedom of speech (i.e.,
not to have one's speech restricted), and a right to assembly and travel
(i.e., not to be denied the freedom to meet whom one wants or travel
where one would like). For Christians, these rights express what it means
for people to be created in the "Image of God"(Genesis 1:26–7). This
means that humans share in a special way something of the Creator. In
the patristic period, Augustine insisted being made in God's image meant
human rationality which reflected the wisdom of God, while Athanasius
wanted to emphasize our unique potential for relationship with God.
When we talk about the "Image of God" it is important to retain both
of these strands and to identify those human qualities that make these
strands possible. So the Image is: Human rationality and relationality that
depend on (a) the capacity for language, which is the distinctive gift of
the rational faculty, (b) the capacity for love and intimacy, supremely with
God, (c) the gift of freedom, and (d) our moral awareness. The Image
requires that we are afforded certain basic dignities that enable us to take
responsibility for the privilege of being created.

The obvious problem with negative human rights is that for many
people such freedoms are luxuries that they are not in a position to appreciate. Karl Marx complained that "none of the so-called rights of man
goes beyond egoistic man, man as he is in civil society, namely an individual withdrawn behind his private interests and whims and separated
from the community."[4] Negative human rights, explains Marx, are
intended for the anxious capitalist who is desperate to protect his property. For the homeless or starving, freedom of speech or assembly mean
very little. The capacity to enjoy these rights depend on a certain basic
standard of living. This is recognized repeatedly in the Christian tradition,
a long time before Marx. The prophet Isaiah writes:

> Ah, you who make iniquitous decrees,
> who write oppressive statutes,

to turn aside the needy from justice
and to rob the poor of my people of their right,
that widows may be your spoil,
and that you may make the orphans your prey!
What will you do on the day of punishment,
in that calamity that will come from far away? (Isaiah 10:1–3)

The poor according to Isaiah have their right which the rulers and the rich deny them. So we need positive human rights, which are nicely defined by Raymond Plant as follows: "A positive right would be a right to a resource of some sort, health care, education and social security for example."[5] These minimum positive human rights consist in the satisfaction of certain basic needs to exist and to flourish.

A version of natural law might be able to help us identify that minimum. We can observe that humans have certain basic needs that need fulfilling if they are going to develop their full potential. We need accommodation, sufficient to eat, an education to develop the mind, and some form of work. These are the positive human rights that are protected in the Declaration.

This sort of argument has been endorsed by Pope John XXIII in his encyclical of 1963, *Pacem in Terris*. Pope John XXIII's argument makes natural law central. He writes, "But the Creator of the world has imprinted in man's heart an order which his conscience reveals to him and enjoins him to obey: This shows that the obligations of the law are written in their hearts; their conscience utters its own testimony."[6] Natural law which shaped the language of human rights is, for Pope John XXIII, the best reason for continuing to affirm human rights.

In the subsequent paragraphs, he argues that the innate dignity of people entitles them to all the basic human rights. So he affirms the right to life, to bodily integrity, and adequate support for development of life (paragraph 11); the entitlement for respect and the right to freedom in searching for truth (paragraph 12); the right to enjoy culture and education (paragraph 13); and the right to worship God (paragraph 14); the right to marry and work (paragraphs 15 and 18); and the right to property, movement, and juridical protection (paragraphs 21, 25, 27). Primarily the argument in almost every case is grounded in the natural law acknowledgment of the dignity of all people. The Pope provides a Roman Catholic justification of the Declaration on Human Rights.

Links can be made between the Roman Catholic justification of human rights and the Eastern Orthodox traditions. Both share a conviction that as creatures created in the Image of God so we are granted the capacity to recognize certain fundamental constraints in our treatment of each other. According to the Greek Fathers, this natural law is best embodied in the Ten Commandments, although equivalent statements are found in other cultures and religions.[7] From the Decalogue, certain human rights are implied. Stanley Harkas explains:

> At the heart of this Eastern Christian view of natural law is fair and equi-table treatment, a right to which all persons appeal on the basis of their humanity. The natural law establishes criteria which, when seen from the perspective of the object of the law's provisions, become rights. "Do not murder" recognizes the right to life. "Do not steal" identifies the right to hold property. "Do not commit adultery" establishes the right to the invi-olateness of the marriage relationship, and so on.[8]

Arguments that persuade the Roman Catholic and Eastern Orthodox tra-ditions, do not necessarily appeal to Protestants. Historically Protestants have tended to feel less happy with natural law, although there are signif-icant exceptions. Central to Reformed theology is the doctrine of the Fall. All people have sinned, and one of the consequences of human sin is the distortion of human reason. Sin makes it difficult for us to always recognize what is right. So, although Protestants would not want to defend human rights on natural law grounds, they do have their own arguments. Protestants are equally committed to the dignity of all people. After all, explains J. Robert Nelson, "God created each one; God loves each one; and Jesus Christ died for the sins of each one that each might be saved. Inasmuch as you did an act of mercy for one of the least of these persons, you did it for Jesus Christ. One of the least! No one is left out. The Creator who marks the fall to earth of each perishing sparrow surely holds dearer by far each human person. These and similar biblical insights and affirmations are fundamental to the religious and moral perspective held by Protestants.[9]

Jürgen Moltmann is probably the best-known Protestant defender of human rights. His argument is overtly Trinitarian and theological. Moltmann's argument is grounded in the Bible. He outlines the central biblical themes which he describes as liberation, covenant, and claim. In the Hebrew Scriptures, God **liberates** the people from slavery; God forms a **covenantal** relationship (one requiring both rights and duties) with them, and through this relationship God **claims** humanity to realize their original destiny. In the New Testament these themes are developed through the i.e., forming power of Christ. Moltmann writes:

> The biblical witness to liberation, covenant, and God's claim leads to a cor-responding Christian practice and theology. The universal presupposition of the particular history of God's dealing with Israel and with Christianity is found in the reality that the God who liberates and redeems them is the Creator of all human beings and things. Thus in God's liberating and redeeming action the original destiny of human beings is both experience and fulfilled. In the "image of God" concept, the divine claim upon human beings is expressed. Human rights to life, freedom, community, and self-determination mirror God's claim upon persons, because in all their rela-tionships in life − human beings with each other and creatures with the creation − they are destined to reflect the image of God.[10]

From this thoroughly biblical basis, Moltmann goes on to defend both negative and positive human rights. Moltmann also argues that this foun-dation places an obligation to witness to the universal truth about God's activity, by calling on all people to observe these fundamental human rights.

The Christian tradition, therefore, provides three ways to justify human rights language. One from creation and natural law; the second from the nature of the Decalogue; and the third from the biblical themes of liber-ation, slavery, and claim. Naturally these arguments overlap and they should not been as mutually exclusive. Instead they provide a firm basis for human rights.

At this point some Christians might object that talk of rights is human arrogance. It is absurd for puny humans to talk about rights. After all, we do not have any rights over against God. God can do whatever God likes with us, or as St. Paul puts it: "Hath not the potter power over the clay, of the same lump to make one vessel with honor, and another with dis-honor"(Romans 9:20–1). Bishop Richard Harries considers this objection when he writes, "[T]he conclusion is not what Paul would have us believe. For the potter has not just tossed off the pot. He has worked at if for day after day, indeed for eon after eon. He has literally sweated blood over it. He has, literally, put his heart and his soul into it. The pot that is pro-duced, flawed though it may be, is infinitely precious to the creator. Or we can put it another way. God creates and at once recognizes the value of what he has created. Here is the foundation for a consciously Christian approach to human rights: God makes man in his own image and respects the worth and dignity of what he has created."[11] At this point, Harries brings the Christian arguments together: it is the fact that God has created us, loved us, framed commandments for human behavior, and promises us continued life beyond the grave that requires recognition for the fundamental human rights of all people.

Using the language of human rights is not a concession to modernity. Christians committed to the truth of the tradition can find entirely orthodox reasons for supporting the United Nations Declaration on Human Rights. Granted the behavior of the church has not always recognized this; it has in the past and continues in certain places in the present to fail to recognize the inherent dignity of all people, especially those who disagree with her. But the intolerant and cruel are the betrayers of the Christian tradition, not the upholders of it.

One major irony of modernity is that the secular West has made the language of rights central to its social discourse while at the same time undermining any possible justification of such language. If ultimately humans are nothing more than complex bundles of atoms emerging from a blind and random process and facing extinction when we die, then it is difficult to see how we can affirm the inherent dignity of people. At best, it becomes a subjective decision: despite the meaninglessness of it all, I will affirm people. The problem arises with those who are not interested in affirming people: those who do not recognize human rights and are willing to violate them. To simply exhort them to behave better is not going to persuade. Humans need reasons. Secularization when it feeds on naturalistic assumptions about the world cannot provide a reason. Theism is essential for such talk to endure. The task now is for the theistic traditions of the world to build an alliance. We need to witness to the reality of God that recognizes the intrinsic dignity of all people and therefore calls on all people to respect the fundamental human rights.

One postscript is necessary for this chapter. The task of engagement and assimilation has revealed the importance of a theistic underpinning of human rights discourse. In other words, when it comes to human rights, Christians are on strong ground. We should be using the language with self-confidence. It is therefore tragic that some Christian groups, in the United Kingdom, felt it necessary to oppose the Human Rights Act (passed into law in October 2000). Martyn Percy is entirely right when he explains that a condition of participation in civil society is that one can affirm these fundamentals. So he writes:

The Human Rights Act offers the opportunity for churches to recover their public role, and rediscover their prophetic voice in the political realm. In this sense, churches need to move beyond a simplistic dichotomy in which they either say an uncritical "yes" to the Act, or seek to secure a potentially damaging legal exemption. A wiser approach to the culture of rights enshrined in the Act would be to go with the flow of the legislation, with a combination of passion and coolness, recognizing that it is only when public participation has been assented to that the prophetic can flourish when it is needed.[12]

The assimilation of human rights discourse into Christianity does have implications. These almost certainly include internal practice within the church, but also there are implications for other issues and positions that the church should take. The dynamic of assimilation followed by further engagement is the issue to which we turn next.

5

RESISTANCE: THE HERESY OF STATE SOVEREIGNTY AND THE RELIGIOUS IMPERATIVE FOR INTERVENTION TO DEFEND HUMAN RIGHTS

In the last chapter we documented how Christians should be able to assimilate the language of human rights. The act of assimilation, I shall now show, carries implications. This dynamic assimilate and think through the implications is a vital part of engagement. I shall now show that the discourse of human rights has implications for the concept of state sovereignty.

The argument of this chapter is therefore this: the concept of absolute state sovereignty, which was born in the seventeenth century when nations denied the higher authority of the papacy,[1] is now, at long last, coming to an end due (among other factors) to the acknowledgment of the higher authority of human rights.[2] Many would want to interpret this as a triumph for modernity and classical liberal individualism. However, if the argument of the previous chapter is accepted, then this change is best interpreted as a triumph for a religious view, because the justification of human rights needs religion. I shall show that this change is best interpreted as a triumph for a religious worldview, because the justification of human rights needs religion.

1 Origins of State Sovereignty

It is generally agreed that the conflicts between the centralizing monarchies of Europe (especially the Tudors in England, the Valois and the Bourbons in France, and the Habsburgs in Spain) and the authority of the Roman Catholic Church are the trigger for the concept of state sovereignty. Two key writers are responsible for explicitly formulating the idea. Jean Bodin (1530–96) explained in his *The Six Books of the Commonweal*[3] (1583) how social and political stability requires an absolute sovereign who makes the law. Law, for Bodin, literally reflects the will of the sovereign and the sovereign is, technically, above the law, although interestingly still constrained by natural law. The other key writer is Thomas Hobbes on whom it is necessary to dwell at rather more length.

Hobbes was born in 1588 and died 91 years later in 1679. He was living in turbulent times: he witnessed "the accession to the throne of three British monarchs, beginning with the first Stuart, James I; the Civil War and the execution of Charles I in 1649; the establishment and dissolution of Cromwell's Protectorate; and the Restoration of 1660."[4] Perhaps it is because he lived in such turbulent times that he insisted on the sheer necessity of the absolute power of the sovereign. Skeptical of the existence of an active deity and utterly unpersuaded of the legitimacy of the language of rights, he argued for absolute sovereignty. *Leviathan* starts with a striking anthropology: humankind is basically a complex machine involving certain physical interactions. He documents the survival instinct and then insists that all people are involved in a basic power struggle. He summarizes thus:

> So that in the first place, I put for a generall inclination of all mankind, a perpetuall and restlesse desire of Power after power, that ceaseth onely in Death. And the cause of this, is not always that a man hopes for a more intensive delight, than he has already attained to; or that he cannot be content with a moderate power: but because he cannot assure the power and means to live well, which he hath present, without the acquistion of more.[5]

It is from this rather depressing anthropology that he gets a rather depressing analysis of what the world would be like if there were no absolute ruler. And it is here that we get the famous quote:

Whatsoever therefore is consequent to a time of Warre, where every man is Enemy to every man; the same is consequent to the time, wherein men live without other security, than what their own strength, and their own invention shall furnish them withall. In such a condition, there is no place for Industry; because the fruit thereof is uncertain: and consequently no Culture of the Earth; no Navigation, nor use of the commodities that may be imported by Sea; no commodious Building; no Instruments of moving, and removing such things as require much force; no Knowledge of the face of the Earth; no account of Time; no Arts; no Letters; no Society; and which is worst of all, continuall feare, and danger of violent death; And the life of man, solitary, poore, nasty, brutish, and short.[6]

The solution is simple: we must transfer all our rights to the sovereign. We must agree to live under the complete authority of the sovereign. So Hobbes writes,

The only way to erect such a Common Power, as may be able to defend them from the invasion of Forraigners, and the injuries of one another, and thereby to secure them in such sort, as that by their owne industrie, and by the fruites of the Earth, they may nourish themselves and live contendedly; is, to conferre all their power and strength upon one Man, or upon one Assembly of men, that may reduce all their Wills, by plurality of voices, unto one Will: which is as much as to say, to appoint one man, or Assembly of men, to beare their Person; and every one to owne, and acknowledge himselfe to be Author of whatsoever he that so beareth their Person, shall Act, or cause to be Acted, in those things which concerne the Common Peace and Safetie; and therein to submit their Wills, every one to his Will, and their Judgments, to his Judgment. This is more than Consent, or Concord; it is a reall Unitie of them all.[7]

It was, of course, the Reformation which had afforded the opportunity for this doctrine to be implemented most clearly. The Reformation disentangled the rulers and princes from the "interference" of the Roman Church. Luther provided the theological justification for the nations; Calvin provided the justification for the cities. However, at this stage, it is a "landlord spirit" sovereignty. In other words, the people and land are, ultimately, a possession of the ruler.[8]

But the modern sense of national sovereignty had to wait until the nineteenth century.[9] The doctrine that a people, coming to be seen as those identified with a particular culture,[10] are entitled to determine their own destiny without outside interference required the French Revolution. Rousseau (1712–78) was a key influence: he was responsible for rejecting the authority of the monarch and displacing it with the "will of the people," expressed in the legislator, hard though it is to give sense to his theory of the "general will," it proved all to easy for it to function as the justification for dictatorship, whether of Robespierre or Napoleon.

Naturally there are a whole range of difficulties involved in this account of sovereignty. The history of Germany illustrates some of the key difficulties. What exactly is culture? One obvious answer is that it is a shared language. However, if that is the case, then it was almost inevitable that the idea of the "greater Germany" was going to emerge. Nevertheless we now have an idea of a people, sharing a certain culture, living in a certain place should have complete control over their own affairs. It is this account of sovereignty that came to dominate international law. David Forsythe, the eminent political theorist, insists that a very strong account of international law exists right up until 1945. He writes:

> Prior to 1945, the relation between an individual and the state controlling "its" citizens was a matter for that state alone. The state was sovereign in an almost absolute sense, exercising supreme legal authority within its jurisdiction. International law existed primarily to keep states apart, and thus prevent conflicts, by confirming separate national jurisdictions.[11]

It is worth at this point noting the significant theological factors that lie behind or may be said to be implicit in these developments. The first is a deeply pessimistic anthropology. Hobbes' pessimistic view of humanity has much in common with some of the convictions in the Reformed tradition. However, of course, the older and more Catholic anthropology insisted that the Image of God is not eradicated by the Fall. Although we have propensities to selfishness, the fact we are made in the Image of God and therefore have the capacity to reason and evaluate morally means that we still have the capacity, even in our unredeemed state, for goodness. Second, we note the theological aspect of the displacement of the Roman Catholic Church by state sovereignty, with its potential for tyranny.[12] It became customary in Protestant circles to justify this by appeal to Romans 13:1. But this is to ignore the much more substantial theme of "responsible rule" developed in the writings of the eighth-century BCE prophets. In the Hebrew Bible, the prophetic tradition (e.g., Amos, Micah) took a much less absolute view of rulers' powers, e.g., imposing on them certain duties towards the poor. And in medieval discussion, there was much

thought about the rights and wrongs of limiting the power of unjust monarchs. The sense of an unanswerable "sovereign ruler," who is entitled to
do absolutely anything, is not found in the Christian tradition.

However, at this point, it is necessary to turn to three contemporary
challenges to the concept of national sovereignty.

2   The Challenge to State Sovereignty

These three case studies explore different aspects of how the concept
of national sovereignty is now under challenge. The first is the Kosovo
conflict, which I shall interpret as **direct military** defense of human
rights; the second is the participation of Herr Haider in the Austrian
coalition, which led to a **diplomatic** defense of human rights; and the
third is the attempted extradition of Senator Pinochet to Spain, which is
a **legal** challenge to state sovereignty, based on consideration of human
rights.

Probably the most familiar example is the Kosovo conflict. Therefore
this will only be discussed briefly and the focus will be on responding to
the critics. However, more interesting, partly because they are less discussed, are the Pinochet extradition case in the United Kingdom and the
Herr Haider participation in the Austrian coalition.

The Kosovo conflict

We start then with the Kosovo conflict. Kosovo has been a small province
and part of Serbia since 1989. (Although it was part of Serbia prior to
this date, in Tito's time it had a measure of autonomy.) The vast majority
of the population are Albanian Muslims (90%), although the province has
various special historical and religious associations for the Serbian minority. The NATO action was intended to assist the Kosovan Albanian whose
rights had been grossly violated in recent years: the strategy was to launch
an air war against Yugoslav military activity against the Albanians. The conflict started on 24 March, 1999 and concluded on 9 June, 1999.

There are a number of striking features about this conflict. First, NATO
was taking military action for the first time in its history. The traditional
military alliance, constructed to oppose the Eastern Communist bloc, has
been increasingly involved in what were classified as strictly peace-keeping
activities since the end of the Cold War. Second, human rights was the
justification invoked for the military action. This, Forsythe notes, is an

interesting extension of the concept of national self-interest or "vital interests." Forsythe writes:

> In Kosovo in particular, NATO member states defined their vital interests to include a liberal democratic "neighborhood" in Europe. Just as European states had considered human rights important enough to merit two supranational regional courts that restricted state sovereignty in the name of human rights, so they, plus Canada and the United States, considered repression of ethnic Albanians in Kosovo important enough to merit military intervention – having come to feel highly uncomfortable with not undertaking military intervention in Bosnia during 1992–4.[13]

The central complaint from critics of the action in Kosovo is that (a) the United States and its allies showed themselves very selective about which "conflicts" to embark on by way of military action, and (b) the action exacerbated the humanitarian crisis. Noam Chomsky is a representative voice. On the first complaint, Chomsky draws parallels between Serbia and Turkey: the Serbs abused their power with Kosovan Albanians, while the Turks have treated the Kurds equally badly. The United States and Britain have continued to support their ally Turkey, but insisted on attacking Yugoslavia. In my view, Reinhold Niebuhr taught us that the multiplicity of factors that determine the behavior of a nation are never going to be "pure" or "uncomplicated."[14] "Mixed motives" on the part NATO were inevitable. In addition examples of comparable situations, where perhaps military action ought to be taken simply means that more military action is needed in this world not that the Kosovo conflict was wrong. To be unable to remedy all "ills" is no reason to remedy none. On the second, Chomsky writes, "With full awareness of the likely consequences, Clinton and Blair decided in favor of a war that led to a radical escalation of ethnic cleansing along with other deleterious effects."[15] This is tendentious. The simplest explanation for the decisions of Blair and Clinton was, as Forsythe notes, their own growing sense that they should have taken military action on behalf of the Bosnian Muslims, and not confined themselves to a peace-keeping role. War inevitably provokes questions about comparative outcomes: inactivity earlier did not help the Bosnian Muslims (that was information Blair and Clinton already had) and it was not wrong to hope that military activity might help the Kosovan Albanians. One could argue that perhaps the military action did, initially, exacerbate the refugee crisis, but in the longer term it is likely that the total problem was mitigated by the military action: most refugees returned to their homes (though many Kosovan Serbs felt pushed into exile in their turn). These are, of course, the difficult choices that face world leaders.

I find myself sympathetic to the NATO action. The major difficulties with the military operation were more linked to competence than to justification. The bombing of the Chinese embassy in Belgrade on 7 May, 1999 is a good example of military error. However, when it comes to justification, the key factor was human rights. Although Kosovo was a province of Yugoslavia, NATO powers decided not to tolerate a tyranny which was abusing the rights of a minority population. Human rights were held to override the traditional doctrine of national sovereignty.

Turning now to two further and less obvious examples (one diplomatic, the other legal), we find the same movement of opinion and behavior. Respect for human rights is undermining national autonomy. The first is the reaction of the European Union to the inclusion of the Freedom Party into the Government of Austria.

Herr Haider and the Austrian government

Jörg Haider was the leader of the right-wing Freedom Party from 1986 until March 2000. From a stronghold in Carinthia, where Haider is the state governor, he had created a significant national presence. Indeed in October 1999 the Freedom Party picked up 27.22 percent of the vote, while the ruling Social Democrats had 33 percent, and the conservative People's Party, the junior partner in the ruling coalition, 26.9 percent. The Social Democrats and the People's Party found it difficult to form a new government. So on Friday 4 February, 2000, the Freedom Party joined the People's Party and formed a coalition. President Thomas Klestil, who was unhappy at the development, required the two parties to make a clear declaration, which included the following:

> Austria accepts her responsibility arising out of the tragic history of the 20th century and the horrendous crimes of the National Socialist regime.
> . . .
> Our country is facing up to the light and dark sides of its past and to the deeds of all Austrians, good and evil, as its responsibility. Nationalism, dictatorship and intolerance brought war, xenophobia, bondage, racism and mass murder. The singularity of the crimes of the Holocaust are without precedent in history. . . .
> The federal government stands for respect, tolerance and understanding for all human beings irrespective of their origin, religion or philosophy.
> . . .

The federal government works for an Austria in which xenophobia, anti-Semitism and racism have no place.[16]

At this point, one might wonder exactly what the difficulty was. The answer was that while Herr Haider turned out to be happy to sign such declarations, he had long sent contrary messages to his supporters. It was clear that Haider had some "affection" for the Nazis. He took the newspaper *Kurier* to court claiming that it was "correct and respectable" to describe the concentration camps as "punishment centers." A case, incidentally, that he lost.[17] His parents were very committed Nazis and he expressed frequently his sympathies for those who fought for the Nazis in the World War Two. Most recently he told a group of World War Two veterans who fought in the Austrian army with the Nazis that "it is unacceptable that the past of our fathers and grandparents is reduced to that of criminals." And he continued to insist that the veterans were "good citizens who sacrificed their youth for Austria."[18]

In terms of manifesto commitments, the most sinister theme is the strong position taken on immigration. Two chapters of the Program of the Austrian Freedom Party slowly develop the argument against immigration. Chapter 3 is called "Austria first"; and chapter 4 is called "the right to cultural identity." Having stressed the entitlement of Austria to be proud of its past, the Program insists on the preservation of existing cultural traditions and then culminates in the insistence that the country is too small to absorb further immigration. So the Program and uncontrolled immigration to Austria. The protective requirement of this fundamental right to a home country makes clear that Austria because of its small size, its density of population and its limited resources cannot be a country of immigration."[19] The next chapter developed a religious justification for cultural homogeneity, namely that Christianity is central to the cultural life of both Austria and Europe.

Leaving aside the Nazi sympathies of Haider, it was understandable that many Europeans felt uncomfortable with this Program. The Foreign Secretary of the United Kingdom spoke for many when he said: "We have made clear our deep concern and distaste at the inclusion in the Austrian Government of a far-right party which appeals to xenophobia. The measures which Britain agreed on Monday with thirteen other EU Member States will come into force as soon as the new coalition takes office."[20]

The actual sanctions introduced by the European Union were almost entirely diplomatic. Austrian ministers would not be "received" by other EU members and no EU member would visit Austria. So, for example,

Prince Charles, on advice from the British Foreign Office, canceled a planned visit to Austria. Washington and the United States government took comparable action.

The sanctions by the European Union finally came to an end in mid-September. In July the European Union referred the issue to the European Court of Human Rights and a panel of three was sent to investigate the situation. Although they found that minorities were not treated badly, indeed in some respects better than in some other European Union countries, they were very critical of the Freedom Party and deplored Haider description of the Nazi concentration camps as punishment camps. Overall, however, the report concluded that it would be unhelpful to continue the sanctions: the message that human rights mattered had been sent, and to continue the sanctions would, it was felt, heighten a sense of "persecution" that was developing in Austria. In the light of this recommendation, the view taken by the European Union was that the seven-month sanction campaign was "useful," but the time had come to bring sanctions to an end.[21]

For my purposes it is important to note the following. First, we see the difference between pre-1945 and post-1945 dramatically illustrated. Whereas the pre-war sentiment was that no nation was entitled to interfere in the elections of another, this quite definitely was not the case here. Other European powers felt that the potential parallels and echoes between Hitler's doctrines and Haider's sympathies formed grounds for strong diplomatic pressure and isolation. It is worth noting that they only eased the sanctions when they were persuaded that the human rights of minorities were being protected. Second, the European Union is an example of an international quasi-federation which has certain legal powers to challenge the policies of the elected governments of its members. Undoubtedly one significant driving force behind the European Union is the prevention of a further war within Europe. The language of human rights, therefore, is enshrined in European Law. The initial action was completely compatible with the nature and purpose of the European Union. It is interesting to note that the entitlement to "interfere" was not challenged as much as the "legitimacy" of the criticisms. In other words, Austria accepted the entitlement of other European Union governments to ask the questions, it simply insisted that there was no danger to the rights of Jews and other minorities from the Freedom Party's inclusion in Government.

We see, then, a diplomatic challenge to national sovereignty from human rights. Unlike the military action, this route uses intergovernmental mechanisms and diplomatic pressure. The inclusion of a "right-wing" party in a national government, democratically elected, was challenged by the European Union. This union of member states has made human rights central to its legal standing and therefore correctly chose "human rights" to make a challenge. To that degree and in this case, it showed itself enough of a political entity to override the normal claims of a member's sovereignty. Many of its members would hesitate or refuse to take the doctrine much further.

The General Pinochet trial

The final case study involves General Pinochet. This was a legal challenge to state sovereignty. The history of Pinochet is well known. The highlights are as follows: he came to power in Chile in June 1973. Almost immediately he suspended the constitution, dissolved the judiciary and congress, and imposed strict press censorship. He also took prompt action against his opponents: Amnesty International estimated that by the end of 1973, some 250,000 Chilean people had been placed in concentration camps. In 1974 the Directorate of National Intelligence was created, with a wide-ranging brief, even going outside Chile itself. Indeed it was the overseas assassinations that the Spanish judges invoked when asking for General Pinochet's extradition from Britain, namely, the Buenos Aires car bombing of General Carols Prats (Pinochet's rival), the shooting in Rome of Bernardo Leighton, and the car-bombing in Washington DC of Letelier Moffitt. It was in the late 1970s that Pinochet started to modify his policies. A new constitution was drawn up, which included his own status as a senator for life. In 1989, Patricio Aywin was democratically elected President, while Pinochet remained the head of the armed forces, a role that Pinochet finally relinquished only in 1998. Confirmation that Pinochet had ruled over exceptional abuses of human rights emerged in the 1991 Chilean National Commission for Truth and Reconciliation, which documented over 3,000 motivated killings and countless torture cases.

It was the Progressive Association of Prosecutors, founded in 1996, in Spain that started work on attempting to bring certain key military figures to justice. With Pinochet in London for surgery, magistrates in Spain invoked the European Convention on the Suppression of Terrorism and Spain's extradition treaty with the UK, and asked the authorities in Britain to arrest the General for extradition. On the 16 October, 1998 Senator Pinochet was arrested on the basis of a provisional warrant issued by the Bow Street magistrate and this was confirmed with an additional warrant issued on 22 October 1998. On 28 October, the Divisional Court quashed these two warrants, on the grounds that Pinochet, as a former head of state, was immune from prosecution. Pinochet would have been free to go at this point, save that an appeal against the Divisional Court judgment went to the House of Lords and was heard on the 25 November.

It was an extraordinary case. The five Law Lords hearing the case were Lord Slynn of Hadley, Lord Lloyd of Berwick, Lord Nicholls, Lord Steyn, and Lord Hoffmann.[22] The central question was whether a former head of state was immune from arrest, especially for alleged crimes that took place while head of state. There were two relatively minor questions that all five agreed upon: first, was Pinochet ever actually head of state in Chile? The suggestion here was that his status was unconstitutional and therefore Pinochet had no Chilean legal legitimacy. However, all five rejected this argument, on the grounds that he was recognized as head of state by other states. Second, was Spain entitled to ask for the extradition of Pinochet who was not a Spanish national? On this the judges largely agreed (Hadley had most reservations) that under English Law the location of the crimes of torture and hostage-taking does not actually matter. Wherever these crimes took place and against whomever, they were still crimes against English Law.

Disagreement between the five judges hinged on the substantial question: is Pinochet entitled to immunity as a former head of state? The crucial laws here were the State Immunity Act 1978 and the Diplomatic Privileges Act 1964. The problem was that they do not explicitly refer to former heads of state. Clearly an existing head of state is entitled to a range of protections, but should these extend to a former head of state? The crucial divide (between Lloyd and Steyn) arose over the question of "official duties." This becomes key because section 20 of the State Immunity Act 1978 reads: "Subject to the provisions of this section and to any necessary modifications, the Diplomatic Privileges Act 1964 shall apply to − (a) a sovereign or other head of state. (b) members of his family forming part of his household; and (c) his private servants, as it applies to the head of a diplomatic mission, to members of his family forming part of his household and to his private servants." Then turning to Schedule 1 of the Diplomatic Privileges Act 1964, which is the Vienna Convention on Diplomatic Relations, we find Article 38 (1), which reads: "Except in so far as additional privileges and immunities may be granted by the receiving State, a diplomatic agent who is a national of or permanently resident in that State shall enjoy only immunity from jurisdiction and inviolability in respect to official acts performed in the exercise of his functions."

On this basis, Lloyd argued that:

> In committing the crimes which are alleged against him, was Senator
> Pinochet acting in his private capacity or was he acting in a sovereign capac-
> ity as head of state? In my opinion there can only be only answer. He was
> acting in a sovereign capacity. It has not been suggested that he was per-
> sonally guilty of any of the crimes of torture or hostage-taking in the sense
> that he carried them out with his own hands. What is alleged against him
> is that he organized the commission of such crimes, including the elimina-
> tion of his political opponents, as head of the Chilean government, and that
> he did so in cooperation with other governments under Plan Condor, and
> in particular with the government of Argentina. I do not see how in these
> circumstances he can be treated as having acted in a private capacity.

For Lloyd, then, we are talking about the actions of a head of state. Therefore the immunity of the person in post extends to the person who is
no longer in post, especially in respect to crimes alleged during that
person's rule. Steyn, however, argued that the relevant part of the 1978
Act "should be read as providing that a former head of state shall enjoy
immunity from the criminal jurisdiction of the United Kingdom with
respect to his official acts performed in the exercise of his functions as
Head of State." But torture and hostage taking are not exercises appropriate to the functions of a head of state. Therefore immunity does not
extend to these actions and once one has the opportunity to bring a
former ruler to court to answer for such heinous crimes, then that opportunity ought to be taken.

Digging a little deeper, one discovers that the key difference between
the two judges who wanted to allow the appeal (i.e., return Pinochet to
Chile rather than extradite him to Spain) and the three judges who wanted
to refuse it (i.e., wanted to allow the extradition request) is the vexed
question of national sovereignty as opposed human rights. Lord Slynn
explains:

> The original concept of the immunity of a head of state in customary inter-
> national law in part arose from the fact that he or she was a Monarch who
> by reason of personal dignity and respect ought not to be impeded in a
> foreign State: it was linked no less to the idea that the head of state was,
> or represented, the State and that to sue him was tantamount to suing an
> independent State extra-territorially, something which the comity of nations
> did not allow. Moreover, although the concepts of State immunity and
> Sovereign immunity have different origins, it seems to me that the latter is

an attribute of the former and that both are essentially based on the principles of Sovereign independence and dignity.

Does the growing corpus of international law that challenges such an account of sovereignty suffice as grounds for extraditing Pinochet? The answer given by Lloyd is No. Lloyd explains:

> Movements towards the recognition of crimes against international law is to been seen also in the decisions of the National Courts, in the resolution of the General Assembly of the United Nations 1946, in the reports of the International Law Commission and in the writings of distinguished international jurists. It has to be said, however, at this stage of the development of international law that some of those statements read as aspirations, as embryonic. It does not seem to me that it has been shown that there is any State practice or general consensus let alone a widely supported convention that all crimes against international law should be justifiable in National Courts on the basis of the universality of jurisdiction.

Lord Nicholls simply disagrees. For him, since 1946, there could be no doubt. "From this time on, no head of state could have been in any doubt about his potential personal liability if he participated in acts regarded as international crimes against humanity." On the issue of where to draw the line, Nicholls is firm that it must be drawn, with torture and genocide on the wrong side of it. When discussing the arguments of the Lord Chief Justice from the divisional court, Nicholls continues:

> The Lord Chief Justice observed that a former Head of State is clearly entitled to immunity from process in respect to some crimes. I would accept this proposition. Rhetorically, the Lord Chief Justice then posed the question: "Where does one draw the line?" After a detailed review of the case law and literature, he concluded that even in respect of acts of torture the former Head of State immunity would prevail. . . . Collins J.[23] went further. He said: "The submission was made that it could never be in the exercise of such functions to commit crimes as serious as those allegedly committed by the applicant. Unfortunately history shows that it has indeed on occasions been state policy to exterminate or oppress particular groups. One does not have to look very far back in history to see examples of the sort of thing having happened. There is in my judgment no justification for reading any limitation based on the nature of the crimes committed into the immunity which exists." It is inherent in this stark conclusion that there is no or virtually no line to be drawn. It follows that when Hitler ordered

the "final solution" his act must be regarded as an official act deriving from the exercise of his functions as head of state."

Nicholls then goes on to suggest that international law does provide a line: "[T]he development of international law since the Second World War justifies the conclusion that by the time of the 1973 coup d'etat, and certainly ever since, international law condemned genocide, torture, hostage taking and crimes against humanity (during an armed conflict or in peace time) as international crimes deserving of punishment. Given this state of international law, it seems to me difficult to maintain that the commission of such high crimes may amount to acts performed in the exercise of the functions of head of state." Finally, Nicholls insists that it makes no difference that Pinochet didn't actually do the acts of torture himself. It is "an elementary principle of law, shared by all civilized legal systems, that there is no distinction to be drawn between the man who strikes, and a man who orders another to strike."

This extended discussion of the Law Lords' arguments over Pinochet serves to demonstrate that here we have a legal challenge to the concept of state sovereignty (and in this case the related concept of immunity from prosecution of a head of state) from the vantage point of human rights. Legally, it is irrelevant that Pinochet was subsequently returned to Chile by the Home Secretary for reasons of Pinochet's medical condition. Amnesty International was correct when they said: "The fact that Augusto Pinochet was arrested while traveling abroad – almost unthinkable just 16 months ago – has sent a powerful message: no one is above international law, even when national laws protect you from prosecution."[24] Amnesty is right: the concept emerging here is crucial: rulers of states are answerable to a higher law.

3   Nations Answerable to a Higher Law

These three case studies all point in the same direction. We find that the nation-state must answer to an authority higher than the state. A loose parallel that can be drawn with the relationship between national cultures within medieval Christendom. Before the Reformation, the secular had to heed the sacred. For all the ambiguities of the complex relation between the rulers and Rome, the concept that a people had to acknowledge a power transcending the state was firmly recognized.[25] As we enter the third millennium, we find a comparable, indeed preferable, mechanism emerging. The language of human rights provides a comparable standard by which the conduct of nations and rulers must be judged.

In the last chapter the case was made that the language of human rights can and should be assimilated by the Christian tradition. Indeed one could go further: the language of human rights needs the Christian tradition. Using this assimilated standard, Christians should resist the discourse of state sovereignty. We resist it because it reflects a problematic elevation of the State over the universal demands of morality.

4   Conclusion

The argument of this chapter is that the diminishing concept and reality of "state sovereignty" and the increasing significance of human rights is a development that Christians should welcome. However, one question remains: the title of this chapter implies that the concept of state sovereignty is heretical: is this true?

I have suggested that theology was key in the development of the concept of state sovereignty. In Hobbes a pessimistic view of humanity made it advisable that we give the ruler all the authority which that person needs to keep order. The Reformers supported the vanity of their own local princes (see for example Cromwell's[26] support of King Henry VIII in England) in their quest for an alternative way of being Christian. The pessimistic anthropology and the support for local rule for domestic religious reasons is, in my view, a cluster of theological errors. Indeed it is tantamount to heresy.

For at the heart of the Christian doctrine of humanity is a sense that all people are dependent for their being upon, and must answer to, God. For a culture or nation on earth to claim absolute "sovereignty" is, in traditional language, an act of sin. Christians should welcome the erosion of national sovereignty. For all the ambiguities embedded in International Law (for example, the propensity of powerful nations to use the legal levers in selective ways), this is a significant step forward in realizing a more appropriate way of ordering the world.

6

ASSIMILATION: THE IMPORTANCE OF THE BLACK AND FEMINIST PERSPECTIVES

There is an obligation on a theology of engagement to engage with everything: which, needless to say, is very difficult! From time to time various pleas will be made for the theological community to attend rather more effectively to this or that issue. So Anne Primavesi explains that the ecological issue facing our world makes this a theological priority;[1] and James Cone is sharp and biting about the inability of white theology to worry about racism in America.[2] It might be objected that we cannot possibly expect every theologian to cultivate sufficient expertise to engage with all these matters. And of course that is true. But we can expect that the Body of Christ will generate groups of theologians that can and should engage with both of these – and other – vitally important issues.[3]

The focus for assimilation in this book has been secular (human rights) and later we shall look at interreligious issues (Nursi on globalization). In this chapter we look at a harder candidate for assimilation: the challenge of assimilating into our theology the appropriate acts of repentance and modification (perhaps even transformation) necessary to overcome the Christian tradition's propensity for oppression. Specifically, we are considering here two significant contemporary movements: feminist and black theologies.

It is importance to recognize that the word "assimilation" in this context does not mean the simple absorption of the other, but repentance and modification as a result of interchange. Many feminist theologians would, not surprisingly, find the idea of "absorption" problematic.[4] In the sense I am using the term, assimilation actually assists in the task of paying greater attention to diversity, both within and outside the Christian tradition. It does not act to "domesticate" challenges by appropriating them into the dominant discourses. It points to a real and potentially transformative engagement.

I come to this as a white, middle-class, married, English male, now living in America and the temptation at this point is to keep silent. After all, how can a person like me write effectively about oppression? But the challenge of the theology of engagement is that the task cannot be evaded. The difficult questions raised by the perspectives of feminism and black theology need to be confronted.

Naturally there are other comparable perspectives that are important. The exclusion of the poor, the gay, and neglect of other animals and the environment have all become increasingly important, and raise issues that are, in various ways, comparable. However, to make this discussion manageable, we shall focus on feminism and black theology, primarily because they pose in a very direct way the twin challenges of repentance and modification. And this is the route that assimilation in these cases needs to take.

The structure of this chapter will proceed in the following way. First, we shall look at feminist theology. Here we will consider the methodological use of experience, paying particular attention to Rosemary Radford Ruether's seminal work, and then turn to ecofeminist perspectives. Both of these are important features in feminist theology which ought to receive more widespread serious attention. Then we shall go on to discuss black theology, and demonstrate just how crucial it is to engage with the implications of racial oppression. In both cases, the thrust of the argument is that we betray the gospel if we are indifferent to social injustice and to theological complicity in its perpetuation.

1   Feminist Theology

> Every three minutes a woman is beaten
> every five minutes a
> woman is raped/every ten minutes
> a little girl is molested . . .
>
> every day
> women's bodies are found
> in alleys and bedrooms/at the top of the stairs . . .[5]

I take the oppression of women by men as a given. This ground is well trodden. The relegation of women to secondary citizenship and restriction to specific, gender-curtailed roles can easily be demonstrated in historical purview. So, too, can a distressing tendency of violence and abuse towards women.[6] In many cultures, men have practiced institutional and domestic cruelty as of right. Some cultures have practiced infanticide of daughters; and if she survived, the options for the daughter have often been – and still are – severely limited. For centuries, in the West, daughters were often denied formal education, even on the limited scale that was available to sons. Expectations were largely confined to the role of a dutiful daughter to a father followed that of a dutiful wife to a husband. The lifestyle options were often very limited and revolved around the primacy of the male. Now it is certainly true that women in certain parts of the globe have made considerable gains in the twentieth century. However, it can be argued that the ideology of patriarchy remains deeply embedded in Western culture, and that, in world terms, there is still much to be done.[7]

Christian theology has at its most benign treated women as invisible; and at its most wicked, it has provided a justification for this cruelty. Even though women comprise slightly over half of the human race, they often do not appear to view within our scriptures and our tradition.[8] (The main exception is the Blessed Virgin Mary who provides an ambiguous celebration of virginity and motherhood.) The main characters in the Christian drama are male kings, male prophets, a male savior, and male apostles. With a few exceptions (e.g., Deborah or Ruth), women have walk-on parts as mothers or sisters. Men, many of whom were celibate, developed the subsequent tradition; and almost all were persuaded of the inferiority of women. When it comes to justifying cruelty, Eve was given a prominent role. Even though Genesis 1:27 teaches that in God's image both male and female are created, this disappears behind the second creation story where Eve is presented in the history of interpretation as the villain. She, it is claimed, is the one who initially disobeys God and lures Adam into temptation. Themes of the disobedience of women and of woman as the temptress of the male have dominated the tradition. The author of 1 Timothy, almost certainly not Paul, develops the argument that sustained centuries of oppression, when he writes: "Let the woman learn in silence with all submissiveness. I permit no woman to teach or to have authority over men; she is to keep silence. For Adam was formed first, then Eve; and Adam was not deceived, but the woman was deceived and became a transgressor." (1 Timothy 2:11–14. NRSV). Tertullian brings out the implications in his famous statement of hostility against women when he writes:

The sentence of God on this sex of yours lives in this age: guilt must of necessity live too. *You* are the Devil's gateway. *You* are the unsealer of that forbidden tree. *You* are the first deserter of the divine law. *You* are she who persuaded him whom the Devil was not valiant enough to attack. *You* destroyed so easily God's image man. On account of *your* desert, that is death, even the Son of God had to die.[9]

There is of course a deep irony in the dominant patriarchy of the tradition. Jesus repeatedly behaves in a counter-cultural ways when dealing with women.[10] And Paul gives eloquent expression to the Gospel implications for gender when he writes in Galatians (3:28): "There is neither Jew nor Greek, there is neither slave nor free, there is neither male nor female: for you are all one in Christ Jesus." The temptation, of course, is to stop there, especially if you are a male theologian. We want to hide behind the claim that male misogyny is a betrayal of the true Christian tradition and attempt to reclaim the insights of Jesus and the vision of Paul in Galatians. (Paul performs less well in 1 Corinthians.)[11] However, this will not do. A theology of engagement needs to go further. The damage is too deep – the patriarchy too pervasive – to allow the Christian tradition not to think more effectively about it all.

And here, of course, theologians in general can learn from feminist theologians in particular. Just how does a Christian committed to the equality of women deal with a tradition which seems steeped in patriarchal, misogynist, and androcentric tendencies? – a tradition which is not only symptomatic of social oppression of women, but has also served to uphold and legitimate it?[12] A classic response was articulated by Rosemary Radford Ruether, author of *Sexism and God Talk*.[13] Ruether determined that the critical principle of feminist theology is, simply:

> the promotion of the full humanity of women. Whatever denies, diminishes, or distorts the full humanity of women is, therefore, appraised as not redemptive. Theologically speaking, whatever diminishes or denies the full humanity of women must be presumed not to reflect the divine or an authentic relation to the divine, or to reflect the authentic nature of things, or to be the message or work of an authentic redeemer or a community of redemption.[14]

This is, then, a criterion that many theologians would recognize as valid. That which comes from God is good, therefore that which is not good does not come from God. To use the criterion of justice to distinguish the true from the false prophet is wholly appropriate.[15]

This does, however, beg the question. By what means does one discern what is just, good, and true? And here we see, once more, a methodological turn to experience as both source and norm. Experience is seen to be central to the whole theological enterprise. Ruether writes:

> Human experience is the starting point and the ending point of the hermeneutical circle. Codified tradition both reaches back to roots in experience and is constantly renewed or discarded through the test of experience. "Experience" includes experience of the divine, experience of oneself, and experience of the community and the world, in an interacting dialectic. Received symbols, formulas, and laws are either authenticated or not through their ability to illuminate and interpret experience."[16]

Ruether notes correctly that this emphasis upon experience is not exclusive to feminist or liberation theologies. It is a commonplace that the proper way to understand the Bible is to recognize that it is an interpretation of a people's experience of God in history and life.[17] However, Ruether explains: "The uniqueness of feminist theology lies not in its use of the criterion of experience but rather in its use of the woman's experience, which has been almost entirely shut out of theological reflection in the past."[18] This is important. It is a methodological emphasis that seeks to correct the silence of the Christian tradition and respond to its oppressive aspects. The use of women's experience in particular, opines Ruether, explodes as a critical force.[19]

Feminist theology thus makes much methodologically of the experiences of women. It should be noted though that third-wave feminism[20] is particularly aware of the dangers of repeating the patriarchal gesture: that is to say, universalizing the experiences of a specific group as normative. Early critics of second-wave feminism noted that this was not a movement "owned" by all women, but one largely from the perspectives of white middle-class women. As Audre Lorde trenchantly expressed it at a 1979 feminist conference in New York:

> If white American feminist theory need not deal with the differences between us (black women and all women of color), and the resulting difference in our oppressions, then how do you deal with the fact that women who clean your houses and tend your children while you attend conferences on feminist theory are, for the most part, poor women and women of color? What is the theory of racist feminism?"[21]

Thus there has increasingly been a recognition in feminist methodologies that "women's experience" cannot simply be employed in a unitary and essentializing way.[22] Differences exist along a wide range of material axes: not only that of gender, but also race, economic status, geographical location, and sexual orientation. Furthermore, while remaining committed to the reality and pervasiveness of women's oppression, this is more and more seen to be not simply along dualist lines, such that men are oppressors and women oppressed. As the above quotation by Audre Lorde underscores, women can oppress women. It is recognized that oppression is more like a pyramid in structure.[23] Of course, this diversity does not evacuate the notion of commonality among women of all content. It is precisely in the structural oppression of women as women that feminism takes its starting point. Yet that commonality is also marked by plurality.

The diversity of experience may lead to the contention that it cannot function normatively within a theological paradigm. Feminists, though, argue that it is the very specificity and particularity of experiences which are the point. Experience is neither universal nor transhistorical, but profoundly contextual. It is also communal as well as simply individual, and reflective rather than only prelinguistic. Ruether further refines her own understanding of how women's experience functions in theology as follows: "by women's experience as a key to hermeneutics or theory of interpretation, we mean precisely that experience which arises when women become critically aware of these falsifying and alienating experiences imposed upon them as women by a male-dominated culture."[24]

A variety of methodological proposals have been put forward to deal with the complexity of experience as category. Sara Ruddick argues for a cumulative analysis of women's experience which thus takes account of plurality but avoids meaningless fragmentation.[25] Sharon Welch suggests it is precisely in engagement with actual contexts of resistance and solidarity that our ability for genuine critique emerges.[26] Linda Hogan concludes her study of the use of women's experience in feminist theology:

> It is absolutely vital, in my opinion, that feminist theologians place a hermeneutic of difference at the core of their theory. So too is it essential that they be attentive to the ambiguity of using experience and praxis as resources and yet claiming validity for the feminist agenda. . . . This is neither to choose anarchy nor to adopt relativism. It is, however, to adopt a risk-filled and thoroughly honest stance in relation to the universalizing potential in our theology.[27]

And, in determining which of conflicting experiences are to be priori-tized, it is usually held to be the experiences of those women who are benefiting least in existing social, economic, and ideological systems. The epistemological privilege of women's experience is, on this understanding, rooted in pragmatic rather than ontological grounds.

Centralizing experience as theological tool raises all sorts of questions about how experience and tradition interact in the formulation of theol-ogy. As Ruether insists, and we have seen elsewhere in this book, this is hardly a "problem" with feminist theology as such. It is part of the task of doing theology at all. Theology is contextual and draws from a range of sources. Ruether herself identifies five areas of "cultural tradition" that can provide "usable tradition." These are: "(1) Scripture, both Hebrew and Christian (Old and New Testaments); (2) marginalized or "heretical" Chris-tian traditions, such as Gnosticism, Montanism, Quakerism, Shakerism; (3) the primary theological themes of the dominant stream of classical Christian theology – Orthodox, Catholic, and Protestant; (4) non-Christian Near Eastern and Greco-Roman religion and philosophy; and (5) critical post-Christian world views such as liberalism, romanticism, and Marxism."[28] She articulates a correlation between feminist theology and prophetic biblical religion: it is the self-critical, prophetic principle which enables biblical religion to undergo correction and be called to repentance. Sexism is another deformation of God's agenda for liberation and justice, which the feminist critical principle calls on us to denounce and move beyond.[29]

Ruether's methodology is an engaged methodology. Once again, she shares with much traditional theology a use of many sources (some Chris-tians and others non-Christian). Ruether goes far in her attempt to show how feminist theology as experiential is in fact true of all theological texts and traditions. However, I would add that in other respects she overworks the contrast between feminist theological method and the classical method. She implies that the latter is a world of static "authority," while, as we have seen in earlier chapters, this is not true of Augustine and Aquinas. Instead of drawing the contrast in terms of many sources and authority, a more appropriate contrast is in the very application of the feminist critical principle.[30] In other words, as the lens through which we engage in theological reflection: in this case, the task of exposing the oppressive and patriarchal principles at work in the tradition.

At this point it is worth pausing. Two points need to be made clear: first, there is absolutely no reason why most theologians sympathetic to the methodologies of Augustine and Aquinas cannot embrace this feminist methodology. The stress on experience is true, to one degree or another, of all theology; the recognition that we use an ethical criterion to distinguish between truth and falsity in theology is also widely recognized; and the use of a range of sources to shape theology has been widely practiced in the tradition. The only point of resistance will be the priority given to the feminist critical principle. So this leads to the second point. The church needs to repent because of our failure to recognize the centrality of the feminist critical principle. On Ruether's criterion, this simply judges as inadequate any theology which is not fully inclusive of women, or treats women as less than fully human.[31]

I hope, pray, and trust that for most of us the feminist critical principle is a discovery that we now all recognize. The argument can be made that it is embedded in the opening chapter of Genesis, in the life and teaching of Jesus, and Paul's famous declaration of equality in Galatians 3:28. Yet despite this, the lesson was really only grasped as the church engaged with the best of Enlightenment thought and its implications. Feminism is a child of modernity. This is not a reason to resist its insights, but to repent. Repentance is needed for two reasons: (a) the church managed to circumvent the truths of feminism that are implicit in our tradition and (b) God had to use modernity to teach the church the lesson. We repent because this double failure led to immeasurable suffering and harm.

As we start the process of repentance so we can start the second stage, that of modification. The use of inclusive language in liturgy and other Christian speech is only a start. We should care about our words because our words betray how we think. One cannot think without words: thinking, by definition, is the task of interpreting experience. And when we are surrounded by men, especially in the priesthood or business or the academy, it is easy to assume that men are the norm. By consciously using inclusive language, we remind ourselves and our hearers that we recognize that gender diversity is part of our world.

Although this is important, it is also trivial. The modification or even transformation of our theology needs to go much further. We need to examine its roots to detect anthropologies and structures which, despite our rhetoric of equality, continue to betray a profound and unjust differentiation according to gender. One of the most deeply embedded such anthropologies is the identification of male with God and woman with nature.[32] Ecofeminism grew out of a critical awareness of connections between the oppression of women and the exploitation of the environment.[33] This is another aspect of feminist theology in which Ruether has been prolific. As she puts it:

> Ecofeminists discern both a symbolic and a structural connection between
> the mistreatment of women and the mistreatment of nature in patriarchal
> cultures and social systems. . . . Patriarchal cultures have seen the bodily
> world as something both inferior and evil and have imagined a higher, male,
> spiritual world where this lower world could be both escaped and domi-
> nated from outside. Thus, for ecofeminists, the struggle against ecological
> devastation is interconnected with the struggle against patriarchy.[34]

The steps in this argument need to be set out with some care. The key
lies in the nature of patriarchy as a system of inequitable power relations
valorizing domination and built upon hierarchical dualisms. And, if we
examine these dualisms, all the qualities typically associated with the ruling
male are assigned to the positive pole: thus, for example, male, mind, intellect, white, spirit, culture are held to be superior to female, body, emotion,
black, matter, nature. When we look at the Christian tradition, God is
spoken almost exclusively as a "he" or in stereotypically male roles (e.g.,
king). In addition the attributes of God are qualities that males (in a patriarchal culture) celebrate: so God is complete power and complete knowledge (i.e., the supreme rational principle). In so far as God is love, the
tradition has always insisted that the love runs parallel with justice, which
in practice means that "he" is willing to send most people to hell to satisfy
the demands of justice. Furthermore God is spirit: God does not have a
body; God does not menstruate or get dirty. We have pushed matter away
from God; in much the same way as a celibate ascetic male wants to distance himself from the physical. It looks as if men have projected this celibate, ascetic maleness into the skies. Women, however, primarily because
of their capacity to give birth to children, have become identified with
nature. They are linked with the physical and with the sexual. Males find
the monthly cycle of menstruation difficult to handle, hence the menstruation taboos. They worry about female sexuality and need it to be
controlled (hence the importance of a patriarchally managed marriage).
And for salvation, males need women to disentangle themselves from their
bodies and sexuality and to cultivate their "spirit." In so doing, they require
women to become like men.[35]

Hence this antagonism to matter is not simply responsible for patriarchy but also, the argument goes, for our abuse of the environment and
is connected to a host of other prejudices which have their roots in a
desire to divide up the world oppositionally.[36] The patriarchal drive is to
control, abuse, manipulate, and exploit. It has led to an indifference to the
damage caused to nature. It is because nature has no status: it does not

matter. It is only our invisible "soul" that will survive death. (The resurrection of the body is an awkward embarrassment to many male theologians.) So we worship the god of economic growth and in the process destroy "mother" earth. A patriarchal Christian theology gives birth to an ecological destructiveness of massive proportions.

As one sketches the argument, all too briefly, one can see the scale of transformation that is being proposed. As Anne Clifford puts it: "Ecofeminism therefore presents an invitation to something radical: conversion of mind and heart from a largely unchallenged hierarchical dualism and androcentric anthropocentrism to a new egalitarian holism."[37] The implications for theology and thinking the divine are far-reaching. It is just this holistic, mutualistic vision which Sallie McFague has striven to articulate in her numerous works which relate how we think about God to the ecological well-being of our planet, at the heart of which is a reemphasis upon both God's immanence and relationality.[38]

What are we to make of this proposed transformation of Christian theology? Our first response is to engage in the conversation. Given we are in the business of repentance, we must listen with considerable care. Our second response is to link this perspective with other perspectives of struggle as we seek to create a nonoppressive celebration of God in God's world.

Feminist theologians are providing a "suggestive narrative" which tells us why and how the Christian tradition became so patriarchal. Rethink our model of God, the narrative suggests, and we will find right relations between the genders and with nature. In this respect, feminism and process thought enjoy a mutually enriching conversation in the project of rethinking God. Like feminism, process thought rejects the notion of autonomous, self-sufficient selfhood and places relationality at the core of its ontology. Elsewhere in this book, I have already defended certain insights from process theology. It is both more coherent than a traditional timeless God and explains more effectively the experience of most Christians, if we think of God as goodness and love at the heart of the universe enabling everything to be and sustaining everything that is. Such a God does indeed embrace matter. In much the same way as the mother carrying her child has an independent life within her, which can kick and move and yet is also totally dependent on her, so God has within Godself an independent creation of creatures endowed with free will that are also completely dependent on God. Such a God cannot be envisaged as an external autocrat, interfering or leaving be at some inexplicable whim, but is rather the God of promise, of cocreation, and of loving relations. This

does not negate the transcendence or aseity of God but takes seriously
God's own covenant with humanity and elected immanence within our
world. As with God, so we need to modify our Christology (we should
resist all flirtation with docetism). And as with Christology, so with the
life to come: we should and can affirm the resurrection of the dead.

Yet even with these changes in the Christian story, I suspect patriarchy
will endure. The difficulty is that there are many traditions in the world
that are pantheist and affirm the female in the deity, but are still deeply
patriarchal.[39] Perhaps a distinction between "conscious challenge to patriarchy" and "unconscious unexplored implications" which *could* challenge
patriarchy might help here. The conscious challenge runs parallel with
repentance and forces Christians to make justice a priority. The unconscious unexplored implications mean that a tradition has not started thinking through the implications of a metaphysic for just relations between
the genders. My hope is that feminist theology provides a "conscious"
modification of the Christian story and that this will ensure that the modification runs parallel with repentance and therefore enable the modification to work. In other words, the feminist "suggestive narrative" for
Christianity might effectively undermine patriarchy, but the patriarchy in
Hinduism, for example, which should be undermined by the metaphysics
of certain strands of that tradition, have not been linked, even in theory,
let alone in practice, with the problem of patriarchy. In Christianity the
connection has been made explicit; in Hinduism there is a disconnection.

Methodologically, feminist theological insights should be easy for the
Christian tradition to accommodate. The method of Ruether is, in fact,
fairly classical. The resistance from male theologians is likely to be a
problem of sin or determined conservatism. It is a refusal to recognize the
crime coupled with a refusal to share power. This is the reason why repentance is so important. And as we repent, so we can recast our story so
that it more accurately represents what we know about the God revealed
in Jesus.

As already explored to some extent, the challenge of repentance and
modification is not only needed in respect to gender but also in respect
to race. It is to the challenge of black theology that we turn next.

2 Black Theology

For any white person living in America there is a deep puzzle at the heart
of the American experience. Almost all the settlers were Christians. The

Founding Fathers recognized the importance of God in the Declaration of Independence and spoke about the equality of humanity. Yet it is a country that, for a whole host of reasons, perpetrated the evil of slavery against black people and continued to tolerate the evil of institutional and legally entrenched segregation until the late 1960s.

The racism of America is an export from Europe. It was the European powers that created the trade in slavery; it was the European settlers who brought a theology of superiority that was indifferent to the nonwhite. As with feminism, I take it as a given that we know of the heinous crimes of the white man against the nonwhite. However, the words of James Cone provide the white theologian with a brutal reminder:

> How do we account for such a long history of white theological blindness to racism and its brutal impact on the lives of African people? Is it because white theologians do not know about the tortured history of the Atlantic slave trade, which according to the British historian Basil Davidson, "cost Africa at least fifty million souls"? Have they forgotten about the unspeakable crimes of colonialism? Author Eduardo Galeano claims that 150 years of Spanish and Portuguese colonization in Central and South America reduced the indigenous population from 90 million to 3.3 million. During the twenty-three-year reign of terror of King Leopold II of Belgium in the Congo (1885–1908), scholarly estimates suggest that approximately 10 million Congolese met unnatural deaths – "fully half of the territory's population." The tentacles of white supremacy have stretched around the globe. No people of color have been able to escape its cultural, political, and economic domination. Two hundred and forty-four years of slavery and one hundred years of legal segregation, augmented by a reign of white terror that lynched more than five thousand blacks, defined the meaning of America as "white over black." White supremacy shaped the social, political, economic, cultural, and religious ethos in the churches, the academy, and the broader society.[40]

It is important to remember the sheer extent of the suffering that these figures hide. Slavery was a cruel and wicked trade. Perhaps we need a witness to remind us of the suffering. This description from a slave on a Portuguese ship is typical:

> The stench of the hold while we were on the coast was so intolerably loathsome that it was dangerous to remain there for any time, and some of us had been permitted to stay on the deck for the fresh air; but now that the whole ship's cargo were confined together, it became absolutely pestilential.

The closeness of the place, and the heat of the climate, added to the number
in the ship, which was so crowded that each had scarcely room to turn
himself, almost suffocated us. This produced constant perspirations, so that
the air soon became unfit for respiration. . . . This wretched situation was
again aggravated by the galling of the chains, now become insupportable;
and the filth of the tubs, into which the children often fell, and were almost
suffocated. The shrieks of the women, and the groans of the dying, ren-
dered a scene of horror almost inconceivable.[41]

While we might feel able to distance ourselves from the crimes of the
1730s, the recent past is much harder to handle. This is just one of thousands of stories from the civil rights campaign. This particular one dates
from the summer of 1963 and Mrs. Hamer is recollecting the case of a
young girl who had been arrested at a voter registration workshop:

June Johnson, a fifteen-year-old black teenager who had attended the voter
registration workshop, was the next person led by Mrs. Hamer's cell in this
grim parade of tortured bodies. "The blood was runnin'" down in her face,
and they put her in another cell." In the booking room, whence Johnson
was coming, the sheriff had pulled the young girl aside for his own personal whipping. He asked her whether she was a member of the NAACP.
[National Association for the Advancement of Colored People.] She told
him yes. Then he hit her on the cheek and chin, and when she raised her
arms to protect herself, he hit her on the stomach. He continued to ask
her questions about the NAACP – "who runs that thing?" "do you know
Martin Luther King?" Soon the four men in the room – the sheriff, the
chief of police, the highway patrolman, and another white man – threw
Johnson onto the floor, beat her, and stomped on her body in concert. The
men ripped Johnson's dress and tore her slip off; blood soaked her tattered
clothes.[42]

For many of us today, this is so obviously wrong and incompatible with
the Christian gospel that there seems to be little more that needs to be
said on the topic. Indeed with the abolition of slavery and then the passing
of the Civil Rights Act of 1964, many assume that these injustices have
been rectified. However, this is untrue for several reasons. Although there
has been progress, the problems of racism and the oppression of African-
Americans continue to the present day. There are more blacks than whites
in poverty; there is a disproportionate number of blacks over whites in
prison and on death row. The political right argues that the problem is
the behavior of the African-American community; they point, for example,

to the higher number of single mothers. The solution, they argue, is a revival of the Protestant work ethic. Cornel West is right when he writes:

> Conservative behaviorists talk about values and attitudes as if political and economic structures hardly exist. They rarely, if ever, examine the innumerable cases in which black people do act on the Protestant ethic and still remain at the bottom of the social ladder. Instead, they highlight the few instances in which blacks ascend to the top, as if such success is available to all blacks, regardless of circumstances. Such a vulgar rendition of Horatio Alger in blackface may serve as a source of inspiration to some – a kind of model for those already on the right track. But it cannot serve as a substitute for serious historical and social analysis of the predicaments of and prospects for all black people, especially the grossly disadvantaged ones.[43]

Every white person knows that West is right. We know it just isn't true to say that "if a black person decides to work hard, then they will succeed." We know it is false because we know too many white people, often very respectable, who are still racist. And we know that when a black person complains that they still find white society racist, it is true. Even those of us who pride ourselves that we are progressive on such issues have sat with our "friends" and heard and tolerated (for fear of creating "an atmosphere") the critical remark, the racist joke, and the criticism of "mixed marriages." And if we are honest we suspect that there are cab drivers who prefer to find a white passenger or employers who prefer someone "familiar" or promotion boards that decide they don't want white people reporting to a black manager (of course this will not be the explicit justification). West complains about the propensity of many to see "black people as a 'problem people.'"[44] The truth is that the problem people are the white people who are still quietly racist (almost politely racist) even though they know about the evils of slavery and segregation. Somehow it has not got through how evil racism is. Those who question this quiet middle-class racism are accused of "political correctness" or being "humorless." It is as if these intelligent nice racists have forgotten how many lives were killed and damaged through racism. And as with feminism, Christianity often provided the justification for a racist worldview. Although it seems obvious to many that Christianity and racism are incompatible, many do not see it. Black theology is not simply for the African-American, but also a vitally important challenge for any theology of engagement.

There are six aspects of black theology that a theology of engagement must assimilate. But before developing these, it is worth clarifying the precise meaning of black theology. James Cone explains that the term "black theology" is a merger of the insights of Malcolm X and Martin Luther King. He writes, "The word 'black' in the phrase was defined by the life and teaching of Malcolm X – culturally and politically embodied in the Black Power movement. The term "theology" was influenced by the life and teaching of Martin Luther King, Jr. – religiously and politically embodied in the black church and civil rights movement."[45] For many historians, Malcolm X and Martin Luther King are viewed as opposites: Malcolm X is depicted as the militant (and some allege a "black racist") and Martin Luther King is the moderate. For most theologians involved in black theology there is a growing consensus that this reading is wrong. Malcolm X provides a stronger analysis of the extent of the racism, while Martin Luther King remains the great theologian who detected the Christian obligation on this matter. James Cone explains:

> Martin and Malcolm embodied in their lives and work the African-American struggle for identity in a society that is not sure what to do with us. There is a little bit of Martin and Malcolm in all African-Americans . . . We should not listen to Martin's "I Have a Dream" speech without also listening to Malcolm's answer in his "Message to the Grass Roots." "While King was having a dream," Malcolm said, "the rest of us Negroes are having a nightmare." Without confronting the American nightmare that Malcolm bore witness to, we will never be able to create the beloved community articulated so well by Martin King.[46]

The important point is that any theology of engagement must confront the militancy of Malcolm as well as the vision of Martin.

The first aspect is methodological. As with feminist theology, it is the argument of this book that the sources that are central to black theology are entirely compatible with the sources that shaped the mainstream Christian tradition. In a working paper prepared by the Kelly Miller Smith Institute at Vanderbilt University, black theology is described as (a) story, (b) story of our faith in God, (c) story of our faith-understanding and our freedom struggle, (d) biblical, and (e) contextual.[47] There is a strong claim, implicit in this list, to see black theology as the authentic theology of the Christian tradition. Along with the liberation theologians, black theology believes that the Bible is about liberation from oppression. Therefore the Bible belongs to the African-American community. Gayraud S. Wilmore is broader when he suggests that there are three sources for black theology. The first is the existing black community, "where the tradition of black folk religion is still extant and continues to stand over against the institutional church."[48] The second is "the writings and addresses of the black preachers and public men of the past."[49] These are people like Nat Turner, Richard Allen, and Martin Delany. And the third sources is "the traditional religions of Africa, the way those religions encountered and assimilated, or were assimilated by, Christianity, and the process by which African theologians are seeking to make the Christian faith indigenous and relevant to Africa today."[50]

Black theology is at these points operating with the same methodology as the more dominant theologies of Augustine and Aquinas. It is a theology of engagement. It is grounded in the Bible and takes seriously the combination of experience (the story of oppression) and the insights that can be derived from the "non-Christian" traditions that shaped the African-American story.

The second aspect is the insight that the gospel is about liberation. Thanks to the Latin-American Liberation theologians, this is now accepted by many Christians. The pietistic gospel about individual salvation and the eternal destiny of the soul does not convey the message of the prophets and the teaching of Jesus. Instead, if we read the Bible through the eyes of those who suffer, we see more clearly that God cares about injustice, oppression, poverty, and obliges us to work for the liberation of those suffering. The theme of liberation is one of the earliest themes of black theology. Back in 1969, the statement by the National Committee of black churchmen speaks of:

> black theology is a theology of black liberation. It seeks to plumb the black condition in the light of God's revelation in Jesus Christ, so that the black community can see that the gospel is commensurate with the achievement of black humanity. Black theology is a theology of "blackness." It is the affirmation of black humanity that emancipates black people from white racism, thus providing authentic freedom for both white and black people.[51]

The gospel must mean a changed world, in which the curse of racism no longer destroys and dehumanizes the black person.

The third aspect is the centrality of "self-love." Cornel West has made this a central theme of his work. There is a crisis of nihilism: men and women are giving up hope. West explains that this nihilism takes the form of a "profound sense of psychological depression, personal worthlessness, and social despair so widespread in Black America."[52] And the appropriate response is a conversion. West writes:

> New models of collective black leadership must promote a version of this
> politics. . . . [T]here is always a chance for conversion – a chance for people
> to believe that there is hope for the future and a meaning to struggle. . . .
> Nihilism is not overcome by arguments or analyses; it is tamed by love and
> care. Any disease of the soul must be conquered by a turning of one's own
> soul. This turning is done through one's own affirmation of one's worth –
> an affirmation fueled by the concern of others. A love ethic must be at the
> center of a politics of conversion.[53]

One aspect of Christianity that can be deeply problematic to an oppressed
people is the idea that "love involves selflessness" or even "love is self-
giving." The danger here is that one starts to believe that the Christian
duty is to be constantly available to the oppressor and, as an act of love,
to tolerate the abuse. When in 1 John we find the expression "we love
God because God first loved us," we find a more appropriate model of
love. To love others, one needs a self to love with. "Love you neighbor as
yourself" carries the same self-affirmation. We need to start loving ourselves before we have any chance of loving anyone else. For an oppressed
people, this is especially true. Imagine what it is like to be ignored, stared
at for daring to walk into a predominately white restaurant, or passed over
for promotion. When society does not provide the affirmation, indeed
does the opposite, it is vitally important that the person finds the resources
for "self-love."

The fourth aspect is the stress on a "contextual theology." The located
nature of theology is often recognized theoretically but often ignored
when it comes to preaching and teaching. How do we think of Christ
when we are preaching? Many churches take the white Christ of European Christianity. This is both wrong historically and wrong theologically.
Historically, Albert Cleage is right in at least this respect when he writes:
"Jesus was a nonwhite leader of a nonwhite people struggling for national
liberation against the rule of a white nation."[54] Theologically it is wrong
because as Matthew 25 teaches us we find Christ in the oppressed. And
black people are oppressed in America. James Cone makes the point thus:

> [W]hether whites want to hear it or not, *Christ is black, baby*, with all of the
> features which are so detestable to white society. . . . If the church is a con-
> tinuation of the Incarnation, and if the church and Christ are where the
> oppressed are, then Christ and his church must identify totally with the
> oppressed to the extent that they too suffer for the same reasons persons
> are enslaved . . . Therefore Christ is black because he is oppressed, and
> oppressed because he is black.[55]

Christ becomes black in America because that is where the oppression is. In the same way that we should contextualize our Christology, so we should contextualize our understanding of God. In line with the sympathy with process theology that has been articulated at various points in this book, it is important to listen to a critique from the perspective of black theology. Theodore Walker, Jr. has reflected on the relationship between the two. He picks up the criticism that process theology often talks of God's love as unconditional, indiscriminate, and universal. The difficulty with this is that black theology needs to think of God not as on everyone's side but as on the side of the poor. But, as Walker goes on to show, if God experiences the damaging impact of oppression on the personhood of both the oppressed and the oppressor (and every act of cruelty to another person destroys the character and well-being of the oppressor), then God must be working for liberation of the oppressed.[56] This is an example of engagement that leads to a significant modification of process theology.

The fifth aspect is the impact on our view of suffering, theodicy, and justice. It was William R. Jones who asked the question in a brilliant essay: is God a white racist? He provides a critique of three theologians: Joseph Washington, James Cone, and Albert Cleage. He examines their implicit theodicies. Washington builds on the suffering servant theme and suggests that in much the same way as the Jewish people were called to witness to "one God," the blacks are called to "witness to the one humanity of the one God."[57] And as the Jews suffered for their calling, so the blacks will suffer. Jones disagrees strongly with the implication that this suffering might be in perpetuity. Similarly, Cone makes the black people an "oppressed people" with whom God identifies. However, the difficulty with this, explains Jones, is that it is not obvious that liberation will come: yet surely God would want to bring such liberation about? As for Cleage, he overcomes the accusation that God is a racist by making God and Jesus both nonwhite; this God allows the oppression and suffering because it is "deserved punishment": all suffering in the universe is a response to earlier cosmic sins. Jones correctly identifies the difficulty with this explanation, namely the extent of black suffering and the comparative lack of white suffering.

This is a challenging article for several reasons. First, our standard treatments of theodicy tend to be very undifferentiated. We talk of "natural suffering" (earthquakes, illness, etc.), and "moral evil" (acts of violence and war against each other). Jones is forcing us to admit that there is "group suffering." Moral evil would work as a category if each group in the world had a virtually equivalent number of individuals who suffer and who do not suffer. However, the truth is that power in history has privileged certain groups. And with the advent of modernity, white Europeans have been especially privileged. If we are going to talk about an active God in human history,[58] then we do need to provide some explanation for the uneven experience of different groups in respect to suffering.

The final aspect is the emergence of "womanist" theology. Kelly Delaine Brown Douglas writes:

> Black women in the United States have given voice to a new theological perspective: womanist. Although the meaning of the term "womanist" orig-inated with Alice Walker's interpretation of the Black cultural expression, "You acting womanish," it goes beyond her words. It points to the rich-ness and complexity of being Black and female in a society that tends to devalue both Blackness and womanhood.[59]

It is undoubtedly true that the experience of the double oppression has been especially challenging. The experience of this double oppression opens up contrasting ways of understanding the nature of oppression and therefore of the processes necessary for liberation.

Much more could be said about all these points. The exercise is intended to demonstrate the task of modification necessary for a theology of engagement. However, given as a white theologian, it seems more important for me to conclude this chapter by examining the demands that are necessary in terms of repentance.

James H. Cone writes:

> Is there any hope for the white church? Hope is dependent upon whether it will ask from the depths of its being with God: "What must I do to be saved?." . . . It must own that it has been and is a racist institution whose primary purpose is the perpetuation of white supremacy. But it is not enough to be sorry or to admit wrong. To repent involves change in one's whole being. In the Christian perspective, it means conversion. . . . For the white churches this means a radical reorientation of their style in the world towards blacks. It means that they must change sides, giving up all claims to lofty neutrality. . . . A racist pattern has been set, and the church has been a contributor to the pattern. Now it must break that pattern by placing its life at stake.[60]

This is challenge we have a duty to attend to. The explicit racist argu-ments of Sam Bowers (Imperial Wizard of the White Knights of Ku Klux

Klan and suspected of "orchestrating at least nine murders, seventy-five bombings of black churches, and three hundred assaults, bombings, and beatings,"[61] between 1964 and 1967) have been, on the whole, disowned by the white church. His capacity to link the civil rights movement with godless communism represents a particular brand of American paranoia. Other western nations were much more nuanced in their evaluation of Marxism and communism. His passion for neo-Nazi literature and the novels of Thomas Dixon (who portrayed the black man as a sexual degenerate) provided a pseudoscientific and non-Christian justification for racial purity. Christianity, ironically, provided the apocalyptic framework in which Bowers saw himself with a mission to save the world and to engage in this war against the forces of darkness with any means possible. This statement is typical of the cosmic dualism underpinning his worldview:

> We Knights are working day and night to preserve Law and Order here in Mississippi, in the only way it can be preserved: by strict segregation of the races, and the control of the social structure in the hands of the Christian, Anglo-Saxon White men, the only race on earth that can build and maintain just and stable governments. We are deadly serious about this business. . . . Take heed, atheists and mongrels, we will not travel your path to a Leninist Hell, but we will buy YOU a ticket to the Eternal if you insist. Take your choice, SEGREGATION, TRANQUILLITY AND JUSTICE, OR BI-RACISM, CHAOS AND DEATH.[62]

Although almost all church leaders would repudiate, unequivocally, this worldview, the church still needs to confront the climate that permitted this distorted worldview to flourish. Charles Marsh sets out the theology of such a church in his critique of Douglas Hudgins. (Hudgins was a Southern Baptist Minister in Mississippi through the 1950s and 1960s.) This theology was a combination of a focus on personal conversion and sanctification that made civil rights irrelevant coupled with a residual sympathy for white supremacy. Marsh explains, "As the shepherd of First Baptist's highly influential congregation, Hudgins preached a gospel of individual salvation and personal orderliness, construing civil rights activism as not only a defilement of social purity but even more as simply irrelevant to the proclamation of Jesus Christ as God. The cross of Christ, Hudgins explained at the conclusion of a sermon in late 1964, has nothing to do with social movements or realities beyond the church; it's a matter of individual salvation."[63] A theology of neglect was a convenient device to preserve power and maintain oppression. It is so simple to insist that

Christianity is confined to the redemption of the soul that leaves a body crying out for food and justice. It is such a betrayal of the biblical witness that it defies belief that exponents of such theology had read their Bible with any real attention. A partial explanation, explains Marsh, is the impact of residual doctrines of racial superiority. So Marsh writes:

> In 1912 the Home Mission Board of the Southern Baptist Convention – the agency in charge of religious instructions for minorities and the poor – called on white Christians to help blacks reach their full potential as a separate race, for in so doing, the report stated, "we shall save Anglo-Saxon supremacy." Far less charitable was the writer of an article in Mississippi's *Baptist Record*, who argued that God intended for the white race to rule supreme over blacks, because "a race whose mentality averages on border-line idiocy" is quite obviously bereft of any divine blessing. . . . White supremacy was the "divine law," intoned the *Laurel Leader Call*, "enacted for the defense of society and civilization."[64]

If this doesn't move a reader to state of rage, then we are in a state of sin. And this is the reason why continuing white racism must be actively resisted and challenged by the white church. It should be the theme of our preaching. It must be named and confronted. The residual impact of such arguments should be forbidden. The jokes that hide implicit racist assumptions should be condemned as evil. These arguments have shaped behavior and theology and in so doing led to death and suffering on a vast scale. Zero tolerance is our only way forward.

The latest device to evade the task of repentance is the charge of "political correctness." Apparently, with these injunctions to forbid racism from our churches, we are simply being "politically correct." But the logic of accepting the charge is to make we make an intelligent discussion of social problems impossible. We must not evade the challenge of repentance. Those who want to be "politically incorrect" often want to be racist. They do not want to recognize the crime that has been committed and the remorse we need to show.

Although explicit sympathy with "white superiority" has in fact largely disappeared, the pietist gospel that insists that social justice is not part of the message continues to flourish. It is important to note that there are evangelicals who recognize that an acceptance of the authority of the Bible entails an acceptance that Christ should be Lord of all aspects of our lives, including the political and social.[65] A theology of engagement believes a gospel indifferent to social justice is a betrayal of the tradition we have inherited. The assimilation of the political dimensions of the gospel is an imperative for us all.

Two other aspects to the demands of repentance need to be noted. First, it was James Cone who explained the "fallacy of colorlessness." He writes:

> It is to be expected that white theologians, clinging to their own sense of worth as defined through identification with whiteness, will not endorse black theology enthusiastically. Some will ignore it while others will respond with the dictum: Theology is colorless! Such judgments are typical of those who have not experienced the concreteness of human suffering inflicted because of color, or who are very comfortable with a theology that is "colorless" only if "white" means absence of color.[66]

Part of the repentance must involve a recognition of the contextual nature of all theology. Theology is rooted in communities. It is expressed in language. It is lived in lives. To ignore this dimension to theology is to ignore its power. Much as we may like to imagine that the doctrine of the Trinity has no connection to earthly life (it is simply a description of God's inner life), we are mistaken. The truth is that the doctrine of the Trinity, properly perceived, connects with a total worldview that shapes our presumptions about the world in which we live. It is a doctrine that tells of the eternal God's ultimate involvement in and identification with the life of humanity and of the world via the person of Jesus and the action of the Spirit. These presumptions express themselves in how we view each other. As with feminism, the task of unmasking the way life is shaped by our theology is an imperative that involves us all.

The second aspect to repentance is an appreciation of how exhausting well-meaning "white males" can be. And please allow me at the point to indulge in a short personal recollection. I remember vividly chairing a research seminar at which a distinguished feminist philosopher of religion was giving a paper. There were about 20 people at the seminar and I was the only male in the room. In the discussion after the paper the speaker was asked: is it possible for a man to be a feminist? Without hesitation, the speaker replied: "it is very difficult. It is only possible if he has tasted oppression in some form. If he is black, or disabled, or gay, or old or poor." At the time I was aggrieved: I felt excluded; I was (well I still am) a white, able-bodied, married, young, and middle-class male. Yet of course she was right. Knowledge, in some cases, does depend on experience. I can enter imaginatively into the tragedy of an oppressed life, but that is not the same as coping with the oppression each and every day. And my reaction of hurt was wrong. Repentance involves understanding that we do not deserve gratitude for having the moral sensitivity to understand a massive injustice. Repentance involves recognizing that we have much to do before we can really expect to be entitled to join the conversation as an equal partner. The speaker hurt my feelings: but that is nothing compared to the hurt that thousands upon thousands of white males have done to women and black people everywhere.

7

OVERHEARING: CLASH OF DISCOURSES – SECULAR IN THE WEST AGAINST THE SECULAR IN INDIA

Thus far we have two examples of assimilation and one of resistance. It is now necessary to explore the third category of engagement "overhearing." The idea here is that by listening to the internal debates within other traditions, there are lessons that we can learn. Even though the basic idea is simple, the actual operation involved in "overhearing" is difficult. First, we will need to make a selection. Which debate of the millions happening in other traditions should we pick to overhear? Second, there is the problem of "decency." We are outsiders writing about the debates of another tradition: is this appropriate?

When it comes to selection, we are searching for an external problematic that can illuminate an internal problematic. The problematic that will provide the justification for this case study is the relationship between church and state (or more broadly the relationship between a dominant religion and the state). To confine the debate simply to Christian cultures is to limit the conversation unnecessarily. By taking a different religion, set in a different country, a different slant on the debate emerges. To illustrate this, this chapter will explore the problem of the secular in modern India.

The second issue of decency is an interesting one. In a recent essay on "Violent Faith" written in the light of September 11, the Christian theologian Kelton Cobb opts to illustrate the intrinsic link between faith and violence by reflecting on the sources embedded in the scriptures and tradition of Islam and Judaism.[1] My question here is whether it is appropriate.

An engaged theology depends upon a positive answer to that question. We are entering imaginatively into each other's world. We are allowing ourselves to be shaped by the other both positively and negatively. Naturally we run certain risks: the outsider can easily misunderstand. Therefore the task comes with an obligation to be theologically serious and work extremely hard to understand the other. But the risk of distortion is always there; however, given the potential benefits arising from the overhearing, the risk is worth running.

So with these preliminaries established at the outset, we turn to India. In the next two chapters we shall engage with the dynamics of political debate in India. In this chapter we shall look at the issue of "secularism." In the next chapter we shall explore the theology of inclusivity that we find in Hinduism. From all this, we shall reflect on the possible implications for the Christian tradition.

Given that the issue of the "secular" has attracted so much attention, it is perhaps helpful to state briefly the argument that I propose to develop over the course of these next two chapters. In this chapter, I intend to join a rather crowded debate about the relationship between Western understandings of the "secular" and those found in India.[2] It will be shown that, as many commentators have noted, Indian understandings of the secular owe a clear debt to Western understandings, yet have developed in a contrasting way. Indeed the Indian understanding of the secular (as interpreted in the courts, for example) exposes certain key difficulties in Western liberal tradition. The key difficulty is at the level of assumptions: the liberal tradition in the West operates with an autonomous, rational individual who opts into society, making a careful distinction between the public sphere and private life. In a deeply religious nation such as India, this distinction is not recognized in this form. Therefore as a result once "the secular" entered Indian life and thought under Western influence the discourse of secularism was justified in Indian political discourse in different ways. In fact the difficulties are so significant that it is moot point whether to talk about "secularism" is helpful at all. So this chapter concludes that we should recognize that it is possible to think in terms of religious communities (even though they are often difficult to delineate) as the defining unit in India rather than in terms of the individual (as in the West).

If we believe toleration, and justice, especially for minorities and women, are key values that all religious people should affirm, then the project for safeguarding them should move from stimulating appropriate legislation to providing cultural and theological justifications for these values that will persuade even conservative adherents of religious traditions. This is the theme of the next chapter. We shall concentrate on the distinctive Hindu justifications for toleration. It will be noted that some of these justifications are grounded in the "famous Hindu principle of inclusivity" (for want of a better term).[3] Inclusivity, it will be shown, is an inevitable outcome of any system committed to a realist account of truth; in that respect, it is appropriate and understandable. However, Hindu justifications expose a potential danger: that these different convictions from one's own simply become a subset of the greater system. To avoid this danger, we need an inclusivity that allows for the genuine possibility that the other has truth that is simply not found in one's own tradition.

This is an exercise in comparative philosophy. The task in this chapter is to analyze and compare different world views or the term I prefer "world perspectives." A world perspective is any attempt to place, understand, and locate people in respect to the past, present, and future and in relation to other people and other communities and includes the economic, social, and cultural elements. So in this respect, the Lockean liberal tradition (conversation partner number one) is a world perspective as are the other participants, which include the Indian constitutional tradition, and the Gandhian Neo-Hindu tradition. As with all comparative philosophy, one is required to simplify complex and diverse traditions to make the conversation manageable. For any oversimplifications or errors, I apologize right at the outset and welcome correction.

This chapter will now start with a brief summary of our first conversation partner: the liberal Lockean tradition.

1   The Secular in the West

Most would agree that the "secular" has its roots in the liberal tradition, which emerged supremely in the writings of John Locke. His achievement was to articulate a growing consensus rather than frame it from scratch. The acceptance of a single religious metanarrative as the basis for a shared culture of England was no longer an option. European Christendom had long since been undermined by the Protestant reformations: religious dissenters needed some sort of accommodation. With Cromwell's Protectorate and the Restoration of King Charles II in 1660 very much part of the context for Locke's work, religion as a deeply divisive and destructive force in society was well understood.

The concept of the secular then emerges in a context where religion needs to be managed by the state. The secular achieves this by refusing to admit any absolute power to any particular religious perspective. In his *Two Treatises of Government*, Locke explains how political obligation can be justified without reference to the Bible. His argument ran as follows: humans are by nature free and independent. They can, however, acquire obligations to obey political authorities that restrict their freedom, by consenting to them. The founding of political society is an agreement of all the members to accept restrictions on their freedom. From then on those members are required to comply with the rules of their society because they have consented to do so in the original contract. The original members give their explicit consent and all subsequent generations give their tacit consent.[4]

Two principal assumptions emerge in Locke's account. The first is that the basic unit of society is that famous character (or is it myth) of the Enlightenment, namely the rational, autonomous individual.[5] Locke offers the outrageous historical myth of a state of nature that was overcome by the rational calculation of individuals and that it is in their interest to surrender certain rights for the privilege of living under law. The second assumption is that it is intelligible to distinguish between one's public and private life. This is made explicit in Locke's *Letter on Toleration*, written in 1689. The cohesion of society is the goal: by distinguishing between the public and private, Locke is able to argue that religious beliefs (held by the individual in private) that differ, in Locke's case, from the Established church can be tolerated. He precludes Roman Catholics because their private belief in the authority of the Bishop of Rome in all matters sacred and temporal has public implications that are potentially destabilizing of the body politic. For Locke, Roman Catholic allegiance takes on political implications. Or as John Dunn puts it: "To worship one's God is a private 'concernment' between oneself and the deity. But to worship one's God in a Catholic rite in a Protestant country amounts to constructive subversion."[6] Less importantly for our purposes, Locke also precludes atheists because you cannot trust their oaths. Atheists are a danger to the state[7] and therefore cannot be tolerated.

Partha Chatterjee helpfully summarizes the implications that this Lockean tradition, as it developed, has had for religion. (It is unclear to what extent Locke would have intended this.)[7] Chatterjee writes:

Three principles are usually mentioned in the liberal-democratic doctrine on this subject. The first is the principle of liberty which requires that the state permits the practice of any religion, within the limits set by certain other basic rights which the state is also required to protect. The second is the principle of equality which requires the state not to give preference to the religious over the non-religious, and which leads, in combination with the liberty and equality principles, to what is known in US constitutional law as the "wall of separation" doctrine: namely, that the state not involve itself with religious affairs or organizations.[8]

Chatterjee goes on to note that the Supreme Court ruling in 1947 is the best example of this US interpretation of the secular and its relationship with religion. The case before the Supreme Court involved a New Jersey law that provided public bus transportation for children going to a Catholic parochial school as well as a public school. In judgment, Justice Black, writing for the majority, argued:

Neither a state nor the Federal Government can set up a church. Neither can pass laws which aid one religion, aid all religions, or prefer one religion over another. Neither can force nor influence a person to go to or to remain away from church against his will or force him to profess a belief or disbelief in any religion. No person can be punished for entertaining or professing religious beliefs or disbeliefs, for church attendance or non-attendance. No tax in any amount, large or small, can be levied to support any religious activities or institutions, whatever they may be called, or whatever form they may adopt to teach or practice religion. Neither a state nor the Federal Government can, openly or secretly, participate in the affairs of any religious organizations or Groups or vice versa. In the words of Jefferson, the clause against establishment of religion by law was intended to erect "a wall of separation between church and state."[9]

It is a moot point whether this interpretation of the US Constitution was intended by the Founding Fathers of America. However, it does capture the logic of the liberal political tradition. All "participation" is strictly forbidden. As we move to the Indian situation, it will rapidly become apparent that the state frequently participates "in the affairs of religious organizations." I shall show that the reason constitutes a fundamental challenge to the view of religion being assumed in this liberal tradition.

2   The Secular in India

One of the major difficulties in offering any analysis of India is its size and complexity. Take for example the relatively innocent statistic that, according to the 1981 Census of India, 82.64 percent of the population are Hindus.[10] "The so-called 'Hindu' percentage," explains Gerald Larson:

> is something of a problem, since it includes Scheduled Castes ("untouch-ables") and Scheduled Tribes ("tribals") that together account for some 23.5 percent of the total population. If one were to assume that many low-status groups would hesitate or prefer not to identify themselves with the category "Hindu," this could lower the "Hindu" total to as low as 500 million, or, in other words, not much more than 60 or 62 percent of the population.[11]

Although of course 60 or so percent of the population is a significant majority, when politics becomes entwined with religion the size of the majority does matter.

It is clear that relationship between different religious groups has bedev-iled India since Independence. The partition of India and the creation of Pakistan, so bitterly opposed by Gandhi, reflects a fundamental Muslim – Hindu divide. While the predominantly Muslim regions of Punjab and Bengal were split of from India to form West and East Pakistan, that still left Jammu and Kashmir with majority Muslim populations. In addition there are Christians, Sikhs, Buddhists, and Jains in India: all are statistically fairly small, although it is worth remembering that, although only 2.5% of the population are Christians, that still means some 20,000,000 people. The management of religious diversity was a key issue for the Constituent Assembly.

The Constituent Assembly adopted the Constitution on 26 November, 1949 and it came into effect on 26 January, 1950. In 1976 the terms "secular" and "socialist" were added to the preamble, but in respect to the term "secular" this was simply recognizing what was already implicit. The preamble of the Constitution now reads:

> WE, THE PEOPLE OF INDIA, having solemnly resolved to constitute India into a [SOVEREIGN SOCIALIST SECULAR DEMOCRATIC REPUBLIC] and to secure to all its citizens:
>   JUSTICE, social, economic and political;
>   LIBERTY of thought, expression, belief, faith and worship;

EQUALITY of status and of opportunity;
and to promote among them all
FRATERNITY assuring the dignity of the individual and the [unity and integrity of the Nation];
IN OUR CONSTITUENT ASSEMBLY this twenty-sixth day of November, 1949, do HEREBY ADOPT, ENACT AND GIVE TO OURSELVES THIS CONSTITUTION.[12]

Those of us living in the West recognize immediately the parallels with the French and US constitutions. As Robert Baird correctly notes, "by highlighting the concepts of *justice*, liberty, equality, and fraternity, The Constitution of India reads like a document with roots in Enlightenment thought."[13] Given this, one might expect a strict separation of religion and the state.

However, the actual articles pertaining to religion exhibit another motive at work. The Constitution wants to disestablish a religion: some of the practices of Hinduism are chiefly clearly in view. So Article 16 prohibits caste being a factor in employment; Article 15 insists that all people should have access to all facilities (e.g., shops and restaurants); and even Article 25 on "The right to freedom of religion" makes clear that the state can still insist that all Hindu temples are open to all classes of Hindus. Marc Galanter is right when he writes:

> The Constitution can be read as the "disestablishment" of the sacral view of caste – the courts can give no recognition to the integrative hierarchical principle; yet it recognizes the religious claims of the component parts. Claims based on the sacral order are foreclosed (in personal law reform, temple-entry, abolition of untouchability, de-recognition of exclusionary rights), but claims based on sectarian distinctiveness or group autonomy are not.[14]

This interpretation is further justified by the ways in which the Supreme Court has interpreted the constitution. Even though Article 25 lays down that: "all persons are equally entitled to freedom of conscience and the right freely to profess, practice and propagate religion," it insists that all this is subject to public order, morality, and health. It is this rider that enables the Supreme Court to interfere extensively in the matters of religion.

Robert Baird helpfully documents the main Supreme Court rulings. The state is entitled to interfere in virtually all matters not directly related to actual religious practice. These include economic affairs, appointment of priests, and certain beliefs, especially in the realm of ethics. On economics, Baird explains:

> In *Commissioner, Hindu Religious Endowments, Madras v. Sirur Matt*, it was conceded that the determination of what rituals were necessary in a temple was a "religious" determination, but that the scale of expenses, being economic, was "secular" and could be controlled by the government without interfering with religious freedom.[15]

On appointment of priests, the Tamil Nadu Hindu Religious and Charitable Endowments (Amendment) Act (1970), which overturned the hereditary system of priestly appointment in South India, was supported by the Supreme Court on condition that "Saivite priests were appointed to Saivite temples and Vaisnava priests to Vaisnava temples."[16] On ethics, the Constitutional pressure for an uniform civil code has meant that both Hindu and Islamic beliefs about monogamy, divorce, and inheritance have been significantly modified. Even though the "Hindu Code Bill" was not passed by Parliament, which would have permitted divorce, provided for intercaste marriage, and change inheritance regulations, the equivalent of that Bill was forced through in a range of different measures between 1955 and 1966.[17]

We have a situation then where the "secular" in the Indian Constitution is not operating in the neutral way suggested by the Lockean liberal tradition, but in an aggressively antitraditional Hindu way. The secular is a weapon to bring about the modification of India and therefore to undermine certain aspects of traditional Hinduism, not least the caste system.

Now there is a significant awkwardness here. On the one hand, we have, bringing, of course, my Western prejudices to the conversation, a laudable desire to create a just society that supports the rights of women and oppressed groups. On the other hand, we have an aggressive secular agenda attacking aspects of religion. For now, we shall simply note this awkwardness and return to it at the end of the chapter.

At this stage, we need to look at two important contributions to this debate. These are Neera Chandhoke's study *Beyond Secularism. The Rights of Religious Minorities* and Partha Chatterjee's *A Possible India. Essays in Political Criticism*. Both tackle the issue from contrasting vantage points, yet both end up discerning a significant difficulty in apply Western liberal assumptions to the situation in India.

Chandhoke's preoccupation is the importance of protecting the rights of religious minorities. This study is partly provoked by the growth and popularity of the Bharatiya Janata Party (BJP), which is committed to protecting the Hindu religion against attack, whether from a secular, Western, or a different religious viewpoint. Therefore much of the study is couched in terms of the clash between majoritarianism and minority rights.

His argument makes much of the importance of communities. He states explicitly, "Individuals are embedded in specific traditions and historical contexts."[18] It is this embedded environment that defines the person. Given this, the community a person belongs to needs legal protection, especially if it is a minority community. As a result of this, Chandhoke does not simply want a celebration of pluralism, but, more positively holds that "if some of these ways of life are decaying or ebbing through want of attention or through deliberate attempts, they should be protected through the grant of supportive measures."[19]

Chandhoke's study is interesting for two reasons. The first is his insight that we need to talk rather more about groups in India and much less about individuals; and the second is his affirmation of a modified secularism. On the first, as I shall show, he is entirely right; on the second he does not seem to appreciate precisely the ways in which the idea of the secular is being used. We will now look at these two aspects in turn.

On the first of his two reasons: Chandhoke stresses that talk of "individual" human rights is an insufficient basis for political society, especially in India. He writes, "[I]ndividual rights alone are not sufficient to safeguard the lives and the liberty of minority groups. This is because individual rights are more often than not transgressed if these individuals belong to communities that have been made the object of hatred and ill will."[20] Chandhoke is right here; and his argument operates on two levels. On the first level, it is a matter of historical and social fact that the so-called negative human rights (the freedoms from interference resulting in freedom of speech, practice of religion, etc.) do not operate effectively if you are part of a minority community that is constantly denigrated and abused. This is because the majority community are without fundamental respect for "another human being" (i.e., the fundamental individual human rights) because of their hostile perceptions of that individual located in the community. To illustrate this, Chandhoke quotes from one of the stories on the Partition of India: "When Lehna Singh reached Islamabad, he found himself in the middle of a violent riot. People of one religion were busy slaughtering people of another religion with the same mechanical efficiency with which his machines chopped grass. Sardar Lehna Singh also pulled out his kirpan and was determined to prove that he was a man by killing the first Muslim who came his way."[21]

Individuals disappear into their religious and corporate identity: this is seen most clearly in those aptly entitled "communal riots." Although a "communal riot" need not necessary need a minority opposed to a majority, it is often the case that there is a dominant majority who create the climate that ultimately leads to the riot.

On the second level, Chandhoke believes that individual human rights are in the end parasitic on group rights. He believes that "the effectiveness of individual rights may be contingent upon the existence of group rights."[22] He explains:

> If . . . communal riots build upon the prejudices which are latent in intergroup relations, then it is not likely that individuals can be respected for what they are, not only in cases of communal violence but also in the practices of everyday life. In some cases it is not enough to demand individual rights in the abstract. We may need to locate the bearers of rights in their affiliative community, and to look at the status or the lack of status of these communities in the wider body politic. If a community suffers from lack of recognition, it is not likely that its members will be able to exercise meaningful rights. We have to then start thinking of the rights of that community to respect and regard, in fact to existence itself, in order to institutionalize preconditions for individual rights.[23]

Chandhoke's vision, then, is that there needs to be a legal recognition of the rights of minority groups because without group rights, individual rights make little sense.

The second reason why Chandhoke is interesting is found in his interpretation of secularism. Chandhoke commends "secularism" in this respect: it is striving towards a neutral state, one that permits all religions and recognizes equality between them. Although he does talk about the limits of secularism, it is confined to the suggestion that the promotion of equality is needed in order to fortify secularism. Chandhoke writes, "The idea of shifting ground from secularism to equality is not meant to devalue the concept. It is meant to strengthen the former by bringing the insights that equality provides us with to secularism itself."[24] Given his stress on "group rights," this use of equality to supplement secularism is not surprising. Equality between religious groups might mean that the state should actively support a minority group, thereby ensuring the survival of that group.

However, Chandhoke's discussion of secularism ignores the way that the concept in the Indian Constitution has been used to (a) support a progressive social agenda, and (b) undermine and interfere in the religion of Hinduism. The BJP believe that the problem is less the protection of minorities, than the denigration of the majority. It is not clear how the group rights claim of the Hindu majority in India will be handled by Chandhoke's proposals.

Partha Chatterjee's discussion of these questions starts from the challenge posed by the BJP. His argument can be broken down into three stages: first, a recognition that the "secular" has been used as a means to the reform of Hinduism. Furthermore the constitution has protected certain minorities (e.g., Islam) from equivalent reform. Second, it is very difficult for liberal political theory to recognize the collective rights of groups. Third, Foucault's idea of governmentality provides a useful tool for analyzing this problem. However, on this model the way forward, would allow groups much greater flexibility in relation to their social arrangements. We shall now look at Chatterjee's argument in more detail.

The first stage of Chatterjee's argument need not detain us very long. This point was established in the first half of this chapter. We should simply note how Chatterjee does recognize the ways in which the minority religion of Islam has been protected against the reforming zeal of the constitution that has had so much impact on traditional Hinduism. The second stage is more important. Chatterjee recognizes a fundamental difficulty for Western liberal thought, which is posed by the religious commitments of India. He explains the difficulty thus:

> The desire for a secular state must concede defeat even as it claims to have discovered new meanings of secularism. On the one hand, the respect for cultural diversity and different ways of life finds it impossible to articulate itself in the unitary rationalism of the language of rights. It seems to me that there is no viable way out of this problem within the given contours of liberal–democratic theory, which must define the relation between the relatively autonomous domains of state and civil society always in terms of individual rights. As has been noticed for many other aspects of the emerging forms of non-Western modernity, this is one more instance where the supposedly universal forms of the modern state turn out to be inadequate for the post-colonial world.[25]

In addition Chatterjee is not entirely happy with Chandhoke's solution, namely to talk of group rights. Indeed, writes Chatterjee, "liberal political theory in its strict sense cannot recognize the validity of any collective rights of cultural groups. Liberalism must hold as a fundamental principle the idea that the state, and indeed all public institutions, will treat all citizens equally, regardless of race, sex, religion or other cultural particularities."[26]

Chatterjee is, in my judgment, entirely right. As we saw at the start of this chapter, the language of the secular is parasitic on certain very important distinctions. It rests on the idea of an individual, who is distinct from the community; and on a distinction between the public and private realms. For the Christian Western mindset, these distinctions are intelligible. We have a strong sense of the particular as opposed to the universal. We are able to disentangle the individual from families and communities. There is, in the West, an entity that has an identity apart from the whole.

However, for Muslims and Hindus, such a distinction is less clear. Within orthodox, traditional Hinduism, in particular, the public and private realms are in acute tension. The relationship between dharma and svadharma is a major theme of the *Gita*. Although there is a private realm, there are endless required connections with the public realm. No where in Hinduism do we find a "state of nature" myth where individuals opt in society. There is an important givenness to our place in the cosmos: we are born into a family, which in turn is located in a community, which in turn is located in a caste and class structure. The entire order of the universe depends on the recognition of this givenness. In short, (far too short you are probably thinking), the concept of an individual is largely a Western construct.

So if the "individual" is a problem for Hinduism, then the public and private divide will also be a problem. This public and private divide makes most sense for those religions that primarily define religious adherence in terms of "beliefs." If religion is primarily a matter of believing a creed, for example, then it is perfectly possible to believe certain propositions in the privacy of one's home. However, given that this probably only fully applies to a semisecularized form of modern Protestantism, it creates a problem for most faiths. And when the defining characteristics of a religion are social or public practice, then this distinction becomes much less clear. In both Hinduism and Islam this is predominantly the case.

All of this is very clearly seen in the debate around a uniform civil code. Returning to Chatterjee, the third stage of his argument brings this out. He uses Foucault to demonstrate that one should not be required to provide reasons for wanting to assert "a right against governmentality, i.e., a right not to offer reasons for being different."[27] This, Chatterjee insists, would be a real, albeit a non-Western, form of toleration. And therefore on the civil code issue, Chatterjee writes:

[M]y approach would not call for any axiomatic approval to a uniform civil code for all citizens. Rather, it would start from the historically given reality of separate religion-based personal laws and the intricate involvement of state agencies in the affairs of religious institutions.[28]

He concedes that this does not help the emergence of a national identity; nevertheless he wants to argue that authentic toleration requires that the uniform civil code be given time to emerge.

Let us now start to bring the threads of the argument together. First, we have an Indian Constitution that clearly owes some form of debt to Western liberal philosophy. Second, the Western liberal philosophy justifies a neutral state in terms of two key distinctions: the public/private distinction and the concept of the rational autonomous individual. Third, the legal interpretations of the Indian Constitution have demonstrated that a religious agenda is operating that is intent on imposing a progressive political agenda on Hinduism. Fourth, as several commentators have noted (and two have been discussed), the emerging position demonstrates how problematic the application of liberal Western assumptions is in the Indian situation. In particular some sort of "group" recognition of religious identities is required.

Larson is therefore right to call for the development of a "multi-religious state." He sees this as the potential "middle way." Larson writes, "There could be merit in exploring the possibility of a middle ground between the extremes of a Neo-Hindu "secular state," on the one hand, and a supposed "Hindu" state, on the other. . . . As a third option which mediates the extremes, consideration might be given to the possibility of developing the Republic of India as a "multi-religious state." No one religious tradition would be favored or established, but all would be recognized (including secularist and agnostic traditions) and "enfranchised," as it were, in matters of public policy, especially in the areas of research, education and communication."[29]

Such a proposal builds on the insight that some sort of "group" identification needs to be the foundation of the State: India is not a matter of managing individuals but groups, all with their own particular world perspective.

However, this leaves us with a significant problem. The motivation of the authors of the Constitution was good. They wanted to challenge certain religious practices that undoubtedly have created problems for significant sections of society (e.g., women and the scheduled castes). There was an affirmation of the intrinsic dignity of all people and insistence that religious perceptions should not be permitted to deny that affirmation. If groups, as opposed individuals, become the base unit in the state, then how do we develop this important politically progressive agenda?

This is to be the question at the heart of the next chapter. However, let us begin to sketch the basics of an answer. It is a theological task: theological in the sense that those of us committed to making sense of the religious traditions we occupy must demonstrate how and why a progressive politics is not alien to our faith but intrinsic to it. Furthermore we need to show that one can be true to one's faith, deeply committed to its tenets, and at the same time able to affirm the equality of all people.

So how, as a deeply committed Hindu do we justify, say, the virtue of toleration? This question, so central in modern-day Indian politics, will be the starting point for our reflection in the next chapter.

8

OVERHEARING: THINKING ABOUT HINDUISM, INCLUSIVITY, AND TOLERATION

Amongst theologians, it is fashionable to decry the concept of toleration. Toleration, explains our Radical Orthodox friends, is rooted in a secular narrative that is non-Christian and opposed to the Kingdom of God. It is a mechanism for the management of power, built on an ontology of violence, which is inappropriate for Christians to affirm.

As we saw in the last chapter, it is perfectly proper to criticize from a religious perspective the narrative of Western secularism. Hindus and Christians have significant difficulties with the assumptions underpinning the secular discourse. We saw how the Indian Constitution, while advocating neutrality ostensibly, is, in fact, deeply partisan: the Constitution is opposed to traditional forms of Hinduism. This contradiction is in part responsible for the continuing religious and cultural instability in India.

Christians and Hindus, then, should not and cannot accept uncritically a secular framework for the organization of society. However, this insight does not permit an overreaction, such as that expressed by those identifying with Radical Orthodoxy. The motives of those who framed the constitution were good: they forced a range of problems that required management. The nature and extent of the caste system, the role of women, and the treatment of religious minorities were all major social issues in India: a way forward for the progressive political agenda needed to be found.

So if we are unhappy with a secular basis to further this agenda, then it is up to those of us who belong to religious communities to suggest an alternative. This is my task in this chapter. Naturally as a Christian, I come to this issue as an outsider. However, as we learnt from the examination of secularism, a critique Hinduism by a Christian will have as a by-product the exposure of issues that the Christian might want to explore within Christianity. To sum up: the Hindu problems with secular assumptions are also problems for certain forms of Christianity: and perhaps the Hindu justification of tolerance will expose potential difficulties or parallels that can be found within Christianity. Being an outsider should not preclude one from offering an analysis.

The argument of this chapter will proceed in the following way. First, we shall examine the concept of toleration: the important point for India is to note that toleration must involve allowing not simply conflicting truth claims, but conflicting lifestyles and values. Second, we develop Gerald Larson's argument that the philosophy of the Constitution owes more to Neo-Hindu traditions than to secular values. Larson is important because he clearly links the "theological" questions with the issues dominating the previous chapter. Third, we shall then examine what I am suggesting we describe as "heretical"[1] adjustment to the Gandhian position, namely the arguments and position of the BJP. There we find a strong affirmation that toleration in Hinduism should be linked to Hindu inclusivity (this will be defined with care). Finally, we conclude by looking at the problems involved in Hindu inclusivity and suggesting that alternatives need to be found. The chapter concludes by commending and returning to the methodology implicit in the "open theology" of Keith Ward. In so doing we are anticipating our discussion of Ward's work in chapter 12.

1   Toleration[2]

For most religious people, at least historically, tolerance is not a virtue. Truth is considered much more important. Truth and toleration, as we shall see throughout the chapter, often appear in tension. To allow those in error to propagate their error and potentially lead others into error seems to the committed religious person an abrogation of responsibility. The arguments against toleration seem much stronger than the arguments in favor.

This is because toleration requires the following:

1   a recognition that one has power but is not going to use it against a minority. Only powerful groups are able to tolerate;

2   a willingness to allow that which one disapproves of strongly to continue to be. The allowance does not simply extend to the teaching of
doctrine but also to the allowance of alternative lifestyles.

It is this latter point that creates some of the major difficulties in India.
While traditional Hindus have to face innumerable restrictions in relation
to social organization (e.g., divorce), Muslims seem to have much greater
freedom. The debate about a uniform civil code is acute in India. Real
toleration has to cope with diversity of lifestyle.

However, while we may want toleration of real diversity, we may well
not want toleration of exploitative practices. The progressive political
agenda is to be given preference and developed. So a traditional lifestyle
that oppresses some groups in society needs be forbidden. This is then a
toleration firmly located within a set of values. A set of values that affirms
the dignity of all people and groups.

This then is our problem. If the secular framework is unsatisfactory,
then an alternative needs to be found. The discourse of "toleration" is
attempting to solve a real difficulty: if we are unhappy with this discourse
then an alternative is needed. Our task is to see whether such an alternative can be formulated.

Framework number 1: the Neo-Hindu solution

Gerald Larson's *India's Agony over Religion* takes an interesting position on
the relation between religion and state. He believes that "the discourse
about 'religion' and the 'state' or 'nation' in modern India is very much
a 'hybrid' discourse."[3] This hybrid discourse is made up of three aspects:
a creation narrative (this is partition), a Gandhian "Neo-Hindu" philosophy, and the implementation of that philosophy attempted by Nehru.
Larson sees these three intertwining in a bizarre mix to create modern
Indian talk about "secularism" and the "nation-state." He explains that such
talk

> must be understood from within the framework of a broadly based Neo-
> Hindu multinational-civilization-state, created by the extraordinary vision
> and person of Gandhi (the creator), sustained by the sophisticated touch and
> person of Nehru (the sustainer), and brought into being by the terrible vio-
> lence and destruction of partition (the destroyer). It is almost as if the high
> gods of the old Indic heritage, namely, Brahma the creator, Visnu the
> preserver and Siva the destroyer were having a last cosmic laugh over the

emergence of India as a modern, "secular" nation-state; and, to follow the analogy one step further, one might well be inclined to say that the lurking tragedy for India as a modern, secular nation-state some fifty years after independence is that whereas the creativity of the Gandhian vision seems to have waned and the sustaining hand of the Nehruvian touch has all but disappeared, the violent and destructive specter of partition is still alive and well on the subcontinent![4]

Larson's exposition is interesting: but will it survive closer scrutiny. Partition, of course, involved a fundamental struggle between Jinnah and Gandhi: a struggle between a vision of India inclusive of Muslims and those who insisted that Muslims needed a separate state. For Larson, this is a religious struggle, culminating in the "holocaust" of partition. Larson writes:

> Finally, the time of the holocaust drew near. By order of the House of Commons in London, two independent dominions were to be created in India between 15 July and 15 August of 1947, with 82.5 percent of wealth and territory going to India and 17.5 percent to Pakistan. Millions of Hindus, Muslims and Sikhs – estimates run as high as ten million – felt constrained to change lands because of the partition. Possibly as many as a million never reached their destination . . . It was a creation-narrative, an epic founding myth, of sheer agony over religion![5]

It is undoubtedly the case that partition had a dramatic impact on the self-perception of Indian national life. It was not simply a matter of the tragedy of the moment, but the fact that two very contrasting constitutions were then written. Pakistan is a robustly Islamic state: India became a "secular" one. For Larson, the explanation for the Indian development lies in the two other aspects of this hybrid discourse.

The second aspect is simply the genius of Gandhi. Larson is right to locate Gandhi as a successor to Neo-Hindu reformist and nationalist traditions emerging from, amongst others, the work of Rammohun Roy, Ramakrishna, and Vivekananda. Gandhi's vision is well known: he believed that all religions were ultimately one. Or, as Nehru reported:

> Gandhi told the Federation of International Fellowships in January 1928 that "after long study and experience I have come to these conclusions, that: (1) all religions are true, (2) all religions have some error in them, (3) all religions are almost as dear to me as my own Hinduism. My veneration for other faiths is the same as for my own faith.[6]

As we shall see, Gandhi has become an important battleground for Hindu views of toleration. Larson claims a Gandhian theology as the basis for the discourse surrounding the constitution, while the BJP will claim the same language to justify some of their difficulties with the constitution.

For now we shall simply note this battleground and press on to examine the third component of Larson's edifice. This is the achievement of Nehru. Larson sees Nehru as the one who was able to take the vision of Gandhi and create a modern state. Larson explains:

> Just as Gandhi had successfully created a mass political movement based on a Neo-Hindu vision of universalism, "firmness in the truth" (*satyagraha*) and non-violence (*ahimsa*) in pre-partition India, so Nehru successful created a comparable mass political movement based on a translation, or perhaps better, a kind of "demythologization," of the same Neo-Hindu vision in terms of "secularism," "socialism," "a mixed economy," "democracy," and "non-alignment" in post-partition India.[7]

Larson is right to see that there is a complex relationship between Gandhi's vision of Hinduism and Nehru's expression of it in terms of political reform. He is also right to describe it in positive terms. However, what he fails to appreciate is that Gandhi's theology does not easily translate into the language of secularism. As we saw in the previous chapter, secular language is grounded in a discourse that makes the autonomous rational individual, who distinguishes between the public and the private a central character. Gandhian discourse would not recognize this personage.

Once this is seen, it explains how the BJP is able to interpret the Gandhian tradition in a way that contrasts markedly with the constitution. It is to this interpretation of Hindu toleration that we turn to next.

Framework number 2: the BJP

The growing political success of the BJP has provoked considerable consternation. The BJP developed out of the RSS (Rashtriya Swayamsevak Sangh), which is a Hindu nationalist movement. The BJP claim that the RSS was simply developing the traditions of Gandhi and others. Indeed the Vice President of the BJP writes:

> In more recent times this torch was picked up by Swami Dayanand and Swami Vivekanada. And in the present century the good work has been carried on by Sri Aurobindo, Lokmanya Tilak, Mahatma Gandhi and others.

The RSS, founded by Dr. Hedgewar in 1925 and consolidated by Shri Guruji after 1940, is the heir to this heroic, historic heritage. It has nothing against Muslim Indians – as distinguished from Muslim invaders. Its position on this issue has all along been: "Justice for all and appeasement of none." But it has no doubt that we were and are a Hindu nation; that change of faith cannot mean change of nationality.[8]

In addition to claiming a proud ancestry, the movement also claims to exhibit Hindu toleration. So the Vice President continues:

The RSS entirely agrees with Gandhiji's formulations that "There is in Hinduism room enough for Jesus, as there is for Mohammed, Zoroaster and Moses" and that "the majority of the Muslims of India are converts to that faith from Hinduism through force of circumstances. They are still Hindu in many essential ways and, in a free, prosperous, progressive India, they would find it the most natural thing in the world to revert to their ancient faith and ways of life.[9]

At this stage I shall simply note the robust assertion of "inclusivity" – an inclusivity that can provide a home for all faiths and an expectation that conversion back to such a wide, inclusive Hinduism would be "natural" – and continue to explore the political development of this movement.

The death of Mahatma Gandhi was a pivotal moment both for India and the RSS.[10] The RSS insists that although they opposed Gandhi's "Muslim appeasement policy,"[11] they supported and admired Gandhi himself. However, given the way Gandhi's death gave impetus to the growth of the developments that the RSS were opposed to, it was felt important to develop a political wing of the movement. This emerged in 1951 as the BJS (Bharatiya Jana Sangh).

During the 1950s and 1960s the key issues were: territorial integrity, cow protection, and advocacy of a nuclear deterrent. Development and growth led to splits and difficulties, which ultimately led to the creation of the Bharatiya Janata Party in 1980. From 1984–95 there was dramatic electoral growth. Finally, real power was achieved. Originally in 1996 and then again in 1998, and most recently on 13 October, 1999, the BJP found itself in government.

The BJP are deeply disturbed by the accusation of intolerance. Much of their literature is dedicated to rebutting the accusation. A sample of their argumentation is found on their website. As this is fairly typical, I propose now to examine the key arguments that are given there in some detail.

S. Gurumurthy of the Center for Policy Studies in Madras has written an article called "Semitic Monotheism: the Root of Intolerance in India." His main contention is that civil society in the West is dominated by the state, while civil society in the East (and by this, he means primarily India) is much more decentralized and self-regulating. The Western emphasis on the state tends to be intolerant, while eastern society is much more inclusive and pluralist.

For Gurumurthy, the issue is power. In the West the state has all the mechanisms of power and anything that wants to compete with state power must organize itself in a way that is similar to the state. So he writes, "Western society . . . became largely a state construct. . . . The Church developed as a state-like institution, as an alternative and a competing institution . . . The result was a society that was at war with itself; a society in which the stately religion was at war with the religious state. The result also was centralism and exclusivism, not only in thought, but also in the institutional arrangements."[12] However, India is entirely different. He writes,

> We had decentralizing institutions, of castes, of localities, of sects belonging to different faiths; of groups of people gathering around a particular deity or around a particular individual. Society was a collection of multitudes of self-contained molecules, spontaneously linked together by sociospiritual thoughts, symbols, centers of pilgrimage, and sages.[13]

The result of this state-free society was a fundamental inclusivity and a willingness to accept difference. So Gurumurthy explains:

> In the East, more specifically in India, there prevailed a society and a social mind which thrived and happily grew within a multiplicity of thoughts . . . Refugee people, refugee religions, refugee cultures and civilizations came here, took root and established a workable, amicable relationship with their neighborhood. They did not – even now they do not – find this society alien or foreign. They could grow as constituent parts of an assimilative society and under an umbrella of thought that appreciated their different ways. . . . This openness to foreign thoughts, faiths and people did not happen because of legislation, or a secular constitution or the teachings of secular leaders and parties. We did not display this openness because of any civilizing inspiration and wisdom which we happened to have received from the West.[14]

Once this rather simplistic distinction is established, the narrative becomes slightly more nuanced towards the end. The target for criticism is Islam.

Gurumurthy believes that while Christianity has adapted and changed, mainly due to economic and technological pressures, Islam has not. Indeed, "the story of Islam is one of 1500 years of unmitigated stagnation."[15] It is for this reason that Hindus need to recover their traditional commitment to inclusivity and challenge the tendencies of Islamic exclusivity. So Gurumurthy depicts the battle thus:

> The encounter between the inclusive and assimilative heritage of India and exclusive Islam, which had nothing but theological dislike for the native faiths, was a tussle between two unequals. On the one side there was the inclusive, universal and spiritually powerful – but temporally unorganized – native Hindu thought. And on the other side there was the temporally organized and powerful – but spiritually exclusive and isolated – Islam.[16]

This is a good example of history being written to make a contemporary political point. Relations between Islam and Hinduism are tense: in addition to relations between Pakistan and India, we have the continuing difficulty over certain holy sites. Gurumurthy concludes his article by making an impassioned plea for Muslims to respect Hindu inclusivity. He writes:

> The assimilative Hindu cultural and civilizational ethos is the only basis for any durable personal and social interaction between the Muslims and the rest of our countrymen. This societal assimilative realization is the basis for Indian nationalism, and only an inclusive Hindutva can assimilate an exclusive Islam by making the Muslims conscious of their Hindu ancestry and heritage. A national effort is called for to break Islamic exclusivism and enshrine the assimilative Hindutva. This alone constitutes true nationalism and true national integration. This is the only way to protect the plurality of thoughts and institutions in this country. To the extent secularism advances Islamic isolation and exclusivism, it damages Hindu inclusiveness and its assimilative qualities. And in this sense secularism as practiced until now conflicts with Indian nationalism. Inclusive and assimilative Hindutva is the socio-cultural nationalism of India.[17]

For the BJP, then, toleration needs to be grounded in a robust affirmation of Hindu theology – on the very ground of its inclusivist possibilities. They are happy to affirm the main themes of a "secular" state, provided it is interpreted in terms of Hindu inclusivity, which means the equality and mutual respect of all religions. Underpinning this is a sense that the majority Hindu population has been treated less well than the other religious groups in India. Two writers, cited approvingly on the BJP website, illustrate this interpretation of secularism: Mihir Meghani and M.V. Kamath. So Mihir Meghani writes, "When Hindus realized that pseudo-secularism had reduced them to the role of an innocent bystander in the game of politics, they demanded a true secularism where every religious group would be treated the same and a government that would not take Hindu sentiments for granted."[18] And M.V. Kamath writes, "The masses were kept in watertight compartments under the sterile theory of secularism. What the proponents of Hindutva are now trying to do is to reverse the process and give to the people a sense not only of unity but of a mission. . . . The greatest danger to our sense of unity and our sense of purpose comes from those who under the guise of 'Secularism' keep the minorities separate and not equal. Hindutva bestows on the minorities total equality under its protective umbrella."[19]

It is worth pausing at this point and examining the argument thus far. The language of secularism, as used in the Indian constitution, involves a certain set of Western assumptions that Indian culture would find problematic. Furthermore, although it ostensibly celebrates the neutral state, the constitution is, in fact, partisan. It is a tool to further a progressive and secularist political agenda.

This lack of neutrality, embedded in the discourse of secularism, has been rumbled and the BJP has been the main beneficiary. The result is a reaffirmation of Hindu nationalism and culture. The claim is now being made that Hinduvta provides a better foundation for toleration because Hinduism is by its very nature able to accommodate fundamental diversity. What we have here, I suggest, is an heretical development of the Gandhian tradition. Where Gandhi advocated a Neo-Hindu tradition that Nehru managed to turn into secular discourse, the BJP are advocating a Neo-Hindu discourse that challenges the problematic aspects of the secular discourse as enshrined in the constitution.

What the BJP's narrative entirely ignores is the wider progressive agenda of the authors of the constitution. Neera Chandhoke, a critic of the BJP rhetoric, makes this point as an aside in a wider attack on the use of Hindu inclusivity as a basis for tolerance. He writes:

> For long, we have been told that the great virtue of Hinduism lies in its tolerance. Its tolerant character is the best guarantor of secularism, argues the Congress(I) in the CWC resolution of January 16. The party [i.e., the BJP] now plans to reappropriate Hinduism from the Sangh Parivar, in order to tell the people what it really means. Apart from the fact that Hinduism

has not precisely been known for toleration of its own people, particularly the so-called lower castes and women, the strategy of the Congress(I) is deeply flawed. For sure, the instrumental use of Hinduism to reassure the minorities who subscribe to different religions cannot but be highly paternalistic and patronizing. Notwithstanding the fact that the religious minorities are as much a part of the body politic as the majority and that they are the equal inheritors of and participants in the nation, they are being told that the majority group tolerates them because that is the nature of the majority religion. What could be more condescending?[20]

Chandhoke is right to note the social agenda: it is always important to make sure that toleration does not extend to the social permission of fundamental injustice. However, the focus of the rest of this paper is the attack which he mounts on the claim to Hindu inclusivity. Is he right to say that this is an insufficient ideological basis for social toleration?

2 Hindu Inclusivity

Let us start by one important qualification. The perception that Hinduism has always been an inclusive religion is probably a post-Vivekanada reading of the tradition, which was developed by Gandhi. There are, it should be noted, plenty of "exclusivist" strands in Hinduism.[21] Nevertheless, given the fact that Gandhian interpretation of the tradition gave birth to the possibility of secular concepts being used in the constitution and the BJP's advocacy of Hinduvta, then for our purposes this has become the significant reading of Hinduism.

A variety of classical texts are cited when talking about inclusivity in Hinduism. The Rig Veda, for example, famously claims, "Truth is one, the learned may describe it differently." Another example is the Gita's instruction, "Behave with others as you would with yourself. Look upon all the living beings as your friends, for in all of them there resides one soul. All are but a part of that universal soul." It is certainly true that such texts were often cited by Gandhi.

J.F.T. Jordens demonstrates this when he explains Gandhi's view of Hinduism: "Hinduism is non-exclusive, or all-inclusive, accepts truth and revelation in all religions, gives room to the worship of all prophets, and admits that all religions are both perfect and imperfect and are able to lead man to his final goal, *moksa*, liberation from the cycle of transmigration and merger with the Absolute."[22] Jordens goes on to illustrate this with the following quotes from Gandhi:

Hinduism is "as broad as the Universe and takes in its fold all that is good in this world," and "what of substance is contained in any other religion is always to be found in it." Not being exclusive, "it enables the followers of that faith not merely to respect all other religions, but also to admire and assimilate whatever may be good" in them. However, Gandhi did not mean to say that Hinduism was but an eclectic amalgam; no, its inclusiveness stemmed from its very nature, from the fact that it was a faith based on the broadest possible toleration.[23]

Sensitive to the criticism that Hinduism is now the best of all religions, Jordens believes that Gandhi modified his teaching to stress "equality" rather than "inclusivity." Gandhi started using a different image: instead of various rivers all heading towards the same ocean, he talked of different branches on a tree.[24] Gandhi was trying to move away from "tolerant" permission to mutual affirmation.

The actual theology, however, underpinning this shift in terminology is largely unchanged. Gandhi still believed that the ultimate unity embracing the diversity of Hinduism also accounts for and includes the diversity demonstrated by the existence of the other world faiths. Both images (the ultimate ocean and the tree) suggest that the particularities of the religious traditions are ultimately subsumed. Apparent truth-claims that suggest otherwise are mistaken (for example, that Jesus is the unique revelation of God and that this belief is essential for salvation). Such claims cannot be true, according to Gandhi, because this would contradict his conviction that all religions are equal and parts of the same tree. His Hindu worldview is clearly taking precedence over the Christian (or any other) exclusivist worldview.

These are the terms on which Gandhi gives birth to Hindu inclusivity. It is worth pausing to distinguish Hindu inclusivity from Christian inclusivity. Christian inclusivity, as understood by Rahner, comes within the framework of Christian soteriology – that is, it is to be understood in the context of God's saving purpose for his human creatures.[25] This is not the case in Hinduism. There inclusivity is better understood as the claim that ultimately the symbol system and dispositions of Hinduism capture ultimate reality more accurately than other world perspectives. In particular, this symbol system provides a better explanation for multiplicity and disagreement. This does not mean that the symbol system of Hinduism is necessarily the last word in any particular area, simply that it is a better one than the alternatives.

The great strength of such inclusivity is the underlying commitment to an universal truth. Gandhi writes, "[T]ruth is the sovereign principle, which includes numerous other principles. This truth is not only truth-fulness in work, but truthfulness in thought also, and not only the relative truth of our conception, but the Absolute Truth, the Eternal Principle, that is God."[26] For all critical realists (i.e., those committed to the view that some descriptions of the world are better than others because they capture more accurately the way the world really is), some form of inclusivity is inevitable. If I believe that my world perspective is true, then this means that I believe my description of the world is more accurate than the alternatives. If this is so, then it must mean that I am able to affirm all those who agree with me (however slight that agreement may be) because they are affirming a truth that I believe I have already discovered and probably can express more clearly.

To take an illustration by way of comparison. Richard Dawkins has a naturalistic explanation for religion. He cites certain features of religious discourse as evidence for his hypothesis which he believes is true. In addition when he encounters other atheistic world perspectives, for example, the Marxist one, he can affirm the atheism, while perhaps rejecting the economic determinism, and insist that his account of atheism clarifies and illuminates the Marxist account. Dawkins' symbol system explains both certain religious features and endorses certain elements of other atheistic worldviews, but in such a way that is, in the view of Dawkins, more accurate than either. In short a commitment to truth will necessarily imply some form of inclusivism as the explanation for such aspects of other world perspectives as agree with one's own. This recognition that a commitment to truth is bound to entail some inclusivity is the great strength of the position.

However, it is at this same point that we find ourselves with a major difficulty. Hindu inclusivity can connect and accommodate any tradition that recognizes that it is only *a* way to truth not *the* way to truth. Or to be more accurate, Hindu inclusivity, when put into practical social terms, accommodates any tradition that can see itself as a way to truth that is really able to be expressed within the language of another tradition, namely Hinduism. In this respect Gurumurthy's rather simplistic contrast between East and West is correct: an exclusivist Islam is at odds with the inclusivity of Hinduism. However, Chandhoke is right: Muslims will find it difficult to appreciate being accommodated, however sensitively, within a Hindu symbol system. (Just as Marxist atheism may jib at being depicted as a subspecies within the larger atheism of Dawkinism.)

A related and more sinister difficulty is that the BJP are using Hindu inclusivity as a weapon in the battle against Islam. Hidden behind the language of "tolerance" is a demand for Hinduism to be privileged. And the danger is then, quite blatantly, that the progressive social agenda will be thwarted. The position of the BJP tends to appeal mainly to the "conservative" Hindu population: they tend to find the positions taken by the BJP on social questions reassuring.

3   A Way Forward

Our examination of Hindu justifications of toleration has now posed an acute dilemma. Hindu inclusivity has given birth to both the exposure of the contradictions and tensions of the discourse of secularism and the aggressive political agenda of the BJP. Yet the great strength of all forms of inclusivity is an underlying commitment to truth.

One way forward is to search for alternative arguments for toleration that can be grounded in Hindu theology. Probably the most attractive contender is the Hindu awareness of the provisionality of all systems. After a careful analysis of the way that Hindu myths function, Julius Lipner writes, "we may regard the pursuit of religious truth in Hindu tradition pardigmatically as assimilative and open-ended."[27] We find in certain strands of Hinduism an awareness that all systems are endlessly displaced and remade. This strong commitment to the provisionality of any particular theology at any time could entail an awareness that an unconditioned commitment to any particular theological insight would be inappropriate. Equally, it would be inappropriate to be overly passionate about opposing theological positions, as if they were absolutes.

Although this alternative Hindu justification for toleration is worth exploring, there is a danger that might lose the possibility of having some approximate knowledge of the way things are. Therefore this chapter will conclude with a brief exploration of how truth, inclusivity, and toleration might combine together.

Keith Ward has attempted to combine the three together in his advocacy of what he calls "open theology." Writing within the context of Christianity, Ward explains:

> One might perhaps speak of an "open theology," which can be characterized by six main features. It will see a convergence of common core beliefs, clarifying the deep arguments which underlie diverse cultural traditions. It will seek to learn from complementary beliefs in other traditions, expecting that there are forms of revelation one's own tradition does not express.

It will be prepared to reinterpret its beliefs in the light of new, well-estab-
lished factual and moral beliefs. It will accept the full right of diverse belief-
systems to exist, as long as they do not cause avoidable injury or harm to
innocent sentient beings. It will encourage a dialogue with conflicting and
dissenting views, being prepared to confront its own tradition with critical
questions arising out of such views. And it will try to develop a sensitivity
to the historical and cultural contexts of the formulations of its own beliefs,
with a preparedness to continue developing new insights in new cultural
situations.[28]

Certain strands of Hindu theology would, I suggest, have no problem in
accepting, in appropriately modified shape, Ward's theological method. His
achievement, in his four-volume comparative theology project, is to
demonstrate that theology in conversation does make a difference. The
presuppositions of his method are worth making explicit. First, Ward
assumes a critically realist framework: he accepts that theology is in the
business of making sense of the complexity of the world in which we live.
Second, unlike Hans Küng's global ethics project, he does not assume that
the task is simply to reach agreement around an ethical core. The task is
both harder and less clear. He constantly admits the diversity of strands
within each religion and the confusing overlaps across traditions. Third,
he rejects the view that the symbol system of any particular religious tradition can subsume the insights of all other traditions.

As our case study in Hindu inclusivity has indicated, it is a remarkable
achievement to hold these three presuppositions together. Ward manages
to do so because he admits that ultimate and definitive truth is only available at the eschaton, even though some traditions at certain times in some
respects are closer to the ultimate truth than other traditions. However,
given that none have complete knowledge of all the truth, then all need
to be open to learning from others. And the truths that other traditions
have to teach us will not necessarily be already contained within our own
tradition.

Ultimately, to use religious terminology, this will mean that religious
diversity is intended by God. Some sort of explanation for the fact of religious diversity needs to be provided. The explanation Ward hints at is that
given the complexity of our subject matter (the relationship of the ultimate with the world), then it is inevitable that different cultures arrived
at different accounts. Therefore we can learn more about the God we
believe in from the perspectives of other faith traditions.

The task is to find some account that is true to the roots of Hindu
theology and yet affirms the progressive political agenda. Gandhi advo-

cated Hindu inclusivity, which was clearly a factor in the theology that shaped the inclusion of the secular discourse that was used in the constitution. However, the BJP use of that tradition exposes certain key difficulties for the progressive social agenda. The alternative, I have argued, needs to be grounded in an "open theology." This is a method that remains committed to truth, yet concedes the complexity of that truth and the need to learn from other sources.

We shall return to Keith Ward later in the book. It is sufficient to note now how the act of "overhearing" is helpful in clarifying a difficulty that Christians might have when it comes to the engagement with other religious traditions. As we have "overheard" the Hindu critique and attitude to Islam, so it might require Christian theologians to revisit our enthusiasm for a theology of other religions that is "inclusivist."

9

ASSIMILATION: CHRISTIANITY AND THE CONSENSUS AROUND CAPITALISM

In the last five chapters we have explored the dynamics of engagement; two have illustrated assimilation, two have involved overhearing and one has involved resistance. However, beyond the simple variety, the more significant discovery that we are making is that dynamics of engagement takes a different form with different issues. So having assimilated the language of human rights, we then find that we are forced to resist the language of state sovereignty. Or having assimilated the insights of feminist and black theology, we are forced to confront the twin dynamics of repentance and modification. Or having overheard from the Hindu critique of Islam, we find a strong imperative to rethink our own language of the religious other. The dynamic of engagement will vary from issue to issue.

Some might object at this point in the argument and point out that the economic realm has been neglected. Yet for many theologians, we have learnt from Marx that this is a primary category for engagement. It is, the argument goes, an issue of resources and power. As will become clear from the next two chapters, I concede that engagement with economics is important (although we must resist the temptation to overstate its significance) and as we do so two discoveries require assimilation. First, we need to assimilate the centrality of the market as a vehicle for effective social organization and management of resources; second, we need to recognize the appropriate benefits that globalization can bring. However, these two discoveries create opportunities for the church. With the first discovery, we should start the task of articulating more clearly our cultural vision for society. And with the second discovery, we need to ensure that the poor and excluded are able to participate more effectively in the processes of globalization.

In this chapter the focus is on the relationship between economics and culture. In the next chapter the focus is on globalization. Here, given the global theme, I treat the issue in conversation with, perhaps what might be regarded as the two important conversation partners, neo-Marxists and Islam. To make this manageable I take representatives: for the neo-Marxists, I am using Michael Hardt and Antonio Negri; for Islam, I am taking the thought of the Turkish thinker Bediuzzaman Said Nursi.

We start then with the argument that a market-orientated form of capitalism needs to be assimilated by the Christian tradition. We need to accommodate the virtual consensus, certainly in the Western world, of the effectiveness of the market. In this case study the point will be that having arrived at the assimilation of the centrality of the market then the task for religious traditions changes. It becomes one of engaging more effectively with the cultural life of a nation.

I shall start this examination of consensus politics by exploring the shift in Roman Catholic Social Teaching, which I shall show has moved from a strong hostility to capitalism to a critical affirmation of it.[1] There is then a rough consensus on the matter involving Thatcher, Blair, and Rome. If there has come to be such a consensus in the economic realm, political debate needs to focus on the conflicting cultural visions available in our society.

We start then with Rome. In two significant encyclicals written in 1891 and 1931, we find a hostile attitude to capitalism. In 1891 *Rerum Novarum* (1891) identified a battle between "capital" and "labor." Capital referred to the rich who are responsible for the misery of the poor. Pope Leo XIII argued that the rights of labor to the conditions necessary for basic human flourishing need to be safeguarded by the state over against capital. *Quadragesimo Anno* (1931) identified a villain called "monopoly capitalism," which behaves like a dictatorship. This dictatorship, Pius XI writes, "is being most forcibly exercised by those who, since they hold the money and completely control it, control credit also and rule the lending of money. Hence they regulate the flow, so to speak, of the lifeblood whereby the entire economic system lives, and have so firmly in their grasp the soul, as it were, of economic life that no one can breathe against their will."[2] This overt antagonism to capitalism is mitigated by the time we get to Pope John XXIII, who in *Mater et Magistra*, sounds almost Keynesian. He argues that it is a duty of the state to achieve the common good, so:

These same developments make it possible to keep fluctuations in the economy within bounds, and to provide effective measures for avoiding mass unemployment. Consequently, it is requested again and again of public authorities responsible for the common good, that they intervene in a wide variety of economic affairs, and that, in a more extensive and organized way than heretofore, they adapt institutions, tasks, means, and procedures to this end.[3]

It took a Polish Pope, especially sensitive to the dangers embodied in the socialist projects of Eastern Europe, to move the earlier engagement with capitalism in a different direction.[4] Admittedly, in *Laborem Exercens* (1981), capitalism is attacked for treating the human worker as a "commodity" and this is not compatible with the Christian doctrine of humans as the *Imago Dei*. However, in *Centesimus Annus* (1991), written in the light of the truly historic event of the Eastern European revolution, the Pope actually commends a form of capitalism. He wants a "society of free work, of enterprise and of participation."[5] He acknowledges the legitimate role of the profit motive. And then he turns to the crucial question: "can it perhaps be said that, after the failure of Communism, capitalism is the victorious social system?"[6] His judgment deserves to be quoted in full:

> The answer is obviously complex. If by "capitalism" is meant an economic system which recognizes the fundamental and positive role of business, the market, private property and the resulting responsibility for the means of production, as well as free human creativity in the economic sector, then the answer is certainly in the affirmative, even though it would perhaps be more appropriate to speak of a "business economy," "market economy" or simply "free economy." But if by "capitalism" is meant a system in which freedom in the economic sector is not circumscribed within a strong juridical framework which places it at the service of human freedom in its totality and sees it as a particular aspect of that freedom, the core of which is ethical and religious, then the reply is certainly negative.[7]

This seems to me completely clear. Pope John Paul II endorses the centrist capitalism of continental Europe: the capitalism of the Christian Democrat parties on the Continent. It is a capitalism which uses the market and encourages competition, yet ensures that there are sufficient in the way of legal safeguards and regulation to protect labor. This interpretation is supported by the Pope's subsequent endorsement of the welfare state, though this is coupled with a warning against excessive dependence. This is a significant shift in emphasis from earlier Vatican attitudes to capitalism, one which has not entirely been taken on board by

Roman Catholic social teachers.[8] The Pope in *Centesimus Annus* has made it completely clear that he is a critical, yet friendly, conversation partner with capitalism.

Now this is not an argument from authority. All it illustrates is that one traditional opponent of capitalism, ostensibly attempting to write from the perspective of centuries, finds itself in agreement with a "consensus" that dominates the Western world. It is important to stress that this is a limited even if significant consensus. My one sentence summary would be as follows: **the consensus affirms that some form of market orientated capitalism, with appropriate legal regulation that is often welfare-motivated, is the best way of organizing the economic life our society.** This, I suggest, is affirmed by the mainstream left and right in both Europe and the United States.

1 The Economic Consensus

Now all of this is contestable. So let us analyze this economic consensus a little more closely. Consensus is, of course, a relative term. It probably implies previous states where there was marked divergence and disagreement. Also there maybe consensus on major questions, while there is continuing disagreement, or different emphases, over the details. Talk today about an economic consensus is only possible because for most of the twentieth century there was an obvious ideological opponent to capitalism. This, as already noted, is the context for *Centensimus Annus*. Marxism, in its strongest proselytizing form, offered an analysis of history, a positive critique of the wealth that capitalism had created, a moral critique of the operations involved in capitalism, and a method to bring about change. It failed primarily for two reasons: the governments who attempted to implement the Marxist vision were totalitarian with the consequences of fear and social sterility. Therefore they became unworkable, especially with freer societies so close. Secondly, instead of sharing the wealth of capitalism amongst the people, Communist societies became relatively poorer. Anthony Giddens puts this failure down to the weakness of the Socialist economic analysis: "The economic theory of socialism was always inadequate, underestimating the capacity of capitalism to innovate, adapt and generate increasing productivity. Socialism also failed to grasp the significance of markets as informational devices, providing essential data for buyers and sellers. These inadequacies only became fully revealed with intensifying processes of globalization and technological change from the early 1970s onward."[9] As Marxism crumbled, so as a small but significant British symptom, clause 4 of the Labor Party constitution had to be dropped. We can indeed speak of an emerging consensus on matters of fundamental economic structures.

Two further illustrations of the consensus come from those clearly defining themselves on the center left. Will Hutton is probably the most eloquent advocate of a Keynesian alternative, which primarily means a stronger role for the state than traditional capitalists would accept. In *The Stakeholding Society*, he chooses to define the apparent consensus as "individualist market capitalism," and presses an alternative involving a reduction in "inequality." Yet note, he writes, "I accept that the price mechanism is the best means we have to allocate goods and resources, and that signals of profit and loss are the most compelling means we can devise to drive both the level and composition of output in ways that correspond to real demand."[10] The centrality of the market is conceded. In my terminology, on the fundamental issues, Hutton is part of the consensus.

Anthony Giddens provides my second illustration. He writes, "Third way politics, it could be suggested, advocates a *new mixed economy*, . . . [which] looks instead for a synergy between public and private sectors, utilizing the dynamism of markets but with the public interest in mind."[11] Giddens is completely persuaded that Marxist Socialism is discredited: the new mixed economy is a regulated market. Precisely what the Pope argues for in *Centesimus Annus*.

However, both Giddens and Hutton believe that there is a significant divide that challenges the consensus. In the passage quoted, Hutton introduces the word "individualist" because it challenges those who are committed to some form of "equality." Giddens is at his most radical when discussing the concept of equality. "Equality of opportunity" is insufficient, he argues, instead we need an "equality as inclusion."[12] However, I want to suggest that Giddens and Hutton are both advocating a different "cultural vision" rather than a different economic one.[13]

2   The Relationship Between Economics and Culture

At this point I want to introduce the whole issue of the relationship between economics and culture. By culture, I mean the set of social assumptions and world perspective that shape the self-understanding of a people. Economic visions are often subsets of broader cultural ones.[14] This has always been so. Thus, Feudal society and culture were parasitic on an agrarian economy. And the whole culture of early expansionist industrial society with its need for maximum markets thrived on minimalist state activity and wide cultural enterprise.

One could indeed argue that "culture" is the primary category. The right-wing journalist, P.J. O'Rouke seems to surprise himself when he discovers that the main requirement for economic prosperity is society's whole fabric of beliefs and assumptions, manifested in, for example, its political and legal institutions. He writes:

> I began this book by asking why some parts of the world are rich and others are poor, and I naturally had prejudices about what the answers would be. I favored the free market . . . I was skeptical about the ability of politics to deliver economic benefits. . . . I was stupidly surprised to find out how important law is. Law, of course, derives from politics. And a political system is ultimately a product of a society's attitudes, ideas, and beliefs – that damned conundrum, its culture.[15]

The relationship between economics, law, politics, and culture is, of course, extremely complex. The point for our purposes is that the existence of a significant economic consensus is not the heart of the matter. Harold Wilson was wrong to believe that the economy determines the result of elections. This belief in a "god-like" status for economics in the public mind reflects a continuing and utterly misguided Marxist sympathy, as if people's economic conditions are the chief determinant of their political views. The truth is much more complicated.

So when it comes to Giddens' and Hutton's stress on "equality," in my judgment, the dominating vision is a "cultural" rather than an "economic" one. Although there is currently a striking convergence on the status of the market, contemporary political debate is dominated by very different social visions. Admittedly the social visions carry different economic implications; for example, one cultural vision might entail a more progressive taxation system. Nevertheless, the "driving force" is a cultural vision not an economic theory. When a person worries about actual inequality, then the underlying anxiety is a sense of the "type of society one is constructing." Those who wish to reduce the gap between rich and poor will place this objective before the all-out pursuit of wealth as a primary goal for society.

3 Relocating the Debate: Culture Displaces Economics

To summarize the argument thus far: there is a remarkable degree of consensus about the central economic framework in which society ought to operate. Some form of legally regulated market-orientated capitalism is seen by most as the best way to organize our society. The market has triumphed: capitalism did win the Cold War. In addition it looks as if this consensus will survive for some time. Its durability can be demonstrated by a simple exercise in futurology, namely, in what ways might it break down?

Those of the Green persuasion see environmental collapse as on the near horizon but the technological benefits of the market are arguably the environment's greatest friend. The traditional Left will cite the continuing and growing inequalities between rich and poor, not only within Britain and America but nationally – despite the best efforts of welfare-minded politicians. Inequalities, they argue, will lead to greater crime and in time the collapse of civil society. I concede that this is a danger. The most significant form of "exclusion" is unemployment, and making sure that the poor are able to participate in the challenge of the market is essential to the survival of the consensus.

Naturally there are scenarios that would destroy the consensus. For example, a massive depopulation of the world due to a hitherto unknown virus would be doomsday indeed. Given the market's need for a significant population to generate the wealth we all participate in, this is a potentially serious problem. However, this is a challenge to the survival of the human race in general and would undermine all forms of economic life. Therefore it is not specifically a challenge to the present economic consensus.

So we are in an interesting period. Our political discourse is undergoing a significant revolution. The old preoccupation with state control as opposed to private enterprise as the determinative forces in the economy will disappear. It will be displaced with contrasting cultural visions. Instead of the economists shaping public policy, the sociologists and cultural analysts will be in demand. The third way requires a vision of society, not details of economic manipulation.

4   Competing Cultural Visions

If we stop thinking in terms of different economic visions, then we can start shaping the sort of world we want to create. The economic question is now resolved: some form of market economy, in which the state can be a participant, is the best economic foundation for society. However, I want to argue that we should not overstate the significance of this fact.

Capitalism still leaves open the question: what sort of society do we want to create? It is often observed that it is difficult to attack "capitalism." Those with the wealth are faceless and untraceable. They are the Chief Executives of large corporations. Indeed, some argue, this is the reason why capitalism provokes riots at a G8 summit: it is the quest to find something that one can identify with the enemy and protest against.

However, this is misguided. Some form of market economy, in which the state can be a participant, still leaves plenty of room for different models of society. Granted, it does have certain implications. It will mean globalization – as we shall see in the next chapter – is something we must accommodate. However, it is also important to see that the individuals participating in the market have the opportunity and the power to shape the future. If we all decide to invest in churches and social organizations, then we will have a strong community orientated vision of the future. If we all decide to go "bowling alone" (to echo Putnam's famous phrase)[16] and watch cable television, then the world will be much more individualist. But the power for these different futures does reside with the decisions of each individual person.

The churches have both a vested interest and a theological commitment to creating a world where humans interact, support each other, create opportunities for sharing and giving. This vision of society is partly realized by making every congregant a part of a subgroup within a church. So for example, the pastor invites every person who steps inside a church to join a group. It could be a house group or a social action group. But participation is the key.

We need to create an inclusive cultural vision, where people enjoy each other. As a part of this it is vitally important that the poor realize the opportunity to work with the market. Tony Blair and Bill Clinton were both right to detect that this consensus on the role of the market will only survive if the poor are included in the collaborative culture of society. Urban regeneration must be a priority. The "New Deal" and the various partnership forums which are implementing an imaginative childcare program are very important. To put it graphically: if a place like Kirkby in Liverpool does not find a way to participate in the working of capitalism, then it is conceivable that the consensus could fall apart.

In conclusion, the argument of this chapter can be summarized thus: first, there is an economic consensus on the fundamental questions. This consensus affirms the centrality of the legally regulated market. Second, this creates an opportunity for the churches. Our task is to construct our cultural vision and persuade the thousands of people participating in the market to make their decisions in favor of that vision. However, it will be objected that this argument is to sanguine about the market. What about the damaging consequences of capitalism? This is the issue that I turn to in the next chapter.

10

ASSIMILATION AND OVERHEARING: RETHINKING GLOBALIZATION – BEDIUZZAMAN SAID NURSI'S RISALE-I NUR, HARDT, AND NEGRI

The last chapter has already made the case that there is agreement that some form of free-market capitalism is the most effective form of social order. This assertion has certain implications for a directly related question – the whole complex issue of globalization. In this chapter, I shall introduce a further dynamic to engagement: it is possible and often proper to utilize more than one aspect of engagement. So here we shall utilize both assimilation (in that globalization is a reality that the church must and should accommodate) and overhearing (that we should do while listening carefully to those in traditions that you might expect to find globalization problematic).

The two traditions chosen are the Islamic tradition (and here the thought of Bediuzzaman Said Nursi shall be taken) and the Marxist tradition (and Michael Hardt and Antonio Negri serve as representatives). I selected Nursi because he is a useful challenge to the striking ignorance amongst Christian theologians about the diversity of Islamic thought. Nursi is an advocate of nonviolent resistance who had a very nuanced view of modernity and is the spiritual inspiration for four to six million Muslims in modern Turkey. I select Hardt and Negri because their book is the best postmodern Marxist critique of globalization. This chapter will start with a brief examination of the meaning of the word "globalization." I shall defend the view that it is important to retain at the heart of the word the idea of market capitalism as the main framework for economic activity. This, I shall suggest, partly explains why globalization is such an issue today. We will then look at Hardt and Negri's *Empire*. This book is a postmodern Marxist response to the economic dynamic underpinning globalization. It will be noted that there are dangers in confining the conversation about globalization to advocates and opponents of free-market capitalism writing largely in the European and American context. Hence there is a need to introduce others into the conversation.

At this point, we shall identify four themes in the work of Bediuzzaman Said Nursi's Risale-I Nur. These four points reintroduce the centrality of the ethical and religious in our dealings with each other in society. From this perspective, the chapter will suggest we need to recover certain basic ethical insights that shape our behavior with each other. In so doing, globalization can be made to work in a constructive way for society.

1   What is Globalization?

Although everyone agrees that "globalization" is a helpful category, there is considerable disagreement about its precise meaning. Many commentators, while conceding an economic aspect to globalization, want to see it defined much more broadly. So Roland Robertson, for example, writes:

> For present purposes, globalization may be defined simply as the compression of the world. This notion of compression refers both to increasing sociocultural density *and* to rapidly expanding consciousness. Globalization itself has been a long term process extending over many centuries, although only in recent centuries has it, with increasing rapidity, assumed a particular, discernible form. Globalization is, it should be clearly recognized, a multidimensional process. In other words, it is simultaneously cultural, economic, and political.[1]

While it is true that the availability of CNN worldwide (media), the growth in international organizations (political) and the MacDonald's fast food option in virtually every city (economic/cultural) illustrate the diversity of factors driving globalization, it is also important to recognize that "globalization" as an issue is linked to the triumph of capitalism in the

Cold War. In other words, Robertson had identified some consequences related to the mobility of people around the world. If this was the main cause of globalization, then it would not account for the hostility that globalization has created. Although Robertson is correct to insist that globalization should not be reduced to free-market capitalism, it is important to recognize the centrality of the economic in our contemporary debates about the nature of globalization.

Kofi Annan (the Secretary General of the United Nations) pointed out that when opponents talk of globalization, they see it as "an ideology of predatory capitalism."[2] This is precisely what provoked the opposition of the demonstrators at the meeting of the eight industrialized countries at Genoa[3] in 2001. So the International Monetary Fund (one of the most hated organizations) is right to put the emphasis on economics, when globalization is defined thus:

> Economic "globalization" is a historical process, the result of human innovation and technological progress. It refers to the increasing integration of economies around the world, particularly through trade and financial flows. The term sometimes also refers to the movement of people (labor) and knowledge (technology) across international borders. There are also broader cultural, political and environmental dimensions of globalization that are not covered here.[4]

The current extent of the hostility to globalization is one reaction to the Eastern European revolution of 1989. Francis Fukuyama in the summer of 1989 talked about the triumph of liberal democracy as the "end point of mankind's ideological evolution."[5] He was not alone; Richard John Neuhaus, the American theologian, saw it as a triumph for the values of capitalism over the dehumanizing tendencies of communism.[6] The Eastern European revolution was a key step in the perception of globalization as the vehicle for the victory of capitalism over all its alternative ideologies. For this reason the definition of globalization suggested by the International Monetary Fund will be used in this paper.

2   Hardt and Negri: *Empire*

Michael Hardt is a Professor in the Literature program at Duke University in the United States. Antonio Negri is currently a prisoner at Rebibbia Prison, Rome. Prior to that, he was a political theorist at

the University of Paris and the University of Padua. This book is important because it is the most substantial post-Marxist attempt to explore the
problem of globalization.

The argument of the book is simple: globalization is a symptom of the
new Empire. The new Empire is a result of the demise of the sovereignty
of the nation state. However:

> throughout the contemporary transformations, political controls, state
> functions, and regulatory mechanisms have continued to rule the realm of
> economic and social production and exchange. Our basic hypothesis is that
> sovereignty has taken a new form, composed of a series of national and
> supranational organisms united under a single logic of rule. This new global
> form of sovereignty is what we call Empire.[7]

Empire, or globalization, is the latest strategy of the wealthy and powerful to control the weak and powerless. It has a number of advantages
over the traditional nation state that it has displaced. First, it has no boundaries. Second, it is attempting to create this myth that it is simply the
logical expression of certain economic laws. Third, it wants to shape
every aspect of human life. And finally, it shelters behind the rhetoric of
peace.[8]

The study makes much of the decline of state sovereignty. It documents
with some care the distinctive set of historical and social conditions that
gave birth to the idea that a particular people within a particular bound-
ary are sovereign over their actions. It notes that this was often a device
that protected a tyranny. Within the nation state, the European powers
worked for ethnic purity, while outside the nation state, these same powers
worked to suppress and control the other. In other words, the European
Enlightenment has strong tendencies towards racism and colonialism.

As national sovereignty declines, however, "Empire" emerges. Where
traditional national sovereignty was grounded in a "transcendent" ruler (for
example, the king over his people), the Empire is now using Capital to
operate on the plane of immanence:

> Capital . . . operates on the plane of *immanence*, through relays and networks
> of relationships of domination, without reliance on a transcendent center of
> power. . . . In the passage of sovereignty towards the plane of immanence,
> the collapse of boundaries has taken place within each national context and
> on a global scale. The withering of civil society and the general crisis of
> the disciplinary institutions coincide with the decline of nation-states as
> boundaries that mark and organize the divisions in global rule. The

establishment of a global society of control that smoothes over the striae of national boundaries goes hand in hand with the realization of the world market and the real subsumption of global society under capital.[9]

Hardt and Negri believe that the socialism of Marx (revolution within the nation state) or the socialism of the "localization of struggles" are over.[10] Instead globalization (Empire) opens up a new option for struggle. They write:

> Empire creates a greater potential for revolution than did the modern regimes of power because it presents us, alongside the machine of command, with an alternative: the set of all the exploited and the subjugated, a multitude that is directly opposed to Empire, with no mediation between them.[11]

In other words, Empire requires a global alliance amongst the multitude against oppression. They note the irony that although mass communication means that we all know about the revolts and strikes in other parts of the world there is no mutual shared ownership by the oppressed people of the world.

> In other words, (potential) revolutionaries in other parts of the world did not hear of the events in Beijing, Nablus, Los Angeles, Chiapas, Paris, or Seoul and immediately recognize them as their own struggles . . . This is certainly one of the central and most urgent political paradoxes of our time: in our much celebrated age of communication, *struggles have become all but incommunicable*.[12]

Nevertheless, the authors do sketch a political program that would be global in intent and organization. The first political demand would be global citizenship. Mobility of labor is a key condition for capitalism to thrive, yet the millions who do relocate often find themselves as illegal aliens in a foreign land, crudely and ruthlessly exploited. Instead there should be "Residency papers for everyone," which "means in the first place that all should have the full rights of citizenship in the country where they live and work."[13] The second demand is "a social wage and a guaranteed income for all."[14] The third is the right to reappropriation, which means "having free access to and control over knowledge, information, communication, and affects – because these are some of the primary means of biopolitical production."[15] Both Augustine's *City of God*, for spotting how the two Kingdoms of good and evil are mingled together, and St.

Francis of Assisi, for insisting on living a life of joy against the abuses of power, are the heroes of the last section of this book.

Although there is much that is perceptive in this book, the major weakness is that it operates with a crude dualism – on the one hand, capitalism and globalization and on the other, justice for the poor. The narrative of the book focuses on power, especially the power shifts from the nation state to global organizations. It takes no account of the argument of those who see that religion (especially, according to Weber, Calvinist religion) is a key factor in generating the capitalist spirit. For Hardt and Negri, the religious component operates in two ways: Augustine provides a framework and St. Francis of Assisi provides an example of counter-cultural living.

However, against this understanding of the relationship between capitalism and religion, we find Max Weber. Weber, in his famous essay *The Protestant Ethic and the Spirit of Capitalism*,[16] argued that it was no coincidence that capitalism evolved in those countries most influence by Calvinism. It was a theological disposition, where one had to live a life of virtue (often interpreted as hard working and frugal) to demonstrate the necessary fruits of the Spirit thereby imparting the self-confidence that one is saved (i.e., part of God's chosen – God's elect), that provided the perfect impetus for capitalism. Now it is not necessary, for my purposes, to accept the details of the Weberian thesis about the role of religion in capitalism. All one need accept is that in amongst the many factors that shaped capitalism there were constructive and good ones. And as it is with capitalism so it is with globalization. To reduce both to the manipulation of resources by the powerful is a crude simplification. Capitalism has generated vast wealth: it has created lifestyle options that previous generations would not have been able to imagine. It has created technological options that can transform life for the elderly and individuals with special needs. Globalization opens up possibilities: it is result of globalization that an English academic can work in the United States and learn from the insights of Nursi in Turkey.

One further reason to reintroduce religious themes into this debate about globalization needs to be mentioned. At the heart of a market economy are a whole set of virtues. The primary one is "trust." The banking system in the West depends on trust: indeed the bank collapses if all savers withdraw their money from the institution at the same time. A contract between the customer and a restaurant is made on the mutual understanding that a healthy product will be served and the customer will pay for the product at the end. V.A. Demant, the English theologian of the 1930s, makes this point well when he writes:

> The period of capitalism . . . has much else in its economic and social structure besides the free interplay of marketable commodities and services. Underneath that, and keeping society together, were ties and responsibilities surviving from the feudal and local social structure. Underneath it, too, were dispositions and spontaneous social disciplines reared in towns and localities, small enough to constitute what the sociologists call an "assessment group" where every member is under moral and social assessment by his community fellows. That wisest father of modern sociology, Frederick Le Play, and his disciple Emile Durkheim, as well as experts like Karl Mannheim, have made clear that only because of this non-capitalist substructure, was the market economy possible on top of it. . . . There was also much religion and the ethics of Christianity informing persons in the capitalist era.[17]

Capitalism is not simply about power over resources, it is also about the relationship of religion and ethics to economic life.

The danger in this debate about globalization is that we allow our reflections on globalization to be confined to the perspectives of the political left (i.e., those with socialist sympathies) and the political right (i.e., those with capitalist sympathies). To prevent this danger, we shall now turn to the work of Bediuzzaman Said Nursi. If I am right in stressing the religious factors at the heart of capitalism and globalization, then we should expect to learn from Nursi.

2   Four Themes in Bediuzzaman Said Nursi

Even with great thinkers it is dangerous to expect to apply their thought to problems that they did not experience. The world of Bediuzzaman (which means Wonder of the Age) Said Nursi (1873–1960) is one that moved from the concluding years of the Caliphate and Ottoman Empire, through the tragedy of the First World War, to the emergence of the Republic of Turkey in 1923 with an initial strong commitment to aggressive secularism. We are all shaped by the world we encounter. For Nursi, he discerned correctly the challenge of modernity to belief and the response was the Risale-I Nur (the Treatise of Light), which provided a strong apologetic for the Qur'an.

Although we should not search for the word "globalization" in the work of Nursi, we do find that there are four themes in Nursi that are relevant. The first is that it is appropriate to build bridges between Western, scientific culture and the Islamic world. Nursi had a very strong sense that the best of modernity is both compatible with and anticipated in Islamic thought. So he writes explicitly about certain technological developments: "Things like the aeroplane, electricity, railways, and the telegraph have come into existence as wonders of science and technology as the result of man's progress in science and industry. Surely the All-Wise Qur'an, which addresses all mankind, does not neglect these. Indeed, it has not neglected them."[18] He goes on to argue that such technological advances are anticipated in the Qur'an. This enthusiasm for the achievements of science underpins his "natural theology" (i.e., his belief that there are good and decisive arguments for God's existence from the world). He lists the sciences of various disciplines before concluding:

through the certain testimony of hundreds of sciences like these, the universe has been adorned with innumerable instances of wisdom, purposes, and beneficial things within a faultless, perfect order. And the order and wisdom given through that wondrous, all-encompassing wisdom to the totality of the universe have been included in small measure in seeds and the tiniest living creatures. It is clear and self-evident that aims, purposes, instances of wisdom, and benefits can only be followed through choice, will, intention, and volition, not through any other way. Just as they could not be the work of unconscious causes and Nature, which lack will, choice, and purpose, so too they could not interfere in them.[19]

Indeed for Nursi the sciences are part of God's intended purposes for humanity. So he writes:

The miracles of the other Prophets (Peace be upon them) all indicate a wonder of human art or craft, and Adam's (Peace be upon him) miracle indicates in concise form, besides the bases of those crafts, the index of the sciences and branches of knowledge, and of the wonders and perfections, and urges man towards them.[20]

His confidence that Islam endorses the technological dynamic of modernity (a major feature of globalization) is reflected in this vision of the future. So one writer on Bediuzzaman writes as follows:

Indeed, as we shall see when examining the Sermon, Bediuzzaman predicted that according to all the signs, Islam and Islamic – or, true – civilization would prevail in the future, and that the majority of mankind would accept and join the religion of Islam. He said: "In the future when reason, science and technology hold sway, that will surely be the time the Qur'an will gain ascendancy, which relies on rational proofs and makes the reason confirm its pronouncements."[21]

The important point is that it is a in a world where reason, science, and technology hold sway, that the truth of the Qur'an will be recognized.

The temptation for many who are sympathetic to religion is to see the emergence of modernity (and its children – the growth of technology and therefore globalization) as evils that religion must oppose. Bediuzzaman argues very clearly that an attitude would be misguided. The achievements of science, modernity, communication, and therefore globalization, need to be recognized. His reasoning is sound: he argues that these achievements represent the best of the human spirit. They demonstrate the creativity of humanity. And they are made possible by the God designed order of the universe.

Themes two to four are much more critical of globalization. The second theme is the need for society to accommodate in a just way the inequalities of wealth between rich and poor. It is interesting to note that he assumes some inequalities are inevitable. However, a "balance" needs to be realized. So he writes:

Yes, the upper and lower classes in human society, that is, the rich and the poor, live at peace when in equilibrium. The basis of that equilibrium is compassion and kindness in the upper classes, and respect and obedience in the lower classes. Now, the first phrase has incited the upper classes to practice oppression, immorality, and mercilessness. And just as the second has driven the lower classes to hatred, envy, and to contend the upper classes, and has negated man's tranquillity for several centuries, so too this century, as the result of the struggle between capital and labor, it has been the cause of the momentous events of Europe well-known by all. Thus, together with all its societies for good works, all its establishments for the teaching of ethics, all its severe discipline and regulations, it could not reconcile these two classes of mankind, nor could it heal the two fearsome wounds in human life. The Qur'an, however, eradicates the first phrase with its injunction to pay *zakat*, and heals it. While it uproots the second phrase with its prohibition on usury and interest, and cures that. Indeed, the Qur'anic verse stands at the door of the world and declares usury and interest to be forbidden. It reads out its decree to mankind, saying: "In order to close the door of strife, close the door of usury and interest!" It forbids its students to enter it.[22]

There are two strategies that keep inequalities in an equilibrium. The first is charity, obligated and required of all, but of course required as a greater percentage on those that are rich. And second the forbidding of usury. Even though Christians are not persuaded of the obligation that all forms of usury are forbidden (after all, if we can sell goods and services, then it seems reasonable to permit those who have purchasing power to "sell" it those who need it). There is an important insight here that we need to accommodate. Economic globalization becomes problematic when the inequalities are not managed. Among the nations there are some that are very fortunate and benefiting greatly from globalization and others that are struggling. As the nations of the world manage these inequalities, this proposal by Nursi has much to commend it. There is an obligation on those that benefit to "give" to those who are struggling; and there is also an obligation that when the IMF provides loans to these developing nations the repayments are not prohibitive. The campaign for debt cancellation for the poorer countries of the world is appropriate, especially in the light of the detrimental contracts negotiated in the middle of the 1970s by Western financial institutions. The overall point is entirely appropriate: inequalities need to be managed with considerable care.

The third theme is that all wealth and property should be ultimately entrusted to God. Nursi tells a story of a King who has two subjects, one of whom allows the King to hold the property in trust, while the other who insists on sole ownership. For the first subject, there are positive consequences; for the second subject, he became an object of pity. The point explains Nursi is this:

> Transient property becomes everlasting. For this waning life, when given to the Eternal and Self-Subsistent Lord of Glory and spent for His sake, will be transmuted into eternity. It will yield eternal fruits. The moments of one's life will apparently vanish and rot like kernels and seeds. But then the flowers of blessedness and auspiciousness will open and bloom in the realm of eternity, and each will also present a luminous and reassuring aspect in the Intermediate Realm.[23]

This is a fundamental religious insight that should shape very fundamentally our view of globalization. The gift of life is a transitory gift: from the perspective of eternity, it is just a moment. Our attitude to possessions can either be deeply preoccupied with them as an end in themselves or they can be seen as a means to a greater end of serving the purposes of God. If it is the latter, then we are searching for ways to make sure that globalization serves the excluded. Globalization should enable us to bring food to the hungry; knowledge to the ignorant; and hope to the hopeless. To make this the goal of globalization is to entrust our possessions to God, who is after all the source and sustainer of everything that is.

The last theme that is worth noting is that Bediuzzaman is not persuaded that we should see all Western achievements as part of the march of progress. There are some very harsh words for those that uncritically support the movement of European progress, especially when it is at the cost of religion:

> O miserable pseudo-patriot who fervently encourages Muslims to embrace this world and forcibly drives them to European industry and progress! Beware, do not let the bonds with which certain members of this nation are tied to religion be broken! If thus foolishly blindly imitating and crushed under food, their bonds with religion are broken, those irreligious people will become as harmful for the life of society as fatal poison.[24]

Extended discussion of this point is not necessary. Suffice to say, it relates to point three, globalization should not become the goal in itself; it should be the servant of a vision of social organization that allows the spiritual dimension of humanity to grow and develop.

This exercise of engaging with the thought of Nursi on globalization has been helpful. Unlike the entrenched positions of Hardt and Negri, we find a much more nuanced approach. To simply interpret capitalism as the tool of the powerful to retain control of as much wealth as possible is a distortion of the reality. The capitalist spirit has its roots in certain religious dispositions. It has generated vast wealth. Although there are many dangers, it must be recognized that there are also many possibilities.

As it is with capitalism, so I want to suggest, it is with globalization. Nursi would certainly recognize as good the technological and scientific underpinning of the globalization project. However, he would also want to make sure that globalization is a force that works for good. Crucially and centrally, there need to be strong safeguards against vast inequalities of wealth emerging. He would have, I am sure, been a strong supporter of the campaign for Western institutions to cancel the debt burden facing the world's poorest countries. In addition, he would have witnessed to the imperative that the economic life of the world is intended to be means to a spiritual vision for humanity. Generating wealth for itself is madness. Generating wealth so that all people can live full God-directed lives is a vision. Globalization might make the latter possibility. It is our task to work toward that end.

These case studies have all demonstrated different aspects of engagement. With human rights, we had assimilation, which then entailed resistance to the concept of state sovereignty; with feminist and black theology, we saw that assimilation entailed repentance and modification; with Hinduism and secularism, we saw that overhearing demonstrated why an "open theology" is important; with economics and globalization, we saw that assimilation and overhearing provides new and positive ways of thinking about the role of religion in the modern dynamic.

We turn now from these case studies to turn to two distinctive theological projects. These are the engaged theologians of today.

11

KEITH WARD: AN ENGAGED THEOLOGIAN

In the next two chapters of this book, we shall explore two examples of engaged theologians. The first is Keith Ward, currently Regius Professor of Divinity at Oxford. The reason for his selection is that he is one of the few theologians that has attempted a systematic theology from an engaged perspective. This chapter will look at his methodology and identify the success of his engaged comparative theology. The second is Pope John Paul II. Pope John Paul II is important for two reasons: one, as the leader of the world's Roman Catholics, his influence is greater than any other Christian leader both on the Christian Church and in the world. And the Pope's own engagement with modernity needs to be explored. However, unlike Ward, he will be criticized because he does not make "engagement" an explicit part of his reflection.

We start then with Keith Ward. My interest in his work is primarily methodological. And to understand Ward's method, one must begin with the logician at the University of Glasgow. Ward is first and foremost a good competent philosopher, able to use the most rigorous of philosophical tools. This has shaped many of his often unspoken assumptions. This meant that as Ward developed his interests in theological questions, he saw the goal of theological study as the quest for a coherent and comprehensive description of the ways things are. He is a critical realist defending the view of truth alluded to in chapter 1. And he uses traditional criteria to determine whether a particular account is true. He writes:

> There are some very basic rational criteria which can be brought to bear upon all claims to truth, in religion as elsewhere. Rationality involves the use of intelligent capacities, including the capacity to register information correctly, to compare similar pieces of information, to deduce and infer in accordance with rules of logic and relate means to ends effectively. A rational

person can act on a consciously formulated principle in order to attain an intended goal. . . . Such simple forms of reasoning are necessary to any form of intelligently ordered social life. They are not, and cannot be, culturally relative.[1]

This means in practice that an account must be internally coherent; if it is coherent, then it is a matter of evidence, explanatory power, and plausibility. He is impatient with those who want to describe different and incommensurable traditions with different rationalities. He explains that:

> if one asks to what "tradition" these basic criteria of rationality – self-consistency, coherence with other knowledge, and adequacy to available data – belong, the answer must be that they belong to the tradition of being human, as such. . . . [T]hey are principles of rationality which are built into the necessary structure of human social life, and thus function as desirable ideals for any community that wishes to survive for any length of time.[2]

It is at this point, he understands, even if he does entirely agree with, the Richard Swinburne project. Richard Swinburne's initial trilogy – *The Coherence of Theism*, *The Existence of God*, and *Faith and Reason* – works with the traditional philosophical paradigm. You demonstrate first the coherence of God, then provide good arguments for the existence of God, and finally demonstrate the relationship of this approach with faith. *Rational Theology and the Creativity of God* is the best example of Ward working within the Swinburne framework. He writes:

> These two tasks – of expounding the idea of God, and of establishing the rationality and moral importance of belief in God – go together. Without a clear idea of God, one cannot be sure of what, exactly, one is looking for reasons to accept. And without a clear account of the reasons for belief, one cannot be sure of what it is that one has established as the conclusion of those reasonings.[3]

Here Ward argues from the assumption of intelligibility to theism at the same time as providing an account of God which is internally coherent.

In terms of philosophical competence, Ward could have easily joined those Christian analytical philosophers of religion who have set themselves the task of defending the central doctrines of the Christian faith, of whom Swinburne is the leading British example.[4] Although Ward has made his contribution to the philosophy of religion debates,[5] this has not proved to be his home. And the primary reason, I want to suggest is his commitment to "engagement." Engagement is an interdisciplinary activity. But in addition engagement cannot simply work within a framework of analytical philosophy of religion. Engagement, which has as its end, a better understanding of God and God's relations with the world cannot confine itself to the limitations of Anglo-American philosophical tradition.

This needs unpacking. In my judgment there is a interesting divergence between analytical philosophers of religion and theologians, which has created a problem for Ward.[6] Philosophers of religion do not read contemporary theologians. Swinburne, for example, discusses the Church Fathers, Anselm, Aquinas, and Duns Scotus. Barth, Moltmann, and Pannenberg are hardly mentioned. For Swinburne, contemporary theologians are conceptually muddled and rationally sloppy. Meanwhile most modern theologians do not read the analytical philosophers. Methodologically, the theologian treats the New Testament as normative or, to be more precise Paul's epistles, especially Romans. For Romans becomes the paradigm of theological argument. As a result, theologians find Barth congenial, because he constructs his arguments in similar ways to Paul, and Swinburne is unrecognizable as "theology." Ward in my judgment has located himself, out of a commitment to engagement, in the middle of these two worlds. This can be most clearly seen in his account of religious language.

In an extended discussion on religious language in *Religion and Creation*, Ward's sympathies with the analytical philosophers emerges when he complains about those theologians who say that nothing literal can be said about God. Ward writes:

> [I]f one uses the word "God" in its proper sense, one is committed to at least one literally true statement about God, namely, that God is an object of supreme value. But this entails many other literally true statements. For example, if one thinks that anything is a value, then God cannot be of less value than that.[7]

At this point Ward's view is similar to Swinburne. Swinburne follows Duns Scotus and believes that many statements about God simply involves taking the mundane meaning of the word and stretching it out to apply to God. However, Ward explicitly distances himself from Swinburne, when he writes: "The reason for hesitation about saying that one can describe God is the immense difference one feels there must be between the creator of all space and time and any finite object in space-time."[8] And later:

> What theologians like Tillich fear is that the concept of God provided by speculation will be so inadequate to its object, so anthropomorphic, that it

will be positively misleading. The theologian's task is to avoid that danger, while providing a characterization of God that is rooted in scriptural tradition and coherent with the best available knowledge of the natural universe. . . . If I claim thereby to produce a literal description of an objective supranatural reality, it must not be forgotten how tentative, analogical, and exploratory such a description must be. When all has been said, the human mind must silently bow before the mystery of self-existent perfection.[9]

Ward finds himself midway between theologians and philosophers because he wants to provide a characterization of God that is rooted in scriptural tradition (a theological methodology) and coherent with the best available knowledge of the natural universe (analytical philosophy).

One further factor in Ward's distant relationship with analytical philosophy of religion was his unfashionable support for certain Wittgensteinian insights. One of his early works *Concept of God* clearly shows a debt to Wittgenstein. He returns to Wittgenstein in *Religion and Revelation*. Here he identifies with Wittgenstein's sense that there are certain "frameworks" that are not justified rationally but simply assumed. Ward writes:

> Worship and prayer, for example, are natural practices by which humans relate to the world of their experience in specific ways. They do not, as such, stand in need of justification, for they are rooted in basic attitudes of awe, reverence, gratitude and dependence, which show themselves in human behavior. They form the basis for developing sets of concepts which aim to provide illuminating descriptions of how the world is and of how humans ought to live. At that stage they become subject to rational inquiry and assessment.[10]

So Ward's more sophisticated account of religious language coupled with his Wittgensteinian sympathy with the community-orientated nature of religious discourse meant that he never reduced the theological task to the reproduction of key doctrines in symbolic logic. Therefore Ward methodology never resulted in Swinburne's rather crude simplification of theological ideas. He understands Swinburne's wish to simplify and clarify religious language, but Ward feels that the confusing nature of elements of the Christian narrative is there for a purpose. Ward in short lives with much greater sense of mystery than Swinburne would ever tolerate.

For Ward then, his methodology involves taking a framework of belief and exploring (a) the coherence of the beliefs within that framework and (b) the arguments for and against those beliefs. He does so sensitive to the distinctive nature of theological discourse. Now this is crucial. An engaged theology needs to be both engaged and theological. The engagement entails handing one or more traditions in conversation with each other. One cannot simply surrender to incommensurable rationalities that makes these traditions unable to speak to each other; nor can one allow one tradition to simply be defined and explained by a different one. It does require the traditional philosopher's conviction that the human gift of rationality does give us the equipment to understand each other. However, conversely, we have to allow the distinctive "music" or "dance" of the theological discourse to thrive. Ramanuja, for example, does not always work with clear premises leading to appropriate conclusions as a result of strict deductive logic. Keith Ward has both the rationality that makes engagement possible and the sensitivity to the distinctive nature of the discourse that makes engagement meaningful.

For a Christian, one of the, perhaps, overstated challenges to engagement is Christology. I say overstated for reasons that will become apparent in chapter 13. However, for now, it is interesting to see how Ward's methodology accommodates the challenge of Christology. It is clear that his understanding of Christ has been modified in three of his books: *Divine Action*, *A Vision to Pursue*, and *Religion and Revelation*. Ward explains the movement from *Divine Action* to *A Vision to Pursue* in his introduction to *A Vision to Pursue*. Since he became a Christian, his instinct was to see Jesus as a human being "who obeyed God fully, knew and loved him intimately, and as a result was able to bring God close to others or even act in the place of God in regard to other people. He was a man wholly transparent to God, perhaps, and thus a perfected vehicle of the divine love."[11] However, he explained he wanted to explore the classical doctrine of the incarnation: he could see certain advantages, and therefore set out to defend an ontological doctrine of the incarnation in *Divine Action*. This is the philosopher Ward speaking: he seems to be saying that *Divine Action* was in part an exploration of a "conceptual possibility" (i.e., the attempt to formulate a good case for a logically possible position). *Divine Action* defends a kenotic version of the Incarnation. Yet even here, he acknowledged the major difficulty that would provoke *A Vision to Pursue*. He writes:

> The intellectual coherence of the doctrine of incarnation, its apparent confirmation by continued experience of the Lordship of Christ in the Church, and its fruitfulness in suggesting illuminating ways of understanding both the nature of God and of human experience in general, all combine to place the gospel accounts within a framework of interpretation which makes them

strong enough to bear the doctrine which has historically grown from reflection upon them. But one major problem remains to be faced. The earliest followers of Jesus saw themselves as living in the "last days," and Jesus as the culminating act of God in history. But the world did not end, and the figure of Jesus has now receded into the past.[12]

Although in *Divine Action*, the problem is resolved by examining the redemption of all time in the eschaton, the problem of Jesus' mistaken knowledge provides the main argument against an "ontological" incarnation in *A Vision to Pursue*. However, he seems to move back to a more incarnational position in *Religion and Revelation*. In a footnote, he explains that any reader of *A Vision to Pursue* "will note a much more pronounced incarnational emphasis in the present work. I have become convinced that such an emphasis is necessary and possible, given a relatively small amendments of the previous analysis."[13] For Ward there was greater consistency than his critics had recognized. He was right; he continued to reject a Jesus who was omniscient, omnipotent, and consciously preexistent. Instead he becomes an advocate of an enhypostatic view of incarnation. Ward explains thus:

> What the life-perfectly-united-to-God shows is the nature and purpose of God. Jesus has a free mind and will, which makes its own decisions and performs its own creative actions. He is united to God in such a way that, in freely obeying his distinctive calling, he expresses what God is, becoming a living revelation of Supreme value.[14]

In short, Jesus is a person completely interpenetrated by the Divine Word.

One must grant that on Christology there is modification. However, methodologically, there are four factors operating here. A respect for the classical definition of Christ, a desire to find a coherent and plausible account of Incarnation, which is compatible with the evidence available in the New Testament and the necessity to have a Christology that is not simply compatible with the expectation that we learn of God from non-Christian sources but makes it an imperative.

Thus his engagement with other faith traditions has introduced a distinctive twist to the Ward methodology. He became an advocate of an "open orthodoxy,"[15] (sometimes described as an "open theology") "which will be true to the main orthodox Christian tradition, yet which will be open to a fruitful interaction with other traditions, and with the developing corpus of scientific knowledge."[16] "Open orthodoxy" makes possible "a committed, open, and developing understanding of faith in the contemporary world."[17] Now it is not entirely clear whether this label is supposed to be descriptive or prescriptive: whether Ward believes that the tradition, at its best, **is** "open" or whether the tradition **ought** to be "open." On the descriptive side, Aquinas is treated as an example of a theologian who took his "interpretative clues from philosophical or cultural factors not confined to Christianity."[18] Yet his description of "open orthodoxy," which by the end of the book is called "open theology" seems rather more prescriptive. Ward writes:

> One might perhaps speak of an "open theology," which can be characterized by six main features. It will seek a convergence of common core beliefs, clarifying the deep arguments which underlie diverse cultural traditions. It will seek to learn from complementary beliefs in other traditions, expecting that there are forms of revelation one's own tradition does not express. It will be prepared to reinterpret its beliefs in the light of new, well-established factual and moral beliefs. It will accept the full right of diverse belief-systems to exist, as long as they do not cause avoidable injury or harm to innocent sentient beings. It will encourage a dialogue with conflicting and dissenting views, being prepared to confront its own tradition with critical questions arising out of such views. And it will try to develop a sensitivity to the historical and cultural contexts of the formulation of its own beliefs, with a preparedness to continue developing new insights in new cultural situations.[19]

This seems prescriptive because, as he admits himself, "no theology is wholly open or wholly closed."[20] This is an interesting issue given my initial emphasis that an engagement with non-Christian tradition is an act of fidelity to the method of Augustine and Aquinas. Perhaps we need to distinguish between "unconsciously open," such as that expressed by Aquinas, and "self-consciously open," which is what Ward is commending. The Christian tradition was "unconsciously open" because it used non-Christian sources without positive celebration of their revelatory origin. Augustine's use of "Neoplatonism" and Aquinas" use of Islamic commentators on Aristotle ran parallel with such fierce denouncements of "Neoplatonism" and "Islam" that the achievement was not recognized. Ward wants the Christian tradition to become "consciously open" (i.e., learn from and positively acknowledge the use of non-Christian sources in our theology).

The important point is that Ward's open theology emerges from a commitment to the Christian tradition. Much in keeping with the themes of the opening chapter, this enables Ward to sound both traditional and liberal because he believes the tradition, at its best and perhaps unconsciously, is liberal. By liberal, I mean the tradition is committed to openness and change. Comparative theology emerges from his commitment to the Christian tradition.

This is the reason why it is wrong to link Ward and therefore any theology of engagement too closely with John Hick. John Hick argues that comparative theology will depend on a "pluralist theology of other religions," which involves a Copernican revolution from a Christocentric tradition to a theocentric one. Instead of exclusivism (Jesus is the only way to be saved) or inclusivism (others are saved through Jesus without realizing it), Hick wants us to cross the Rubicon and become pluralists (all religions are equally salvific).[21] Ward does not see Christ as a problem for a theocentric understanding of religions and is disinclined to cross the Rubicon. Instead Ward underpins his open theology with "soft pluralism." Ward is unhappy with Hick's pluralism because it seems to rest on a "pragmatic theory of truth."[22] Instead Ward does want to talk about more or less adequate accounts of ultimate reality and that all traditions contain some false beliefs. He rejects the label inclusivist because an inclusivist assumes that his or her tradition includes the best of other traditions, while a soft pluralist believes that other traditions have insights not known (or perhaps not known sufficiently well) within Christianity.

Ward's "open theology" approach has been applied to four areas. The first is "revelation" (volume 1, 1994); the second is "creation" (volume 2, 1996); the third is human nature (volume 3, 1998); and the fourth is community (volume 4, 2000). The results are interesting. First, he captures well the diversity of each tradition and the legitimate connections that can be made across traditions. So, to take an example, the study on human nature shows how the nondualistic school of Vedanta – Advaita, which holds the view that human beings are essentially spiritual is also found in certain strands of "Western religious thought which have Neoplatonic roots."[23] Second, for Ward, one must first understand the other before offering an analysis. In this way he then finds that the exercise of understanding provokes an insight which he insists the Christian tradition must take seriously. This is close to my concept of "overhearing." For example, Ward looks at three major interpretations of rebirth within Hindu orthodoxy. Although he notes the problems (for example, Vaishnava rejects the scientific hypothesis of evolution because it is incompatible with the rebirth hypothesis), he insists that "the idea of rebirth does enshrine a hope for the possibility of spiritual progress and development, even for those whose earthly lives seem to make such a hope impossible. That is a hope that must be basic for any religion of devotion to a truly gracious and loving God, and there must be some way of providing for it in any religion of grace."[24]

The theology of engagement that is being commended in this book can work well within a Wardian methodology. And there are five elements to that methodology. First, Ward is a critical realist. The task for the theologian is to provide a coherent account of faith based on sound reasons and compatible with other insights in other areas. Second, he insists that there is no neutral vantage point for evaluation of traditions, yet strongly rejects any talk of different rationalities within different traditions. This is in part shaped by his Wittgensteinian sympathies. Third, the theological task must take other religious traditions seriously. Comparative theology is a historically self-conscious development of traditional Christian methodology. Fourth, comparative theology assumes that it is possible to arrive at more or less adequate descriptions of ultimate reality; Ward is therefore a "soft pluralist." Fifth, the results of comparative theology are (a) greater understanding, (b) connections within and across traditions and (c) the illumination of certain issues that then need to be subsequently accommodated into any adequate Christian theology.

Thus we can see how Ward's distinctive methodology is a methodology of engagement. He rejects the tribal "liberal" and "conservative" positions. Instead his methodology is consistent, albeit sometimes reaching contrasting, and sometimes, preliminary conclusions (see his discussions on Christology). Ward is rightly acclaimed by both conservatives and liberals, and this could create the possibility of an interesting convergence between them. Ward believes the Christian tradition is a liberal one. By affirming the tradition and "orthodoxy," Ward is a conservative; by affirming a liberal methodology, Ward is a liberal. In all these respect, Ward is a model of an engaged theologian.

12

ENGAGING WITH THE POPE: ENGAGEMENT YET NOT ENGAGEMENT

Having explored Keith Ward's methodology as a case study of good "engaged" theology, I now want to turn to Pope John Paul II. This chapter seeks to demonstrate the following features of an engaged theology. First, it is necessary to discern the "trends of an age." Roman Catholicism is one such trend and the remarkable leadership of Pope John Paul II is especially significant. Engaged theology must engage the trends that matter. Second, good engaged theology needs to be messy. We shall find that as engage with the Papal worldview that there is a problem area: his engagement is insufficiently sensitive to the ambiguities of human situations and the complexities of public life.

To establish these two aspects of an engaged theology, this chapter proceeds in the following way. First, we start by attempting to identify the intellectual trends of our age. Here we justify the significance of Roman Catholicism as a conversation partner for anyone interested in an engaged theology. Second, we look in some detail at the vision provided by Pope John Paul II. Without a doubt one cannot but admire the achievement in his work. Third, we offer a critique that introduces the need for an engaged theology to be messy.

1   Intellectual Trends of our Age

Imagine that you are standing on the eve of the twentieth century. It is 1897 and someone asks you to identify the important intellectual trends that will dominate the next century. How would you react? If you're that sort of person, you may seek clarification of the expression "intellectual trend." So, **an intellectual trend is a mode of thought or sensibility that provides an interpretative framework for the evaluation of aspects of life and the world**. Therefore you can exclude from your consideration the emerging technologies of mechanical power, which are going to lead to greater industrialization. You can also exclude some of the social changes that period was already witnessing, for example, the dramatic migration of people to far corners of the globe. You are also not considering the relative success or failure of particular nations – imperially or economically: you are interested in "intellectual trends" – trends of thought that may indeed include these elements within their purview. Second, you will need to know from what standpoint the trends are being identified. It will make a difference whether you are in India or in Britain. Let us take the dominant trend of our own culture (i.e., European-American culture) which, as it happens, is the culture of the most powerful part of the world. With these clarifications, we can attempt an answer to the question: what are the important intellectual trends that are going to dominate the next century?

One could, perhaps, foresee the way that the combination of Darwinian evolution and Hegelian philosophy was going to be, at least for a time, responsible for a Western self-confidence and optimism. It is under the impulse of this trend that much of the scientific and technological revolution will emerge. Marxism is already important and significant. Although I think the revolution in Russia was impossible to foresee (a big shock to Marxist theory itself), we could perhaps guess that its all-embracing critique of capitalist society was going to be a powerful vision in the next century. The potential for psychology and sociology to develop and grow could surely be expected. And under this head countless movements have developed, from management consultancy to holistic medicine. If in 1897 you managed to discern all these movements, then you would have done well, because indeed they all proved significant.

But now we turn to today. The comparable exercise is much harder. Our world seems so fragmented; it is pulling in numerous different directions. Postmodernism is a term intended to describe the breakdown in the hegemony of any one tradition within a given culture: the quest for a universal narrative is over. Instead all we have are many different communities each with their own narrative.

Yet, despite modernity's tendency to fragmentation, there are certain factors that will determine the success of any "intellectual trend." First, it must contend with the victory of free-market capitalism in the Cold War.

Contending with a victor does not mean that capitalism should be simply accepted uncritically. For despite the victory of capitalism over Marxist socialism, the West is subdued. We know it is preferable to Marxist social-ism but do not want it to triumph absolutely. We are worried about our human ecology: we are worried about the growing gap between those rich and fortunate and those poor and unlucky. Second, most intellectual trends need to be embodied institutionally. Ideas that do not emerge from or speak to a community will have little or no impact; ideas that persuade institutions to take a certain set of positions are almost certain to become significant. Finally, an "intellectual trend" needs to be expounded in an elegant and coherent way in a set of texts. Slogans have a short-term impact; an intellectual trend needs to provide a comprehensive worldview, which needs to be available for study and reflection. Granted only a few will read such texts, but their influence will extend out through educa-tion, media, the academy, and popular culture. The most important text for our post-Enlightenment age is Immanuel Kant's *Critique of Pure Reason*, despite the fact that those most influenced by it are also the least likely to have read it. So, given these factors, I want to suggest that the three movements which will dominate the next century are (a) Roman Catholi-cism, (b) Islam, and (c) feminism.

The task of identifying the trends that matter is an essential precondi-tion for any reflection on the links between theology and public life. We are historically conditioned creatures, so we are sensitive to the changing nature of human society. In the Christian context, for example, the attempt to apply biblical principles unchangingly to any and every society is always doomed to failure. Many of the problems preoccupying the writers of the Bible have disappeared, while later times have developed a myriad new ones. The great theologians of the past all succeeded because they found fresh ways of formulating the tradition in a changing culture. We have already seen in chapter 2 how Augustine made use of his Neoplatonic background; and in chapter 3 how Aquinas created the brilliant synthesis of Augustinian Platonism and a rediscovered Aristotle. Both men were sen-sitive to the dominant intellectual trend of their age and even moved it on: both men formulated their understanding of the Christian faith in the light of it.

In the last chapter, we postulated that Augustine and Aquinas did the task of adaptation largely unconsciously, while we are historically self-conscious. Modern history is a discipline parasitic on the Enlightenment. We are now able to see the ways in which cultures change and develop. We can see the movement of "intellectual trends" and the ways in which theology makes the appropriate adjustment. Given this awareness, it is necessary for us to operate theologically with this self-conscious historical sensitivity.

It is for this reason I have elsewhere identified the three modes of ethical inquiry:[1] the theological – that is, its grounding in the Christian tradition; the cultural – that is, sensitivity to the age we are in conversation with; and the practical or applied mode – the implications of our analysis for public polity. Reinhold Niebuhr saw this agenda perfectly; V.A. Demant, Christopher Dawson, Jacque Maritain too were sensitive to the scale of the task, even if they were less able than Niebuhr. Any Christian in conversation with public life needs some sense of where we are as a culture and where we are going.

Our exercise is one of "discerning the signs of the times." It is fraught with difficulties. If we go back fifty years, we find the Anglican theologian V.A. Demant calling his Scott Holland Lectures of 1949, *Religion and the Decline of Capitalism*.[2] Despite the way things now look, it did look then as if "the state principle" (as Demant called it) was winning over the unfettered market; but, since the arrival of Margaret Thatcher and Ronald Reagan in the 1980s (not to speak of the revolution in Eastern Europe) the title looks very odd. Ideally the task of cultural analysis needs to be done slowly, drawing on a range of disciplines, and weighing with care the significant factors that are operating. It is beyond the confines of this book to provide a sustained justification of my selection, nevertheless I shall now briefly outline the main reasons why I suggested that Roman Catholicism, Islam, and Feminism are the three most significant "intellectual trends" for the next century.

Two of the three trends, I have identified, are religious. This might come as a surprise to some. For much of this century, it has looked as if the intellectual trend of secular humanism was in control. In the East, Marxism made secular atheism a part of its creed: in the West, a materialist secularism was spreading fast. Propagating a self-confident story of the gradual demise of religion since the Enlightenment, proponents of secularism celebrated the steady decline in church attendance. In the 1960s, Christian apologists were preoccupied with a "modern man" who was skeptical about the traditional Christian metaphysic and therefore the future lay with a radical version of Christianity, that might even proclaim the death of God himself. In the 1990s there is a quaintness about prophecy that all this might soon lead to the extinction of Christianity. Religion has not only survived but thrived. The vast majority of cultures in the world both historically and today are deeply religious. The most advanced nation in the world by most standards of measurement, the United States, has over 40 percent church attendance and an almost universal belief in God. And even in Europe, where secularism has had the greatest hold, we find the majority of people continue to believe in God, however undeveloped that belief may turn out to be. In Britain a proper appreciation of so-called "folk religion" shows a deep religious strain in our nation. Grace Davie – the sociologist of religion – has argued that although people do not belong to religious institutions, they do believe. She writes, "For most, if not all, of the British retain some sort of religious belief even if they do not see the need to attend their churches on a regular basis. . . . In contrast, secularism – at least in any developed sense – remains the creed of a relatively small minority."[3] Granted many find their faith difficult to describe; hence the famous exchange between a pollster and a person in Islington:

Do you believe in God?
Yes.
Do you believe in God who can change the course of events on earth?
No, just the ordinary one.[4]

It is this belief in the "ordinary God" that means the British still tend to believe that religious education should be compulsory and that, on the whole, children should get baptized. So in Britain, from *Songs of Praise* and *Thought for the Day* on Radio 4 to the extraordinary mourning rituals that developed after the tragedy of 94 deaths at the Hillsborough stadium in Sheffield and the death of Diana, Princess of Wales, we find a national religious disposition expressing itself. Secular humanism, although disproportionately influential in the media and in some of our public institutions, is a cultural aberration. It is true that our secular attitudes have given birth to certain significant offspring, but overall the next century is likely to belong to religion. So why is this?

Religion survives and thrives because it provides an interpretative framework of the kind that human beings need to make sense of their activities. One dominant theme of the twentieth century has been the secular attempt to provide a nonreligious account of all those features of human life that have been traditionally grounded in religion (and, for the West, in Christianity). I have argued in *Truth and the Reality of God*,[5] that this project has failed. Everything that makes human life significant seems to need a religious setting: as Alasdair MacIntyre has shown in *After Virtue*,[6] the language of morality disintegrates when it is disentangled from the religious context which was its source and made it intelligible. As with morality, so, I believe, the assumptions underpinning our concept of truth become unintelligible when we disentangle them from their religious context. Natural theology is no longer a question of persuading a person from a certain set of traditionless premises to a conclusion that all rational people will accept. Instead it is the clarification of the choice: either some form of religious life must be true or everything that matters to humans becomes, in an ultimate and literal sense, meaningless. Most people opt for the former rather than the latter. In short, religion remains the powerful interpretative framework because life without is simply unbearable.

It is for this reason that I include two religious traditions as significant intellectual trends for the next century. Before discussing Roman Catholicism, a brief word about Islam and then feminism, which have been treated at greater length in earlier chapters. There are one billion Muslims in the world; it is the fastest growing religion. It provides a universal message (unlike Hinduism and Judaism which both have strong tribal strands) and can organize itself to powerful political effect. Overtly Islamic political parties are gaining power in Pakistan and Algeria. Nations beset with corruption, sensitive to past colonial abuse, and searching for some economic justice for the poor are turning to Islam as the religion that can transform them and give them cohesion. Its increasing self-confidence and willingness to challenge Western assumptions has best been seen in the tragedy surrounding Salman Rushdie and the novel *The Satanic Verses*. The cherished Western assumption of "freedom to publish" was challenged by a world religion requiring "respect for the sacred."[7] It has left a novelist in hiding and the Western nations of the world bewildered by the significance of Islam for certain people and nations. These aspects of Islam, I suspect, will be more enduring than the links between Islam and terrorism, which of course expressed itself in the tragic events on September 11.[8] There is no future in a long-term terrorist strategy (as seen in September 11) because it is so unclear what are the goals of such action. As such Islam will increasingly distance itself from such actions and will become a more sophisticated conversation partner with Western liberalism. Given all this, it seems like that it is and that it will continue to be a major intellectual player in the next century seems beyond any reasonable doubt.

I have already said that most intellectual trends require institutions to sustain and develop them. Both Islam and Roman Catholicism have strong institutions that ensure they survive and thrive. However, some trends can be so pervasive that they do not need direct institutional support. Instead the trend becomes part of our cultural assumptions. Feminism falls into this category. Feminism is a child of the Enlightenment. Although most women don't call themselves feminists, almost all take advantage of feminism's victories. The power relations between the sexes are at long last beginning to change. Women will no longer tolerate exclusion from employment, education, and power. This trend, already clearly established, in my view will continue, affecting not just politics and the law, but many aspects of social structures and everyday behavior.

2   Roman Catholicism

We return to the first of my three movements. In my view Roman Catholicism concludes this century in remarkably good shape, despite the tensions and decline in parts of Western Europe. It remains the largest Christian (and therefore the largest religious) community in the world; and in the most important cultural battle this century (i.e., the one between capitalism and communism) it demonstrated decisive political power – though not because of any uncritical alliance with capitalism for its own sake. For the election of Karol Wojtyla – a Polish Pope, together with the emergence of Gorbachev in the Soviet Union, provided the inspiration for the Eastern European Revolution.

Some no doubt dispute this. Such recent history is very difficult to assess. At the fringes, you have Carl Bernstein and Marco Politi, who believe that the Pope collaborated with Ronald Reagan to undermine Poland and therefore the entire communist edifice.[9] The Pope himself is much more measured and, as you might expect, he gives the credit to the power of the teaching of the church. In *Centesimus Annus*, he writes, "An important, even decisive, contribution was made by the church's commitment to defend and promote human rights."[10] What seems completely clear is that the combination of a fiercely Roman Catholic country and an intelligent Polish Pope assisted considerably the transition to democracy and the break-up of the command economy.

However, the Pope's legacy will not simply be a political one. The style of his Pontiff has had its impact: he is the most widely traveled Pope ever; he has visited and engaged some of the most troubled nations in the world. However, style is no substitute for substance. In the end, to become an intellectual trend in the next century, we need an intellectual legacy. The output of this Pope has been considerable. Along with his encyclical letters, we have an immense corpus of talks and sermons, which he has given in the course of his pastoral visits across the world, as well as his "Apostolic Exhortations" issued as a result of a series of International Episcopal Synods held in Rome. I shall concentrate on his encyclicals; and I shall show that they provide a coherent analysis of modernity and the basis for continuing Roman Catholic dialogue in the next century. Most commentators have not given the encyclicals the attention they deserve: the tendency has been to take particular encyclicals and become preoccupied with the passing allusion to one issue: for example, to imagine that *Evangelium Vitae* is primarily about contraception is a complete distortion of the entire letter. To understand precisely what the Pope is doing, the encyclicals need to be read as a unity.

Pope John Paul II has issued thirteen major encyclicals since 1979. Of these, four are predominantly doctrinal – *Redemptor Hominis* (1979), *Dives in Misericordia* (1980), *Dominum et Vivificantem* (1986), *Redemptoris Mater* (1987); one encyclical for each member of the trinity and the final one on the blessed Virgin Mary. Then we have a social trilogy – *Laborem Exercens* (1981), *Sollicitudo Rei Socialis* (1987) and *Centesimus Annus* (1991). We have three on the fundamentals of morality – *Veritatis Splendor* (1993) *Evangelium Vitae* (1995) and *Fides et Ratio* (1998). And finally three which concentrate on pastoral and ecumenical issues: *Slavorum Apostoli* (1985), *Redemptoris Missio* (1991), and *Ut Unum Sint* (1995).

This is remarkable intellectual legacy. There is no doubt that the Pope is an "engaged" theologian. His call in *Fides et Ratio* that theology should engage with philosophy illustrates his commitment to such engagement. He writes:

I have reaffirmed theology's duty to recover its true relationship with philosophy. . . . Philosophical thought is often the only ground for understanding and dialogue with those who do not share our faith. The current ferment in philosophy demands of believing philosophers an attentive and competent commitment, able to discern the expectations, the points of openness and the key issues of this historical moment. . . . In concluding this Encyclical Letter, my thoughts turn particularly to theologians, encouraging them to pay special attention to the philosophical implications of the word of God and to be sure to reflect in their work all the speculative and practical breadth of the science of theology . . . This is why I urge them to recover and express to the full the metaphysical dimension of truth in order to enter into a demanding critical dialogue with both contemporary philosophical thought and with the philosophical tradition in all its aspects, whether consonant with the word of God or not.[11]

With this disposition and commitment to engagement, what I shall now show is how the Pope is succeeding in positioning himself as a constructive critic of the modern world whose legacy can scarcely fail to mold the twenty-first century. He reaffirms traditional Roman Catholic teaching that this role of the constructive critic is part of the expertise that the Pope can bring. It is part of the duty of the church, as "an expert in humanity, to scrutinize the signs of the times and to interpret them in the light of the Gospel."[12] There can be no doubt of the power of this Pope's contribution in this area. We attend now to the social and moral aspects of this body of teaching.

Let us turn first to the social trilogy, which can be seen as offering a critical affirmation of the market. On social questions, Pope John Paul II is quite explicit about his method. In *Sollicitudo Rei Socialis*, which was written to celebrate the twentieth anniversary of Pope Paul VI's encyclical *Populorum Progressio*, John Paul II explains that he wants to "reaffirm the continuity of the social doctrine as its constant renewal. In effect, continuity and renewal are a proof of the perennial value of the teaching of the church."[13] Continuity involves affirming the insights of his predecessors while renewal acknowledges a changed situation which needs different teaching.

It is this distinction that enables Pope John Paul II to make a decisive shift of tone in the Papal attitude to capitalism in *Centesimus Annus*, issued four years later. This is a masterly encyclical, which we looked at in chapter 9. Written in the aftermath of the 1989 Eastern European revolution, it provides a profound social commentary. He sees the demise of communism as a vindication of Pope Leo XIII, who one hundred years ago, identified the inherent weaknesses of Marxist philosophy.

In this light, he then turns to capitalism. He wants a "society of free work, of enterprise and of participation."[14] He acknowledges the legitimate role of the profit motive. And then he turns to the crux question: "can it perhaps be said that, after the failure of Communism, capitalism is the victorious social system?"[15] I quote again his answer:

> The answer is obviously complex. If by "capitalism" is meant an economic system which recognizes the fundamental and positive role of business, the market, private property and the resulting responsibility for the means of production, as well as free human creativity in the economic sector, then the answer is certainly in the affirmative, even though it would perhaps be more appropriate to speak of a "business economy," "market economy" or simply "free economy." But if by "capitalism" is meant a system in which

freedom in the economic sector is not circumscribed within a strong juridical framework which places it at the service of human freedom in its totality and sees it as a particular aspect of that freedom, the core of which is
ethical and religious, then the reply is certainly negative.[16]

As I argued in chapter 9, this seems to me completely clear. He is endors-
ing the capitalism of continental Europe: the capitalism of the Christian
Democrat parties on the Continent. One which uses the market and
encourages competition, yet ensures that there are sufficient in the way of
legal safeguards and regulation to protect labor. This interpretation is
supported by his subsequent endorsement of the welfare state, which is
coupled with a warning against excessive dependence. This is a significant
shift in emphasis from earlier Vatican attitudes to capitalism; one which has
not entirely been taken on board by Roman Catholic social teachers. Yet
given that capitalism is the only economic contender, then the future will
lie with those who are willing to engage with capitalism. The Pope in
Centesimus Annus has made it completely clear that he is a critical, yet
friendly, conversation partner with capitalism.

The second major theme, highlighted in the encyclicals on morality, is
the Pope's stress on the relationship between freedom and truth. For him,
the West won the Cold War because of its commitment to human freedom;
this was the strongest weapon in our armory. So it is tragically ironic that
even as the West fought the battle, it was undermining its commitment to
human freedom by the widespread adoption of relativist philosophy.

Veritatis Splendor sets this theme out brilliantly. Many imagine today that
freedom is opposed to identifiable and authoritative truth. To believe in a
right and a wrong, which you ought to obey, sounds like a prison. To
believe that morality is (and should be) a matter of personal preference or
opinion sounds like liberation. However, the Pope rightly shatters this illusion. Relativism is always self-defeating. It is itself a system of thought
emerging from a particular culture. And if absolute truth is impossible
because all systems of thought are relative to a culture and therefore not
unchangeably true, then relativism itself must be false. However, in addition to this incoherence, relativism is also potentially destructive. The Nazi,
who believes that the Jew should be killed; the cannibal who believes that
people should be eaten; the misogynist who believes women are inferior;
all can insist that they are entitled to their cultural perspective and, in so
doing, in effect all destroy morality and freedom as a prime moral value.
Although as I shall argue later certain Papal authoritarian attitudes conflicts with this affirmation of freedom, the Pope is right to argue that

freedom depends on a set of assumptions about the significance of humanity; to undermine that set of assumptions is to undermine freedom.

The Pope's third theme is related: it is his reaffirmation of an objective ethic grounded in natural law. Those who us who believe that there is truth in ethics are then required to provide some description of how we know that moral truth. Pope John Paul II is clear: the answer is natural law. He writes:

> Only God can answer the question about the good, because he is the Good. But God has already given an answer to this question: he did so by creating man and ordering him with wisdom and love to his final end, through the law which is inscribed in his heart (cf. Romans 2:15), the "natural law."[17]

Much of *Veritatis Splendor* is spent explaining why any modification to the traditional understanding of natural law is wrong. All consequentialist ethical theories (i.e., those that take consequences into account when deciding the right way to behave) are mistaken; proportionalism (i.e., the view that you should weigh up the balance of different values and disvalues in deciding the right way to behave) is dangerous. The Pope writes, "Such theories however are not faithful to the church's teaching, when they believe they can justify, as morally good, deliberate choices of kinds of behavior contrary to the commandments of the divine and natural law. These theories cannot claim to be grounded in the Catholic moral tradition."[18]

This is a pity because I am one of a number of Christian theologians who want to weave consequentialist insights into a deontological framework.[19] Nevertheless, I concur entirely with the Pope that any viable Christian ethic needs to make natural law central. It has all the important characteristics: it is objective (i.e., the ethical is a matter of discovery and truth); and it is accessible to all human communities and not dependent on revelation.

The fourth theme is the Pope's indictment of a culture of death. If on capitalism he was a friendly critic of modernity, on human life he is a complete foe. He makes much of the irony: Western culture which stood so firm against communism on the basis of the dignity of the human person, undermines that dignity so completely when it comes to the start and, increasingly, the end of life. Repeatedly he anguishes over this irony:

> On the one hand, the various declarations of human rights and the many initiatives inspired by these declarations show that at the global level there

is a growing moral sensitivity more alert to acknowledging the value and dignity of every individual as a human being, without any distinction of race, nationality, religion, political opinion or social class. On the other hand, these noble proclamations are unfortunately contradicted by a tragic repudiation of them in practice. This denial is still more distressing, indeed more scandalous, precisely because it is occurring in a society which makes the affirmation and protection of human rights its primary objective and its boast. How can these repeated affirmations of principle be reconciled with the continual increase and widespread justification of attacks on human life? How can we reconcile these declarations with the refusal to accept those who are weak and needy, or elderly, or those who have just been conceived? These attacks go directly against respect for life, and they represent a direct threat to the entire culture of human rights.[20]

The Pope is surely right to identify this contradiction. The language of rights implies an entitlement regardless of your power or perceived worth in society. Yet so much discussion about human life at the start, where we assume that it would be better for the unborn child, if the child were dead; at the end, where we imagine that the elderly have nothing to give human community and it would be more sensible if they were gently put to sleep; for the disabled and handicapped, where we assume that their lives are a drain on our limited resources; and even for the poor and uneducated, where talk of eugenics is quietly whispered: in all these respects, the Pope has correctly identified a potentially dangerous contradiction in our modern discourse.

It is because the Pope is persuaded of the seriousness of the crisis that he is impatient about those Roman Catholics who want to disagree with the Magisterium. When it comes to the culture of death, the Pope is at war. And in a war situation, discipline is essential within the ranks. So he writes:

While exchanges and conflicts of opinion may constitute normal expressions of public life in a representative democracy, moral teaching certainly cannot depend simply upon respect for a process: indeed, it is in no way established by following the rules and deliberative procedures typical of a democracy. Dissent, in the form of carefully orchestrated protests and polemics carried on in the media, is opposed to ecclesial communion and to a correct understanding of the hierarchical constitution of the People of God. Opposition to the teaching of the church's Pastors cannot be seen as a legitimate expressions either of Christian freedom or of the diversity of the Spirit's gifts.[21]

Now it is at this point I am least happy. Although I understand entirely the sense that a united front helps the effectiveness of the message, the magisterium seems to be oversensitive and therefore insensitive. It could be argued that this does not preclude "loyal dissent" (or the term preferred by Kevin Kelly "graceful disagreement"[22]) provided it is done discreetly. However, leaving aside the problems that "loyal dissenters" have found, one is still left with an assumption that disagreement is intrinsically unhelpful. Those of us outside the Roman Communion are accustomed to living with disagreement and to seeing the virtues in a variety of positions, and many of us find it liberating. This is a point I shall develop at greater length later in the chapter.

The final theme emerging from these encyclicals is the Pope's plea to build bridges with other Christian communities. The audacity of *Ut Unum Sint* is breathtaking. Here, he is trying to both seize and also create an opportunity. The orthodox Churches of the East are now discovering the West for the first time in sixty years. Under Communist rule, survival was the only issue on the agenda. Since 1989, they are proving a significant force again; in some cases, for example Russia, they have become essential to national identity.

The Pope's global eye can see the opportunity here offered. Without a sacramental theology, to advance ecumenism with the Reformed Churches (the classical Protestants of various kinds) is too difficult. The ordination of women in the Anglican Church has posed a significant obstacle. Yet Rome and the Orthodox Churches agree on so much that the Pope pleads for a bridge to be constructed. He wants the Orthodox Churches, especially, to find a way of coming to terms with Papal authority. He cites his own homily delivered in the presence of the Ecumenical Patriarch His Holiness Dimitrios I:

> I acknowledge my awareness that "for a great variety of reasons, and against the will of all concerned, what should have been a service sometimes manifested itself in a different light. But . . . it is out of desire to obey the will of Christ truly that I recognize that as Bishop of Rome I am called to exercise that ministry. . . . I insistently pray the Holy Spirit to shine his light upon us, enlightening all the Pastors and theologians of our Churches, that we may seek — together, of course — the forms in which this ministry may accomplish a service of love recognized by all concerned.[23]

He then goes on:

> Could not the real but imperfect communion existing between us persuade church leaders and their theologians to engage with me in patient and fra-

ternal dialogue on this subject, a dialogue in which, leaving useless controversies behind, we could listen to one another, keeping before us only the will of Christ for his church and allowing ourselves to be deeply moved by his plea "that they may be one . . . so that the world may believe that you have sent me"?[24]

While the Pope is insisting that the Papacy itself is unnegotiable, he can be taken to say: "Just tell me what I have to do to accommodate the Orthodox Churches and I am willing to do it."

But just imagine: there are one and a quarter billion Roman Catholics in the world. Add a further 170 million orthodox adherents, and the resulting communion would be, by far, the most significant grouping in the world. Approximately 22 percent of the world's population would be in the resulting Catholic body. Furthermore, no part of the globe would be unrepresented. It would be a formidable global force.

So there we have it: the Pope's manifesto for this new millennium involves a friendly conversation with capitalism, a strong affirmation of truth in morality discovered through natural law, a passionate opposition to the "culture of death," and a determination to encourage the universal church to work together more effectively.

3 Engaging with the Pope

It would be churlish not to recognize and admire the achievement displayed in the corpus of Pope John Paul's encyclicals. This is a remarkable set of documents; he has set out an internally self-consistent position which speaks in a profound way to the contemporary situation. In addition there is much that is almost self-evidently right: the need to make the market work on behalf of the poor; the danger of judging all human life on the basis of utility rather than intrinsic value; and the need to witness to the possibility of truth in morals, without which no civilization can survive.

While there is much to admire and accept, there is nevertheless one major defect in the entire position. It seems to me it ignores entirely the revelatory significance of complexity and ambiguity or to put it more directly all engaged theology will end up being messy. In other words, for these encyclicals, for this Pope, the ethical task has become very simple: accept the interpretation of the tradition (of which, natural law is a major part) that is proposed by the magisterium. The complexities of modern life are not conceded: there is no dialogue with external expertise. Ronald Preston is right to point out that the problem lies in the genre of the encyclical:

> They all lay stress on the continuity of teaching, . . . Each contains references to the Bible, to the church Fathers and to previous Popes. Lately there has been an occasional reference to a United Nations document. No other empirical sources are mentioned. No flaws in church teaching are admitted.[25]

It is the tradition interpreted by the magisterium which is in control. As if fueled by a fear of the whole system unraveling, the ethical task is reduced to simple uncomplicated obedience to those who know better. The experience of all those who think otherwise is simply disregarded.

At this point, it might be objected that as I have already shown the encyclicals are intended as "cultural documents," which enable the tradition to converse with the modern world and church, it is unreasonable to expect engagement with expertise and disagreement. Even if this is conceded, we still find the same style being used when the Vatican is attempting to engage with a particular profession. To illustrate what I mean, I shall now turn my attention to a document on *Ethics in Advertising*.

Ethics in Advertising was published on 25 February, 1997 by the Pontifical Council for Social Communications. Let us note right at the outset that all 37 footnotes are to Papal pronouncements and encyclicals, Vatican reports, and the Catechism. Let us also concede that much of the report is good and thoughtful. It is right to say that advertising has the power to influence society; it does not simply mirror cultural values but can determine them. It is good to see an unequivocal declaration about the positive value of advertising, given the historic tendency of the churches to simply link advertising with consumerism and waste. Much of the report draws attention to issues that the industry are already aware; so, for example, it correctly sets high standards in terms of truthfulness. "It is a fundamental principle that advertising may not deliberately seek to deceive, whether it does that by what it says, by what it implies, or by what if fails to say."[26] In the UK, the advertising industry concurs entirely with such expectations: "No advertisement should mislead by inaccuracy, ambiguity, exaggeration, omission or otherwise."[27] And the Advertising Standards Authority (ASA) in the UK spends considerable time evaluating the truthfulness of advertising claims.[28] The ASA require substantiation for any testable claim in an advert: so if a store claims to have a wider choice than any other store, then there must be evidence to show that is true.

However, despite these achievements, there are at least three major difficulties with the report. First, it misses an opportunity. The conclusion seems to imply that overt government regulation is the best means of control. The problem with voluntary ethical codes, the report explains, is that they "are only as effective as the willingness of advertisers to comply strictly with them."[29] Actually this is not true; the Committee of Advertising Practice not only provides the code for the advertising industry but also creates and implements the sanctions against those advertisers who violate the code. However, the report fails completely to see the intrinsic moral value of self-regulation. Self-regulation can be justified on many grounds. Pragmatically, it provides a cheaper and more effective system of regulation. Cheaper precisely because it does not involve the recourse to law and lawyers; more effective because it can make and implement decisions quickly. However, one can also defend it on ethical grounds. Given a choice between legislating ethical behavior or encouraging practitioners themselves to be ethical, then the latter is more enlightened. To be ethical simply out of obedience to the law is less commendable than the creation of an ethical culture.

Coupled with the report's failure to reflect ethically on advertising regulation, we find a comparable failure to identify the major problem with advertising. The report gives most space to the evils of "brand advertising," which I shall show in a moment is not really a problem at all. In actual fact, the problem area of advertising is its exploitative potential. The Advertising Standards Authority is utterly uncompromising with those adverts that exploit vulnerable consumers. The adverts which promise instant and effortless weight loss by taking this expensive course of pills: or more trivially, the promise on the front page of a free trip to France in today's paper, which actually needs a further five coupons that have to be collected over the next two weeks. Both examples are exploitation: they promise something you cannot actually get. Although the report does stress the need for truthfulness and that "human dignity" should not be violated, there is no explicit identification or discussion of this problem.

The third problem area is the inconsistency in affirming the market yet condemning brand advertising. I have already commended the Papal shift in his affirmation of the market. This report echoes this shift, when conceding the intrinsic value of advertising: "Advertising can be a useful tool for sustaining honest and ethically responsible competition that contributes to economic growth in the service of authentic human development."[30] However, it then goes on to condemn consumerism and, in so doing, insists that "brand advertising" is wrong:

> The practice of "brand" – related advertising can raise serious problems. Often there are only negligible differences among similar products of different brands, and advertising may attempt to move people to act on the basis of irrational motives ("brand loyalty," status, fashion, "sex appeal," etc.) instead of presenting differences in product quality and price as bases for rational choice.[31]

Given that the market is about competition and given that competition will inevitably lead to different companies producing similar products, then brand advertising is an inevitable part of the market. Take, for example, the proliferation of Coke cans: along with Pepsi and Cola, we have Virgin cola and numerous supermarket brands. As a result of this competition, we can buy cheaper coke. And although price will be one factor in the advertising (something conceded by the report), it cannot be the only one. To sustain the competition, the market needs the "brand advertising" based on nonrational factors. Unless there is a degree of image association, for example, "Coca-Cola with life," then the choice will cease. In mature economies, such as Britain, there is very little evidence that this "brand advertising" creates any problems for the consumer. Anyway to criticize "brand advertising" sits very awkwardly with the affirmation of the market and competition.

The first problem illustrates insufficient ethical reflection; the second ignorance of the industry; and the third brings the first two problems together, the report is, in the end, inconsistent. Although I am certain that there was considerable consultation, the conventions surrounding the final text meant that the report lost sight of some of the complexities involved in the ethical analysis of advertising.

4   The Need for Engagement to Handle Expertise and Ambiguity

So now we come to the heart of the argument in this chapter. For all the thoughtfulness of the Papal encyclicals, to have an impact on public life, points of contact have to be made. Although some in the world of work are wicked (i.e., they are corrupt or exploitative), most are not. Yet every profession has its dilemmas, which require ethical reflection. However, the guidance needs to be informed; it needs to take into account the complexity of the world; it needs to admit that much of human life is ambiguous and confusing. To simply divide all human experience into "good" and "bad," fails to make contact with all those situations which are in between – those "shades of gray."

The Monkees are responsible for a song that develops this contrast: the lyrics are as follows:

> When the world and I were young, just yesterday,
> Life was such a simple game, a child could play.
> It was easy then to tell right from wrong,
> Easy then to tell weak from strong,
> When a man should stand and fight, or just go along.
> But today there is no day or night,
> Today there is no dark or light,
> Today there is no black or white, only shades of gray.
> I remember when the answers seemed so clear;
> We had never lived with doubt or tasted fear.
> It was easy then to tell truth from lies,
> Selling out from compromise,
> Who to love and who to hate,
> The foolish from the wise.
> But today there is no day or night,
> Today there is no dark or light,
> Today there is no black or white, only shades of gray.
> It was easy then to know what was fair.
> When to keep and when to share,
> How much to protect your heart and how much to care.
> But today there is no day or night,
> Today there is no dark or light,
> Today there is no black or white, only shades of gray.

Allow me to become personal for a moment. When I was twelve, I believed that the car was a polluting luxury that our environment could not afford; now at forty, for the sake of convenience and safety, I drive a Ford Escape. When I was sixteen, I was persuaded that there was a Christian obligation to live simply in the light of a world of need; now at forty, I live in a detached house in West Hartford, Connecticut and consume more than my fair share of the world's resources.[32]

How does one explain these changes? Perhaps it is simply due to sin. The demands of the Gospel, as described in the Sermon on the Mount, call us to a simple lifestyle where we are willing "to give to him who asks" (Matthew 5:42). But the sin hypothesis breaks down because the intent was not to be wicked. Granted it is easy to deceive ourselves into believing that a middle-class lifestyle is the minimum we should expect. And confronting that deception is a moral obligation; revisiting our lifestyle in the light of the Sermon on the Mount is a requirement of the Christian faith. Yet opting out of conventional society is not an easy option; and it is wrong to insist that all of us who struggle to be good within are guilty of compromise and sin.

It is the complexity of human life that leads to ambiguity. **By complexity I mean the interlocking matrix of factors that need to be taken into account when making moral decisions.** This leads to **ambiguity because our intentions have to take so many conflicting factors into account that we end up with less than satisfactory outcomes.** Lying at the heart of this song is a certain image of maturity. In one's youth one has a clarity of vision; as one matures the world is just much more complicated. Let us be honest, sometimes it is the sinfulness of accepting that which it is too exhausting to change. But more often, I want to suggest it is due to the inherent complexity of situations, what I am calling the "ambiguity of human situations."

In my judgment this feature of human experience creates the major problem for a theological ethic of public life. Others seem to concur with this judgment. Reinhold Niebuhr was perhaps the first to identify the problem. In *Moral Man and Immoral Society*, Niebuhr makes much of the tension among worthy individual moralities that become confused by unfeeling and insensitive institutions and nations.[33] Since then many feminist writers have been stressing the ways in which women, to be true to themselves, need to behave in ways that seem (or have seemed) immoral. Often it is a matter of intractable character of power (indeed this is what Niebuhr stressed) but often it is just the confusion of being mortal and human. Kevin Kelly stresses the centrality of experience in moral judgment: it is "in the light of experience some of our principles may need to be revised in order to do justice to our deeper understanding of our ourselves and our world."[34] And it is clear from his work that those experiences include all those where people are confused and muddled. The Anglican theologian, V.A. Demant pointed to the "ambiguity" of much marriage breakdown. One overlooked feature of much debate on sexual morality is that more marriages break down **because** of Christian virtues than because of virtually anything else. Love and honesty, two central Christian qualities, can be deeply destructive. Demant argued that in an age when people used to work, live, and die in the same community, the opportunities for infidelity were fewer and the conventions protecting the marriage were stronger. To talk about Christian love involving discipline and decision was easier. But now, in our global village, where work requires mobility, the potential for significant relationships to develop outside the marriage is so much greater. In among the tragic tales of marriage breakdown, we find men and women discovering significant relationships outside the marriage (which are perceived as loving) and, in the face of inability to live a double, hypocritical lifestyle, the love is admitted and the marriage breaks down.[35] Even if this example is easily open to criticism, literature is packed full of testimonies from tormented men and women trying to handle love and honesty and finding them complex in their demands.

The problem for the theologian is that we have to make contact or engage with these situations. So how best should we proceed? Let us start by recognizing the benefits that this ambiguity can create. First, ethical pluralism (or the term I prefer – ethical plurality) is inevitable. The ambiguity is bound to generate different ethical positions: diversity and disagreement are always going to be with us. Second, "the ambiguity of human situations" inculcates in us the necessity of humility. Although some things are clearer than others, for example the need to protect innocent human life, many things are not so clear. We need to hold our understanding of the truth with humility. And thirdly, this ambiguity encourages conversation and dialogue. We need each other to illuminate the intractable difficulties facing our age. It is in dialogue that truth will be illuminated, contrasts realized, disagreements recognized and, of course, confronted.

It is for these three reasons that I believe that God intended the complexity and ambiguity of the ethical domain. Ethical plurality should be celebrated: diversity and disagreement are part of God's world. The ambiguity is intended because it is God's chosen mechanism to bring about conversation between those who disagree; it is intended precisely because it encourages diversity and disagreement.

The idea that diversity and disagreement are revelatory needs unpacking. At the biblical level the position is not what it may seem. Within the Bible there are passages that resist the notion of human diversity: there is the old story of Babel, seeing variety of languages as a curse inflicted for human hubris, and in the New Testament, some writers are alarmed, as cracks in Christian unity make their appearance. However, for all the overt aspiration for uniformity, it is clear that the Bible reflects significant disagreement and diverse positions. Chronicles sits alongside Kings, even though there are clearly different theological outlooks at work. Matthew, Mark, and Luke are all in the canon, even though they clearly disagree. Paul was at variance on certain crucial matters with the Jerusalem apostles. So although we lack overt verses to justify my desire to celebrate disagreement, the actual form of the Bible clearly supports my claim. It is a book that embraces disagreement and diversity, precisely because of the complexity of its subject matter.[36]

Coupled with these reflections on the Bible, I want to argue that diversity and difference must be intended by God because he (or she because of course God is beyond gender) built it into the creation. The argument needs to be formulated thus: the Christian–Judaeo God is the God of the whole world. This God is responsible for the Big Bang fifteen billion years ago; it is the God responsible for the vastness of space, the diversity of life-forms, and the emergence of different peoples in different parts of the world. It seems a very attenuated view of the cosmic God to imagine that God is only involved in the history of ancient Israel starting with Abraham and then the church as it spread through Europe. It is a very impoverished faith which leaves Satan with most of the world and God dabbling in Israel and then Europe. Given that all good things come from God, then God must have been doing something when Confucius taught in China. God must have been involved somewhere when the Upanishads were being written. God must have not only allowed but delighted in the wisdom of the Buddha.

Yet we feel that all this diversity is confusing, so much so that, as it were, a respectable deity could not be mixed up in it or recognizable through it. We much prefer that God simply provided one clear revelation: Jesus, the apostles, and the magisterium perhaps, rather than muddy the scene with all these different religions.

That God has not made things simple and clear is manifestly true. Even within the Roman Catholic communion, but also elsewhere, magisteria have always had their work cut out: always adjusted, often belatedly, to circumstances and to new kinds of awareness.

Although the remarkable theology of Vatican II made the experience of the laity central and, therefore by implication, believed that dialogue with disagreement was important, the authoritarian tendency embedded in these encyclicals is problematic. You cannot simultaneously concede the possibility that one can learn from others and at the same time exclude

any discussion or dissension. Despite his obvious enthusiasm for the orthodox traditions, it is interesting to note that relations between Rome and
the Eastern Orthodox Church have been worse than in the reign of any
other Pontiff this century, notably since 1989. The orthodox traditions do
not believe that this Pope is really interested in authentic conversation.
Constructive engagement with diversity and disagreement is still needed.

So to sum up this chapter: "shades of gray" are the complexity of
human life and the ambiguities these complexities can create. It is the
argument of this chapter that we cannot move from cultural analysis to
policy prescriptions without taking into account these "shades of gray."
Failure to do so will result in a failure to make contact with those we
need to influence and persuade.

As we shape this new millennium, we find a profound analysis of our
contemporary situation set out in the encyclicals written by Pope John
Paul II. However, I have argued that these encyclicals are marred by their
failure to acknowledge any "shades of gray." The ethical methodology is
traditional: the positions taken are firm and uncompromising; and the
recognition of complexity is rarely conceded. These problems become
more pronounced when the Vatican attempts to move from the cultural
framework provided by the encyclicals to engagement with a profession.
Despite the considerable consultation which probably preceded the report
Ethics in Advertising, the final product fails to make contact with the profession: it comes across as either platitudinous (in its talk about "human
dignity") or confused (in its affirmation of the market running parallel
with its condemnation of brand advertising).

A "Theology of Engagement" makes dialogue (or the term I prefer is
"conversation"; conversations are wider and more varied than a dialogue)
central. To accommodate the complexity and ambiguity, we need expertise. We need to become much more sensitive to the ways in which good
intentions have been either thwarted by institutions or have unforeseen
side-affects. Public life is made of dilemmas, where the right and the good
are rarely clear. There is a danger that the language of morality will be
confined to those who want to sloganize: to avoid that danger it is vital
that the Churches illustrate that moral discourse can meet people where
they are. Moral discourse needs to be able to weigh conflicting goods; it
needs to concede the "ambiguity of human situations."

Calls for the centrality of "conversation" with others in Christian ethics
are often perceived as calls for compromise from the high standards of the
Gospel. Such a response arises from sloppy theology. To converse with
others is not betrayal, but obedience. It is precisely because I believe in

the God revealed in Christ that I admit the complexity of the world we live in. God could have made everything much more straightforward: however, this is not the case. Instead we "see through a glass darkly." To find a way forward, we need each other: we need conversation.

Conversation is not an end in itself. We converse for two reasons. First, we do so because we believe that conversation is preferably to conflict. It is the "ambiguity of human situations" that often leads to the seeds of conflict. If conversation is not encouraged, then conflict is often the result. Second, we do so, in the hope, that conversation will generate new and better options for the way forward. Our goal remains the same – a just society, where all are able to participate. Inspired by the promise of God's kingdom, we are called to transform the present into what God always intended.

An engaged theology is in the business of conversation. We must not allow the conversation to be too polite: difficult disagreements need to be confronted. We need to see the conversation extended to those from other faith communities. Increasingly, it is the cross–faith alliances that can be the most effective; it is these alliances that cut through the indifference of those in power.[37]

13

THE SHAPE OF AN ENGAGED THEOLOGY

An engaged theology is relocating and we need to be perpetually relocated. For many within the church, the use of labels is a way of staying comfortable and located. The label "Christian religion" tends to assume that there is a single entity that can be contrasted with other "religions" and that these religions can each be seen as self-contained. The labels "conservative" and "liberal" are devices that create two contrasting tribes with supposedly different attitudes to the tradition – conservatives affirm the tradition, while liberals want to challenge it. We use these labels to promote divisiveness between ourselves and pride in our tribal identity: they are the means by which conversation is curtailed and stopped. So we find ourselves saying: "we can't affirm that idea; it is practically Hindu" or "but the Church has never recognized the legitimacy of same-sex unions." Further discussion is supposed to be terminated by these assertions.

We have become so familiar with these labels that to think in alternative ways is exhausting and uncomfortable. Many liberal Christians seem to enjoy dissecting the texts of the church fathers to find anti-Semitic or patriarchal statements and then denouncing the tradition. Some conservative Christians love attacking change and then calling for schism when the church dares to modify her position on a particularly contentious modern issue.

The task in this chapter is to stand back from the exercises that have dominated the book thus far and examine the framework surrounding this engaged approach to theology. This framework has four features. First, it recognizes that all religious traditions are interconnected and mutually dependent, and that generalizations about particular religions in their entirety are misguided and unhelpful. Second, it affirms the category of "theism" as logically prior the particularities of the "Trinitarian" account of God. Recognizing this provides an important basis for engagement with other theistic traditions and the best way of challenging a secularist world perspective. Third, engagement is embedded firmly within the biblical witness. Fourth, an engaged theology is a Catholic theology.

1   Many Traditions and Religion

It was Wilfred Cantwell Smith who famously exposed the unhelpfulness of the word "religion." It was, he explained, an imposition that distorted the complexity of the world.[1] Anyone involved in interreligious dialogue knows full well that this is the case. Once a dialogue moves beyond politeness (often expressing itself as the careful avoidance of anything at all sensitive), the group of (for example) Christians and Jews find many odd alliances emerging. It is discovered that certain strands of Christianity have more in common with certain strands of Judaism than they do with some of the strands within their own faith.

For those involved in the history of religions, the explanation for this is easy to provide. The fact of engagement, documented for Christianity in chapters 2 and 3, means that the multifaceted experience of traditions creates some surprising bedfellows. In very broad terms, we can document the following historical patterns and trajectories. Most significant and enduring religious traditions emerged in what Karl Jaspers called the "axial period." It is the period between 800 BCE and 100 CE.[2] The Upanishads are written in India, the Buddha and Confucius lived in the sixth century BCE, and the eighth-century prophets set in train a tradition that gave birth to both modern Judaism (after the fall of the temple in 70 CE) and Christianity. The prophet Mohammed believed that he was best understood as a successor to the prophets of Judaism and the ministry of Jesus. Not only did the shared spark of faith and divine ethical obligations emerged at a similar time (speaking of course in broad terms), but similar factors shaped the traditions. Certainly Judaism (at least for a time) felt with Christianity the impact of Hellenistic philosophy, which subsequently was equally important for Islamic thought. India's own history, a combination of the Indus Valley Civilization and Aryan thought, was giving birth to the diversity of Hinduism and subsequently Buddhism and Sikhism. And so we could go on. The point is this: the great religious traditions have been endlessly cross-fertilized with certain nonreligious traditions and with each other.

To provide a concrete example of the implications of this shared history, we need to return to the "concept of God' debate, which has been extensively discussed in earlier chapters. We saw in chapter 3 how Aquinas (Christian), Maimonides (Jewish), and Ibn Sina (Avicenna) (Muslim) all concur about the nature of God's attributes. They affirmed God as totally other from the world and therefore timeless, immutable, and simple. Conversely, we find many contemporary writers, for example Charles Hartshorne (Christian) and Allama Muhammad Iqbal (Muslim) affirming a contrasting account of God. For Hartshorne and Iqbal, God should be understood as embracing the universe and thus enabling everything to be. Such a God is everlasting, rather than timeless. Indeed we might be able to use the language of panentheism.

Here we have a Christian and a Muslim moving slowly into the territory occupied traditionally by Hinduism. It was Ramanuja, the twelfth-century Hindu thinker, who most famously talked about the world as the body of God. He writes, "The entire world is a body the Self of which is constituted by knowledge abiding apart from its world-body."[3] Charles Hartshorne, the Christian thinker and follower of A.N. Whitehead, speaks in very similar ways when he formulates his account of dipolar theism. He writes:

> God orders the universe, according to panentheism, by taking into his own life all the currents of feeling in existence. He is the most irresistible of influences precisely because he is himself the most open to influence. In the depths of their hearts all creatures (even those able to "rebel" against him) defer to God because they sense him as the one who alone is adequately moved by what moves them. He alone not only knows but feels (the only adequate knowledge, where feeling is concerned) how they feel, and he finds his own joy in sharing their lives, lived according to their own free decisions, not fully anticipated by any detailed plan of his own. Yet the extent to which they can be permitted to work out their own plan depends on the extent to which they can echo or imitate on their own level the divine sensitiveness to the needs and precious freedom of all. In this vision of a deity who is not a supreme autocrat, but a universal agent of "persuasion," whose "power is the worship he inspires" (Whitehead), that is, flows from the intrinsic appeal of his infinitely sensitive and tolerant relativity, by which all things are kept moving in orderly togetherness, we may find help in facing our task of today, the task of contributing to the democratic self-ordering of a world whose members not even the supreme orderer reduces to mere subjects with the sole function of obedience.[4]

This sense of God in everything and upholding everything led to his aphorism that "Cosmic being is cosmic experience, is cosmic sociality or love."[5]

Allama Muhammad Iqbal arrives at an account of the Ultimate Reality "as pure duration in which thought, life, and purpose interpenetrate to form an organic unity."[6] And later he makes the parallel with panentheism when he explains how we must move from our own experience of life to the discovery that there must be a God. He writes, "The operation of thought which is essentially symbolic in character veils the true nature of life, and can picture it only as a kind of universal current flowing through all things. The result of an intellectual view of life, therefore, is necessarily pantheistic."[7] It is clear then that there is a remarkable convergence of view between Ramanuja, Hartshorne, and Iqbal.

Our idea of God is one of the fundamental aspects to belief. To have a Muslim having more in common with Christian process thought and Hinduism than with Al-Ghazzali, his own coreligionist, is both remarkable and noteworthy. If we take a particular issue, this is often the case. On revelation, for example, we find across traditions theologians who take a propositional view of revelation (that in some sense the text or doctrinal formula is the very Word of God) and a nonpropositional view (that the revelation lies behind the text, located within the experience of those who wrote the text). On the propositional side, James Packer (Christian)[8] and Norman Lamm (Jewish)[9] agree, while on the nonpropositional side, John Hick (Christian)[10] and Abraham Joshua Heschel (Jewish)[11] line up together.

Given these alliances and areas of agreement across the so-called "religions," it is necessary to revise the ways in which we think about interreligious relations as a whole. The "God illustration" is interesting. It is fundamental, yet many Christians feel able to circumvent its implications by simply appealing to the fact that "Jesus" is not anywhere mentioned in the Islamic and Jewish accounts. This response is inadequate because "Jesus" is himself a complex image understood differently both across the Christian tradition and beyond. On the one hand, we have some Christians who think of Jesus in ways that are similar to the Islamic view. Leaving to one side Sura 4:152 which talks of Jesus not being crucified, many Christians think of Jesus as a prophet. For many Christians, "Jesus the prophet" is an important aspect of any proper Christology. And as the publication of The Myth of God Incarnate[12] illustrated, there are those who are attracted to a low Christology that stresses the prophetic nature of Jesus. In the Qur'an Jesus is born of a virgin, preaches the rule of God, and performs miracles. On the other hand, those Christians with a strongly Docetic Christology are close to the view of Jesus suggested in certain twentieth-century Hindu Christologies.[13] It is not true, then, that all

Christians can unite around a single view of Jesus. Indeed, those with a low Christology will often find themselves comfortable with a Jewish or Islamic view of him, while those with a high Christology will have more in common with certain Hindu understandings. This might provoked some skepticism. However, as Sandy Martin, who has been actively involved in the Hindu – Christian dialogue, writes this is a real issue:

> There is a paradox about the interreligious dialogue between Hindus and Christians. Mostly such meetings involve liberal Christians and Vedantic Hindus. Liberal Christians tend to emphasize the humanity of Jesus. Vedantic Hindus, placing this humanity with a cosmic Christness, assert the divinity of Jesus.[14]

Elsewhere Martin has documented illustrations of the Hindu attitude to Jesus, this one from Ramakrishna in 1874 demonstrates the high Christology operating:

> Near the end of the third day, as he was walking in Panchavati, he saw, evidently with open eyes, a Godman of fair complexion coming toward him with a steadfast look. Recognizing him as a foreigner, he saw that his eyes and face were beautiful. Sri Ramakrishna wondered who this was. The answer came from his heart, but in words loud enough that he described them as "ringing." "Lord Jesus Christ, the Master-Yogi, eternally one with God, who shed his heart's blood for the deliverance of man! It is He!" The figure embraced the Master and disappeared into his body, leaving the latter in *bhavasamadhi* (a devotional ecstasy).[15]

The fact is that plenty of liberal Christians could easily be Muslims and plenty of conservative ones would happily sit alongside the Hindus.

This means that the sentence "Christianity is a truer religion than Islam" requires a good deal of unpacking. There is no such homogeneous or insulated entity as "Christianity" or "Islam." Not that it is impossible to rank different beliefs. The traditional criteria for the evaluation of different beliefs are still useful, namely coherence and explanatory power. Self-contradictory traditions cannot all be true; and those that explain in a more comprehensive way the complexity of the world are more likely to be true than those that do not.[16] So it is possible to evaluate, with considerable care, two contrasting traditions. However, the problem is that the set – in a mathematical sense – "all Christians" is not sufficiently uniform in viewpoint and approach to the Christian life for the contrast with "all Muslims," who are equally varied, to take place.

When we rank beliefs, in an environment where we recognize the complexity of the different traditions, we might find the following: the God
of Aquinas, Maimonides, and Ibn Sina rests on a disputable assumption
(namely that perfection implies immutability), provokes a range of conceptual difficulties (e.g., the relationship of divine action to timelessness),
and does not address our experience that matter and humanity need to
be embraced within the divine (the point made repeatedly by feminist
theologians).[17] This picture of God is less adequate than the God of the
process theologians, the Upanishads, and of Sufi Islam. Here we have a
more dynamic account of God, who embraces the universe, and affirms
all matter as part of the divine life. It is possible to rank traditions, but
the fact here is that the ranking is interreligious.

The important point is that an engaged theology, with its sense of
ramification, recognizes as intrinsic and inevitable this interreligious complexity. It recognizes the historical roots of the different ideas that shape
our religious traditions. However, there are subsidiary points that emerge
from this analysis of the nature and comparison of religious traditions that
are worth bringing out.

In many ecumenical and interfaith discussions, there is a continuing
presumption that there are fixed entities that share a certain set of beliefs
which contrast with those held by other bodies, whether a church or a
distinct religion. The Roman Catholic attitude to the Eucharist is a good
example. To exclude hospitality to communicant members of other
churches on the grounds that non-Roman Catholics do not affirm all the
teaching of the magisterium of the church ignores the fact that most (or
at least many, especially in America and Europe) Roman Catholics are in
exactly the same position. It is interesting to read the statistics docu-
menting the attitudes of Roman Catholics.[18] They vary considerably in
their "sense of belonging." Some are in the church because they were born
into the tradition and, out of family loyalty, will never leave. Others are
converts attracted to this or that aspect of the tradition. Others are seeking
faith and happened upon the Roman Catholic Church as their initial
encounter with religion. As a result, some understand the creed in a fairly
traditional way, while others do not. Some believe the traditional account
of the Eucharist, while others are inclined to see it as symbolic. Some
appreciate the Roman Catholic teaching on contraception, others have
long since disregarded it. Some believe that women could never be priests,
others are members of pressure groups that campaign for that goal. Almost
all Christians from other churches could find agreeable company amongst
the many viewpoints embraced by the Roman Catholic Church. If the

Roman Catholic Church manages to be in communion with herself, then there is absolutely no reason why she cannot be in communion with the other churches.

It might be objected that I am treating membership of a church as a matter of "ticking boxes," rather than appreciating the more mystical sense of "belonging" in the one body, in which some belong even if they hold "imperfect" views. Although it is true that the church is not a "club," rather a better and biblical analogy is to think of the church as a family, it is careful such reasoning does not underpin a tribal prejudice. For Christians the issue is the extent to which we can recognize the family resemblance even though there are differences of worldview. The point remains that divisions with the Roman Catholic family are as great as the differences that Roman Catholics have with those outside. Therefore perhaps the time has come for the Roman Catholic Church to recognize their brothers and sisters outside the communion.

What is true at the ecumenical level amongst Christians is also true at the interfaith level. If I manage to sit alongside a fundamentalist Christian and trust that God is receiving our worship, then there should surely be no problem about sitting alongside a Muslim or a Jew. Christians have different accounts of God, different expectations of the efficacy of prayer, and different understandings of how Jesus slots in. When I join a Muslim or a Jew, this diversity is no greater. If worship with different Christians is not a problem, then interfaith worship should not be a problem either. I concede that there are problems of vocabulary and liturgy (for example, do you pray, expressly, in the name of Jesus); however, once we recognize the different interpretations found within the Christian tradition, this problem should be relieved.

The first aspect then to the framework of a Theology of Engagement is this recognition of the diversity, and the reasons for it, both within and outside the traditions that make up the Christian family. A Theology of Engagement recognizes this diversity and even enjoys it.

2   Working with Theism

One assumption of an engaged theology, stated briefly, in the opening chapter was the idea that our theistic understanding of God can and should be disentangled from our conviction that God is a trinity. It is now necessary to revisit this debate and look at it in more detail.

Much recent theology, both in America and Britain, has stressed the unique contribution that the doctrine of the Trinity makes to the Christian understanding of God and then the implications for God's activity within the world. Colin Gunton in Britain, for example, has argued for the relevance of "Trinitarian transcendentals for the overcoming of some of the characteristic unease of the modern condition."[19] And Robert Jenson in America has made a similar argument.

Both men are firmly grounded in the Reformed traditions. Gunton is a minister in the United Reformed Church, while Jenson is a Lutheran. Both are inspired by the brilliance of Karl Barth, who argued that all knowledge of God depends upon an encounter with Jesus, which is made possible in the preaching of the Word. Barth is famous for his adamant denial of any knowledge of God outside the revelation of Jesus. This not only tends to exclude natural theology (the view that with an appropriate use of reason it is possible to deduce some sense of God from the world), but also the gross distortions of Nazi Germany with the Aryan Jesus.

When it comes to knowledge of God in other religions, Barth is equally clear. All religion, explained Barth, is unbelief. Barth writes, "We begin by stating that religion is unbelief. It is a concern, indeed, we must say that it is the one great concern, of godless man."[20] For Barth, then, it is an act of human hubris that aspires to have knowledge of God without accepting the revelation of God. How can sinful, insignificant humans located within time and history expect to be able to have knowledge of God *apart from* God disclosing the truth to them? Barth insisted that the choice is always: either accept the revelation of God in Jesus or construct a human system of thought. If we want "knowledge" of God, explained Barth, then we must opt for the former. It is only in accepting God's self-disclosure in Christ that we can have knowledge of God. The latter – opting for a religion or a philosophy – will be a human speculation; it will not enable one to have knowledge of God; therefore it will be tantamount to unbelief.

One further consequence of this approach should be noted. It is incompatible with the form of engaged theology advocated in this book. The Christian revelation of God in Christ is made the sole source of knowledge of God. Everything else is "unbelief" or a "human speculation." Such a view does not encourage a willingness to learn from non-Christian sources (or indeed from several forms of Christianity) and then be shaped by the wisdom found beyond the church. Those sympathetic to this approach tend to view engagement as no more than "location." We looked at this view of engagement in chapter 1. It means that instead of being shaped by non-Christian traditions, one simply "positions" oneself in respect to them.

Attractive though this approach is to many, especially in these post-modern times with the stress being placed on a fideistic decision to live in the community of the church, the difficulties are overwhelming. Many of these are well known and widely documented. However, the entire argument of this book depends on challenging the Barthian approach to theology, so it is necessary to discuss them here. Three objections will be discussed. The first is the problem of religious diversity; the second is the historical development of the Trinity doctrine and its relationship to Jewish monotheism; and the third is the recognition of the purposes of the doctrines of the Trinity and the Incarnation. We start, then, with the first.

The problem of religious diversity: it is much harder to "trust a revelation" when it is recognized that there are many books and teachers claiming to provide such a thing. Indeed every religion in the world is based, in one way or another, on revelation. When Keith Ward discusses the view of Scripture held by Thomas Aquinas, he writes:

> Aquinas' view would be that theological assertions are certain because they derive from biblical propositions which are given by God. There is no better reason for making claims about God than that God reveals such truths in person. God reveals truth to whomsoever God will; there need be no expectation that there will be universal agreement; and one is justified in placing complete confidence in what God reveals. This sounds a fairly convincing argument, until one reflects that it could be, and is, used with equal force by Jews, Christians, Muslims, Mormons, Hindus, and Jehovah's Witnesses. The position depends upon the basic belief that God has revealed the Divine nature to particular human beings – whether to Jesus, Muhammed, Krishna, or Joseph Smith. But can one be certain this is true, especially in view of the fact that so many diverse and conflicting claims to have received direct Divine revelation exist?[21]

In short, we have an epistemological problem as to how we decide which revelation we should trust.

Advocates of a Barthian approach to theology evade this objection by insisting it is unreasonable to expect to exercise choice between "revelations." This, they retort, assumes an Archimedian vantage point that is an illusion of modernity. The Enlightenment project, to use Alasdair MacIntyre's famous phrase, was the quest for a vantage point that transcends different traditions.[22] Such a project was doomed to failure, explained MacIntyre, for the simple reason that no such vantage point exists. Instead the "liberal tradition" emerged which denied it was a "tradition" and imagined falsely that it was possible to survey in a magisterial way all the options and determine which option was true. The fact of religious diversity, the defenders of Barth retort, is simply a testimony to the extent of the human imagination. Belonging to the church is the *gift* of faith; those that have the gift have been confronted with the Word that is Christ and therefore have knowledge of God.

Even if we concede some legitimacy to this response (especially in respect to the absurd expectation that one can exercise "traditionless" reason to make a choice between traditions), the underlying objection, which was summarized by Keith Ward, still has force. It is still true that there are many religions and all claim to be based on revelation. Furthermore the Barthian does concede that faith in the revelation of Jesus is not to be justified in terms of arguments but in terms of a faith decision.

This leads to the second objection. In terms of the history of the Christian story, the Barthian approach is problematic. To see an incarnational understanding of Jesus and a Trinitarian understanding of God as the exclusive means to knowledge of God has obvious implications for one's view of the Old Testament.[23] We saw in chapter three how an anthropomorphic account of God within the Hebrew Bible gradually evolved into a more sophisticated theism. New Testament scholars, working from the synoptic Gospels, are largely persuaded that Jesus had a theocentric message rather than a Christological one. It was a message about God and the reign of God not about Jesus himself. This means that a significant quantity of the text of our Scriptures (our source about the revelation disclosed in Jesus) comes from men and women working with a monotheistic view of God not a Trinitarian one. The Old Testament assumes that knowledge of God is possible through creation and history. The Psalms describe the ways in which creation witnesses to the "glory of the Lord"; and the prophets sought to provide an interpretation of history from the vantage point of the agency of God. In addition the Old Testament is working within a monotheistic framework not a Trinitarian one. After all the doctrines of the Trinity and the Incarnation were not fully worked out until the period from the third to the fifth centuries CE. As the doctrines were not available to the writers of the Hebrew Bible, then they could not use them.

The problem of history in fact extends to the formulation of the doctrines of the Trinity and Incarnation. We saw in chapter 3 that these doctrines are a result of engagement with a range of non-Christian tradi-tions. They were constructed within the complexity of human history: to lift them out of this setting and identify them as the sole means of having knowledge of God is a denial of their origins.

To evade this objection one would have to take a propositional view of revelation and hold to a strong sense of God's providence safeguarding the construction of the creeds. This is the sort of position held by many kinds of conservative Christians. It would need a high view of inspiration because then the authors would need virtually to be scribes of the Holy Spirit. If one took this position, then the Holy Spirit would obviously be within a Trinitarian framework. And it would need a strong sense of God guiding the early church fathers to account for the historical accidents that gave birth to the creeds. However, the problem with biblical inspiration is that the text can only bear such a high view with the utmost difficulty. It is manifestly all too human: the motives of the human authors can be identified and discussed; and as with all human projects, inevitable errors of fact and contradictions creep in.[24] Likewise with Christian doctrine in the early church.

A third difficulty with the role the Trinity and Incarnation are playing in these post-Barthian theologies is that it is a misuse – or at least a novel application – of the doctrine. As we saw in chapter 3, the doctrines emerged as Christians struggled to make sense of the fact that they were worshipping Jesus. God was the primary category that all Christians assumed; and the doctrines of the Trinity and Incarnation were innovative categories setting out to make sense of a distinctive experience of God found in Jesus of Nazareth.

Now it is perfectly proper that the church retains the distinctive sense of our experience of God by continuing to use the language of the Incar-nation and Trinity. Although the precise language used will inevitably change, the ideas intended by the doctrines are important to affirm. We need to explain precisely why Jesus matters to a Christian.[25] Our love for Jesus is at the heart of the Christian liturgical experience. Our ecclesiol-ogy and our liturgy depend on this continuing affirmation that Jesus is God and worthy of worship. But all this should not eliminate the prior category of "theism."

The importance of theism is a point I shall return to in a moment. But first, one last objection to the Barthian approach should be discussed. Its consequences are damaging in a number of ways. We have already noted that theologians of this persuasion are not sympathetic to a theol-ogy of engagement as defined by this book: they would consider it illegitimate to embark on the styles of engagement that have been developed in our earlier chapters. If we have succeeded in demonstrating the value of a theology of engagement, then it is obviously regrettable to arrive at a theological framework that forbids such engagement. However, two other conversations are also in difficulty. The conversation with secular thought needs a natural theology. The discourse with secularism needs to be able to start from within a world perspective of that kind and to illustrate that a certain incompleteness implicit in secularism requires theism. I have argued elsewhere that the secular commitment to arrive at the truth (understood as the goal of arriving at a coherent and comprehensive understanding of our experience of the world) rests on a particular set of assumptions about that world. It assumes stability and the capacity of the human mind to order the world that requires an explanation. And the best explanation available is a theistic one.[26] There is no need here to develop this particular argument further. It is sufficient to note that the explicit Barthian attack on natural theology is the eradication of a form of engagement that is deeply damaging to the conversation with secularism. The same point can be made with respect to other religious traditions. To exclude *a priori* that we can have no knowledge of God from other religious traditions is both implausible and damaging. The question must be answered: why did God allow all this religious diversity? It is implausible to attribute them all to human sin or even human imagination – and to deny such factors in the reception of "genuine" revelation. It seems much more plausible to suggest that the divine pressure touches most human lives and the religious spirit in the world is good evidence of this. If this is the case, then naturally there is much of God that we can learn from these different religious traditions. I hope aspects of this book are a good testimony to that truth.

Our Barthian critic will insist that these damaging consequences are simply consequences that we must live with. Perhaps; but I trust I have made the case that from those of us less convinced that the Barthian paradigm is the only effective one to operate within will find these consequences fatally damaging in so many ways.

The point of all this is that the theology of engagement needs to operate on both the theistic and Trinitarian canvases. And the former should not be reduced to the latter. They can be disentangled. We can and should talk the language of One God creator and sustainer of everything that is. It remains true that we inherited from Judaism a belief that there is one God, the source and sustainer of everything that is. It is also important to stress that we share that understanding of God with Islam.

And indeed the case can be made that theism permeates other traditions, for example strands of Hinduism. The canvas of theism gives us a shared framework for engagement with the thought of those in other faith traditions. Instead of starting with the particularities of the Incarnation and the Trinity, we should return to our roots and use the category of God, upon which there is much agreement.

Therefore, although there is a sense in which the doctrines of the Incarnation and Trinity are true, they should not assume a disproportionate significance. The role of these doctrines is to explain the significance of Jesus. In this respect they are very significant, but there are other assertions, which also are true and very significant. Consider the following sample list:

- humanity is made in the Image of God;
- the ideal is the aspiration to practice infinite compassion with infinite wisdom;[27]
- prayer should be a daily obligation and is essential for our human wholeness;
- Jesus is the incarnation of God.

Now a Christian would want to affirm all these assertions as true. Perhaps they could surely be seen as essentially Christian, although the first was discovered by Judaism, the second is an assertion from the Dalai Lama, and the third is an insight found in the Islamic pillar of salāt (prayer). It is surely wrong to assert that the last statement takes precedence over all the others. Anthropology, compassion, and prayer are also important.[28]

A "Theology of Engagement" wants to encourage the church to recognize the centrality of theism. In so doing we are recognizing that there are many aspects to the Christian world perspective of which the doctrines of the Trinity and the Incarnation are important examples. However, so are many other beliefs, such as monotheism, anthropology, compassion, and prayer. If we talk as much about these other beliefs as we do about the Incarnation and Trinity, then we will be able to work much more constructively with other religious traditions.

3 Engagement as a Biblical Imperative

Thus far much in this chapter we have stressed elements that Christians of a liberal persuasion would find most encouraging. Yet an important theme of this book is that engagement is the theological method which characterized the greatest and most traditional of theologians. We saw in chapter 2 how Augustine of Hippo can be interpreted as a model "engaged theologian." It is important to provide arguments for this approach to theology that enable those with a "conservative" theology to identify with it. Fortunately, there are many such arguments. This section proposes to examine two arguments grounded in the nature of Scripture.

It is important that a theology of engagement can be seen at work in the Bible. This is not an attempt to formulate a "biblical argument" – as if the Bible in its complexity all points in one direction; instead it is taking the Bible seriously and in so doing discovering a biblical connection. We shall examine two illustrations: the first is Acts 15; here we see in the shaping of the church, two traditions engaging with each other. The second is the form of the Bible and for this we shall look at the work of Judy Fentress Williams and Leslie Houlden.

Let us start with the first so-called Council of the Church as described by Luke in the Book of Acts. For Luke this is a pivotal part of his narrative: it is the official endorsement of Paul's mission to the Gentiles. We know from a comparison with Paul's letter to the Galatians that Luke has simplified events considerably.[29] In Galatians, Paul had been converting the Gentiles for fourteen years before this meeting in Jerusalem; in Acts, Paul had a short pilot project (it does not specify the time, but it is clearly brief). Yet despite these differences this meeting is of crucial importance because it is the official exploration of the church's identity.

At the heart of the narrative is a disagreement. On the one hand, the Jerusalem Church led by Peter and James wanted all Gentile Christians to accept the Jewish law, especially in respect to circumcision. Paul, on the other hand, believed (at least at this stage in his ministry) that Christ had freed the Gentile Christian from observance of the law. There are two very contrasting visions of the Christian mission here, which need to engage each other and to be reconciled or assimilated together.

The result, as reported in Luke, is interesting. They agreed that circumcision was not necessary. However, they did introduce four requirements to be laid on Gentile Christians. These are: (a) they must not eat food offered to idols, (b) they must abstain from sexual immorality (or unchasity), (c) they must abstain from meat that was strangled, and (d) they must abstain from meat containing blood. Now there is an interesting question as to the origins of these requirements. Some New Testament scholars are inclined to the view that they reflect four aspects of the seven Noachide laws.[30] The difficulty with this view is why only four of the seven are listed. So perhaps it is better to link this list with Leviticus 17–18. This list corresponds to the requirement of aliens who are resident in the land. However, the precise explanation for this list need not be resolved: it represents a classic compromise between two visions of the church, both of which were in the end accommodated. Or as Howard Clark Kee puts it: "It seems clear, therefore, that Acts seeks to portray James and the Jerusalem apostles as adopting a position that is a compromise between the law-free invitation for gentile participation that one finds in the letters of Paul and a position that transfers to new gentile converts the basic rules binding on nonIsraelites resident in the land as formulated in the final version of the Pentateuch."[31] In other words, there was a fusion, an assimilation, of these different views of the Christian community.

The distinction between "process" and "content" is helpful here. It is especially helpful for those Christians who want to hold the Bible as authoritative but have no problem with the consumption of a turkey (which has been strangled) or a rare steak (which has blood in it). The process of engagement is the significant point of the passage. It may be seen to show that the process of engagement arrived at certain authoritative obligations that were helpful to the church for a limited period of time. (The observation of these food laws seems to have disappeared by the time we get to Tertullian.)[32] Interpreted in this way, the text is not binding in terms of content, but in terms of the process of engagement that it witnesses to.

There are other places where we can see engagement in the text.[33] However, rather than supplement Acts 15 (which is the best New Testament example), I shall now propose to examine an additional and contrasting argument. The very form of the Bible illustrates the obligation for engagement.

This is an argument that Judy Fentress Williams has made. She talks about the dialogical nature of the text. The form of the narratives in, say, 1 Samuel is that different traditions are carefully put into conversation with each other. She sees an almost Bakhtin type narrative emerging. She writes:

> I propose that the literary character of the Bible transforms what we perceive as the babble of different voices into a dialogue that produces theological meaning. This meaning is not fully realized in any single aspect

of the text but is found as the words, phrases, and other units of language
engage in dialogue with each other. . . . Literature, even sacred literature, is
inherently dialogic.[34]

Through a careful analysis of 1 Samuel 2–3, she demonstrates the dialogical nature of both the poetry and prose. Sometimes the dialogue is made
up of contrasting images (that function metaphorically); at other points it
is a result of juxtaposition within the text or an echo that provokes a contrast with an earlier theme. In all these ways, the form of the Bible gives
expression to a dialogical commitment.

Leslie Houlden has made the same point. There is something deeply
puzzling that the Synoptics all survived. The overlap between the three
gospels is considerable. And in addition, one can see how many passages
have been changed and modified by the later gospels. Houlden writes,
"That Matthew and Luke wrote, at least in part, out of positive disap-
proval of Mark and other predecessors is overwhelmingly likely, and, in
the case of Luke, explicit. Yet their diversity of testimony to Jesus survived,
as we can now see inadvertently and by a misconception, for us to
contemplate as exemplifying the theological pluriformity of first-century
Christianity."[35] So for all the problems this created for the church, there
is an implicit commitment to pluralism and difference here. All three are
connected with Apostles (Matthew was believed to be an apostle, Mark
was linked to Peter, and Luke with Paul) and therefore all survived to be
included in the canon.

A "Theology of Engagement" enjoys working with different perspectives. This is the material that needs this theology. The fact that the early
church included these different perspectives is good evidence that the task
of engagement is both needed and intended.[36]

4   A Catholic Theology

For the Western Church the most significant divide is between the Roman
Catholics and the Reformed Churches. Now generalizations about these
two traditions are always difficult; however, there are three disagreements
that have come to symbolize that divide. The Reformed Churches have
a more negative view of humanity; for Calvin such language as "total
depravity" describes the consequences of the Fall. For the Catholic
theologians, the Fall could not and cannot erase the truth that all people
are made in the Image of God. Linked to this, Reformed theologians are

more pessimistic about the possibility of natural theology. Human reason has, they argued, been damaged by the Fall, therefore it is unable to properly encounter the divine, while Catholic theologians are more inclined to see the capacity for humanity to partially appreciate the nature and reality of God as evidence for the continuing presence of the Image of God. This flows into the third area: for the Reformed theologian, knowledge of God outside the church is impossible, while for Roman Catholic theologians the grace of God is at work in every human life and knowledge of God can be found in many and varied places.

As will be clear from the argument thus far in this chapter, Catholic theology has what is necessary to underpin engagement. At the heart of this book is a Catholic theology. The framework I have been suggesting in this chapter can all be deduced from Catholic insights about the nature of God and the activity of God within the sphere of human history.

CONCLUSION

We started by defining engagement as **an encounter that subsequently shapes the theology itself**. Having defended this as firmly rooted in the work of Augustine, Aquinas, and others, we organized the task of engagement into three: assimilation, resistance, and overhearing.

Having worked through a range of exercises that illustrate these three aspects to engagement, we are now in a position to identify the dynamic that often underpins any act of engagement. The dynamic has four elements:

1   Engagement can take the form of either assimilation, or resistance, or overhearing or a combination of the above.

2   Certain acts of engagement will carry certain implications that will require further engagement. This dynamic was seen in respect to human rights: the largely modern discourse of human rights can, should, and has been assimilated by the Christian tradition. However, this is its turn leads to an engagement with the concept of state sovereignty. Here the engagement required will be resistance.

3   The demands of justice generate forms of assimilation that require acts of (a) repentance, and (b) modification. The two examples of this were the assimilation of black and feminist insights.

4   Engagement can involve both assimilation and say overhearing. The example of this was the reflection on globalization and the use of the Hardt and Negri in conversation with Nursi.

To work with the dynamic of engagement will make the task of the theologian much harder. This is, I guess, one of the reasons why such an approach is not popular. It will also disrupt the location of theologian. Rowan Williams writes, "I assume that the theologian is always beginning in the middle of things."[1] By this he meant in the middle of a preexisting community – i.e., the church – participating in the unconscious theological life as expressed in hymns and liturgy and facilitating clarification when a tension is felt. Although this is undoubtedly true and important to remember, theology always belongs to the church, I am suggesting the theologian needs to both in the middle and on the edge. We are on the edge because the Pope is right we are in the truth business. When the Pope talks about relationship between theology and philosophy, he writes:

> [T]he relationship between theology and philosophy is best construed as a circle. Theology's source and starting-point must always be the word of God revealed in history, while its final goal will be an understanding of that word which increases with each passing generation. Yet, since God's word is Truth, the human search for truth – philosophy, pursued in keeping with its own rules – can only help to understand God's word better.[2]

The Pope sees this task as embracing the engagement with culture. He writes:

> [F]aith's encounter with different cultures has created something new. When they are deeply rooted in experience, cultures show forth the human being's characteristic openness to the universal and transcendent. Therefore they offer different paths to the truth, which assuredly serve men and women well in revealing values which can make their life ever more human.[3]

So the theologian needs to be both in the middle and on the edge.

The theologian must be in the middle of the believing community. We are servants of the church. We should not delude ourselves: it is the church that is interested in theology and we depend upon the church for our vocation. However, we must also be at the edge of that community forcing that community to listen to the truth of God as it is in non-Christian traditions. The task of engagement is difficult. In an ideal universe, languages should be learnt. Long and complicated conversations are needed. Silence between traditions needs to be listened to with attentiveness. But we embark on this task believing that, as others have before, there is much of God that we can learn and need to learn from those that disagree with us.

NOTES

Introduction

1 Pope John Paul II, *Fides et Ratio*, 3.33.
2 See John Milbank, *Theology and Social Theory*.
3 Karl Barth, *Church Dogmatics*, vol. 1, pt 2, p.774.
4 This is of course the theme of George Newlands, *Generosity and the Christian Future*.

1 Engagement: What it is and Why it Matters

1 See the statistics in Ian Markham (ed.), *A World Religions Reader*, p. 373.
2 I hesitate to use Karl Barth as my illustration of this position. He is easy to misunderstand. Alan Race in his useful book that introduced the now famous "pluralist, inclusivist, exclusivist" paradigm describes Barth as an exclusivist, which is odd given Barth's universalist sympathies. If all people are saved, then presumably there must some mechanism by which those without conscious knowledge of God's saving power gets saved. This is closer to inclusivism. For Alan Race see *Christians and Religious Pluralism*. David Lochhead rightly stresses that the description that "religion is unbelief" applies to all forms of religion, including Christianity when it functions as a religion. However, Lochhead overstates the case when he writes that the theology of Karl Barth is "is a theology that is open to and affirming of any dialogue with the world." See David Lochhead, *The Dialogical Imperative*, p. 39. Or at least Lochhead's concept of dialogue is not as inclusive as the concept of engagement that I shall develop later in this chapter. We will return to Karl Barth and the problems with his theology in chapter 13.
3 Karl Barth, *Church Dogmatics*, vol. 1, pt 2, p. 771.
4 Ibid., p. 774
5 The alternative explanation for diversity (one that perhaps is implied by Genesis 11) is that it is due to the Fall. The Fall explanation for diversity is

problematic because (a) it contradicts what we now know about the origins of diversity from an anthropological and scientific point of view and (b) it does not take into account the many 'fruits' of diversity, e.g., humility and love (Galatians 5:22).

6   Hans Küng, *Global Responsibility. In Search of a New World Ethic.*

7   John Macquarrie, *Principles of Christian Theology*, p. 21.

8   For an excellent discussion of the whole issue of definition see Peter Byrne and Peter Clarke, *Definition and Explanation in Religion.*

9   David Tracy, *Plurality and Ambiguity*, p. 18.

10 Ibid., p. 23.

11 David Lochhead, *The Dialogical Imperative*, p. 46.

12 Leonard Swidler, *After the Absolute. The Dialogical Future of Religious Reflection,* p. 3.

13 Stung by his former teacher James Gustafson's attack on him, Hauerwas dedicates the introduction of this book to a rebuttal. For James Gustafson see "The Sectarian Temptation: Reflections of Theology, the Church, and the University," in *Proceedings of the Catholic Theology Society* 40 (1985): 83–94. For Stanley Hauerwas see *Christian Existence Today: Essays on Church, World, and Living In-Between.*

14 Stanley Hauerwas, *Christian Existence Today. Essays on Church, World, and Living In-Between,* p. 10.

15 Ibid., p. 11.

16 For John Milbank see *Theology and Social Theory*; for Hauerwas's use of Milbank see Stanley Hauerwas, *After Christendom?*. For my critique of Milbank's theological realism see *Truth and the Reality of God*, pp. 37–41.

17 Stanley Hauerwas, *Christian Existence Today*, p. 11.

18 Ibid., p. 11.

19 Ibid., p. 7.

20 Michael Banner, "Some Comments on Two Critics" in *Crucible*, Jan–Mar, 2002, pp. 20–1.

21 Michael Banner, *Christian Ethics and Contemporary Moral Problems*, p. 44.

22 Ibid., p. 229.

23 Ibid., p. 37.

24 Ibid., p. 38.

25 John Milbank, *Theology and Social Theory*, pp. 327–8.

26 A. MacIntyre, *Whose Justice? Which Rationality?*, p. 355. For a more extended discussion of MacIntyre on truth see my *Truth and the Reality of God*. Some of the following discussion is dependent on my summary of MacIntyre in chapter 2 of that book.

27 Ibid., p. 361

28 Ibid., p. 362.

29 Ibid., p. 356.

30 Ibid., p. 365.

31   Bruce D. Marshall, *Trinity and Truth*, p.xi. I am very grateful for this stimulating and clear statement of the argument against my attempt to disentangle "theism" from the doctrine of the Trinity.

32   For two contrasting views on these issues, see William J. Abraham, *Divine Revelation and the Limits of Historical Criticism* and A.E. Harvey, *Jesus and the Constraints of History.*

33   The choice of these two will be challenged by many. So to defend the selection briefly, the primary reason for the choice is that they are both influential and widely read. Spong is a great popularizer: while McGrath's *Christian Theology. An Introduction* is one of the most widely adopted textbooks in the conservative academy.

34   See my letter in the London *Times* Wednesday 22 July 1998.

35   John Selby Spong, *Why Christianity must Change or Die*, p. 3.

36   Ibid., p. 4.

37   Ibid., p. 17.

38   Ibid., p. 5.

39   Ibid., p. 19.

40   Ibid., p. 20.

41   Ibid., p. 19.

42   Ibid., p. 119.

43   Ibid., p. 31.

44   Ibid., p. 46.

45   Ibid., p. 64.

46   Ibid., p. 233n6.

47   Alister McGrath, *A Passion for Truth. The Intellectual Coherence of Evangelicalism*, p. 3.

48   R. T. France and Alister McGrath, (eds), *Evangelical Anglicans: Their Role and Influence in the Church Today*, p. 4.

49   Alister McGrath, *Evangelicalism and the Future of Christianity*, p. 51.

50   Dispensationalism is an interpretative schema which was developed by J. N. Darby and popularized in the Scholfield edition of the Bible. For a critique of dispensationalism see James Barr, *Fundamentalism*. See also the substantial article in Alister McGrath's *Encyclopedia of Modern Christian Thought.*

51   Alister McGrath, *Evangelicalism and the Future of Christianity*, p. 59.

52   Alister McGrath, *A Passion for Truth*, p. 35.

53   Alister McGrath, *Evangelicalism and the Future of Christianity*, p. 94.

54   Alister McGrath and John Wenham "Evangelicalism and Biblical Authority," in R.T. France and Alister McGrath, (eds), *Evangelical Anglicans: Their Role and Influence in the Church Today*, p. 27.

55   Alister McGrath, *The Genesis of Doctrine*, p. 137.

56   Ibid., p. 37.

57 Alister McGrath, *A Passion for Truth*, p. 155
58 Alister McGrath and John Wenham "Evangelicalism and Biblical Authority,"
    p. 29
59 Alister McGrath, *A Passion for Truth*, p. 96.

2 Augustine's Theological Methodology

1   John Milbank, *Theology and Social Theology*.
2   Augustine, *De Natura et Gratia* 4.4–5.5.
3   See Anne Primavesi, *From Apocalypse to Genesis*. It is a moot point the extent
    to which these criticisms are justified. A. Hilary Armstrong makes a strong
    case that both Christians and Platonists have a much more positive view of
    the body and the material universe than opponents give them credit for: he
    writes, "Augustine in particular is often more balanced and positive – and
    not, as sometimes seems to be assumed, more unbalanced and negative – in
    his attitude to the body, sex and marriage than most of his Christian con-
    temporaries." (See A. Hilary Armstrong, *St. Augustine and Christian Platonism*,
    p. 11.)
4   See Augustine, *Confessions* 11 and *The City of God* 5.9.
5   *De animae quantitate* (On the greatness of the soul) 13. Unless otherwise stated
    all translations of St. Augstine are taken from *The Fathers of the Church*.
6   *De trinitate* 15.1.
7   Etienne Gilson, *The Christian Philosophy of St. Augustine*, p. 29.
8   *Retractionarie*, Prologue.
9   *De vera religione* 25.45. Translation taken from St. Augustine, *On True
    Religion*.
10 *Contra Academicos*. 3.20, 43.
11 Ibid., 3.15, 34. The term "samardocus" is an African word meaning a
    conjurer and trickster.
12 *Confessionies* 6–7. Translation from St. Augustine, *Confessions* trans. by H.
    Chadwick (1991).
13 For an example of an interpretation of Augustine that makes much of the
    Cartesian parallel see Etienne Gilson, *The Christian Philosophy of St.
    Augustine*, p. 42.
14 Rowan Williams, "The Paradoxes of Self-Knowledge in the *De trinitate*,"
    p. 125.
15 Ibid., pp. 130–1.
16 Wayne Hankey, "Ratio, reason, rationalism," p. 698.
17 St. Augustine, *Confessions*, trans. by R.S. Pine-Coffin (1961) p. 5.
18 Ibid., p. 62. It is interesting to note that as Augustine looks back on his admi-
    ration with Manichaeism he blames "reason"; he writes, "My own specious

reasoning induced me to give in to the sly arguments of fools who asked me what was the origin of evil, whether God was confined to the limits of bodily shape, whether he had hair and nails, and whether men could be called just if they had more than one wife at the same time, or killed other men, or sacrificed living animals."

19   Peter Brown, *Augustine of Hippo*, p. 51.

20   St. Augustine, *Confessions* trans. by R.S. Pine-Coffin (1961) p. 104.

21   Augustine writes, "I preferred to excuse myself and blame this unknown thing which was in me but was not part of me. The truth, of course, was that it was all my own self, and my own impiety had divided me against myself." See Ibid., p. 103.

22   *De dono perseverantiae* 21.55. There is an interesting discussion of this in G. Lawless, "Augustine of Hippo and his critics," pp. 14ff.

23   One complexity not so far discussed is Augustine location of "reason" within a theistic framework. In *The Problem of Free Choice* he develops his natural theology, which involves the striking claim that one cannot believe in truth unless one believes in God. Although this is deeply rooted in his Neoplatonism, it is worth noting the sophistication of his argument. He admits very clearly the critically realist insight that mind sometimes misinterprets the world (for example, to use his own illustration a stick in water will appear bent even though it is in fact straight). As the hierarchy of truths develops so he arrives (in good Neoplatonic fashion) at a conception of truth which requires a unifying factor which is God. This argument is explored in my *Truth and the Reality of God*.

24   See G. Quispel, *Eranos-Jahrbuch* (1951) pp. 115–40 as cited in John J. O'Meara, *Understanding Augustine*, p. 92.

25   Alfred Matthews sets out the debate with some care. His response to the difficulties, I largely find persuasive. See Alfred Warren Matthews, *The Development of St. Augustine from Neoplatonism to Christianity*, pp. 7–10.

26   St. Augustine, *Confessions* trans. by R.S. Pine-Coffin (1961) p. 59.

27   Ibid., pp. 144–5. (7.9)

28   John J. O'Meara, *Understanding Augustine*, pp. 84–5.

29   Etienne Gilson, *The Christian Philosophy of St. Augustine*, p. 234.

30   Ibid., p. 234.

31   *De vera religione* 3.3–4. Translation taken from St. Augustine, *On True Religion*.

32   *Civitas Dei* 8.11

33   Sabine MacCormack, *The Shadows of Poetry*, p. 226.

34   *Civitas Dei* 7.18, p. 178.

35   John Rist, *Augustine*, p. 3.

36   St. Augustine, *Confessions* trans. by R.S. Pine-Coffin (1961), 8.12, pp. 177–8.

37   A. Hilary Armstrong, "Reason and Faith in the First Millennium AD" in A. Hilary Armstong, *Plotinian and Christian Studies*, p. 108.

38   A. Hilary Armstrong, *Plotinian and Christian Studies*, p. 107.

3 Assimilation, Resistance, and Overhearing

1 Martyn Percy, *The Salt of the Earth*, p. 20.

2 It might be objected that the criteria that Aquinas uses to assess legitimate engagement contrasts markedly with the criteria I am using. On this point I refer the reader back to the conclusion of chapter 2, where I respond to the equivalent objection concerning Augustine. I concede that Aquinas would dissent from many of my modern assumptions. However, there is a generosity in the thought of Aquinas that is easily obscured.

3 There are many other illustrations of the process of learning from non-Christian sources that I could have used. Roger Johnson in a recent paper delivered to the New Haven Theology Group makes a powerful case for Nicholas of Cusa (1401–64). For Roger Johnson see 'The Beginnings of a Modern Theology of Religions: Nicholas of Cusa', unpublished paper.

4 G.B. Caird, *The Language and Imagery of the Bible*, p. 174.

5 Ibid., p. 175.

6 Jonah 3:10: "When God saw what they did, how they turned from their evil way, God repented of the evil which he had said he would do to them; and he did not do it."

7 Keith Ward, *Images of Eternity*, p. 90.

8 Thomas Aquinas, *Summa Theologicae*, vol. 1, Part 1, Question 4, Article 1. p. 21.

9 Ibid., p. 21.

10 Ibid., Part 1, Question 3. Article 8. p. 19.

11 Ibid., p. 19.

12 Ibid., Part 1. Question 9. Article 1. p. 38.

13 Ibid., Part 1. Question 10. Article 2. p. 41.

14 Henry Chadwick, Introduction of Origen, *Contra Celsum*, p. ix.

15 Ibid., p. ix.

16 Ibid., pp. 192–3. Origen is fairly representative of many church fathers in his view of the divine Jesus and suffering. St. Cyril makes the implications of such reasoning explicit when he suggested that Jesus "suffered impassibly." This would mean that Jesus would have felt the "attack" of the nails, but not the "grief."

17 Ibid., pp. 193–4.

18 Larry Hurtado, *At the Origins of Christian Worship*, p. 39.

19 Richard Swinburne, *The Coherence of Theism*, pp. 290–1.

20 Christopher Stead, *Philosophy in Christian Antiquity*, pp. 202–3.

21 I am grateful for many illuminating conversations with Martyn Percy on this point.

22 David B. Burrell, *Knowing the Unknowable God*, p. 109.

23 David B. Burrell, "Aquinas and Islamic and Jewish thinkers," pp. 60–1.

24 Ibid., p. 65.

25 Gavin D'Costa, "Christ, the Trinity, and Religious Plurality," p. 23.
26 It is with some nervousness that I point out the Trinitarian structure embedded in this model of engagement. It is easy to misuse and overwork the links. For some of the difficulties with this approach to theology see my discussion of the St. Andrews' Statement on Homosexuality in "Ronald Preston and the Contemporary Ethical Scene."

4   Assimilation: Engagement with Human Rights

1   The nations abstaining were: Byelorussia, Czechoslovakia, Poland, Saudi Arabia, South Africa, Ukraine, Soviet Union, and Yugoslavia. The Eastern bloc countries, as they were then, were largely opposed to its individualism; South Africa and Saudi Arabia worried about its potential use.
2   Jeremy Bentham, *Anarchical Fallacies*, pp. 52–3.
3   Raymond Plant, *Politics, Theology and History*, p. 237.
4   Karl Marx, "On the Jewish Question," p. 147.
5   Raymond Plant, *Politics, Theology and History*, p. 237.
6   Pope John XXIII, *Pacem in Terris*, paragraph 5.
7   For a fuller discussion of this point, see Stanley S. Harakas, "The Natural Law Teaching of the Eastern Orthodox church," pp. 215–24.
8   Stanley S. Harakas, "Human Rights: An Eastern Orthodox Perspective," p. 19.
9   J. Robert Nelson, "Human Rights in Creation and Redemption: A Protestant View," p. 3.
10 Jürgen Moltmann, *On Human Dignity. Political Theology and Ethics*, p. 22.
11 Richard Harries, "Human Rights in Theological Perspective," in *Human Rights for the 1990s*, (eds) Robert Blackburn and John Taylor.
12 Martyn Percy, *The Salt of the Earth*, p. 134.

5   Resistance: The Heresy of State Sovereignty and the Religious Imperative for Intervention to Defend Human Rights

1   This is especially true of England, although perhaps less true of other nations. In England, Henry VIII did have a full-blown theory to explain the relationship of the ruler to Rome, namely England is an "empire" and therefore, now the legend of the Donation of Constantine had been exploded, England should take responsibility for its own affairs. The legend, of course, had said that Constantine had subordinated himself to the Pope. It is interesting to note how the English had its own legend about Constantine's mother, Helena, that she was a descendent of a British King.
2   This is not to deny that there are not other factors that limit state sovereignty, for example, international agreements etc.

3 See Jean Bodin, *On Sovereignty*.
4 Arnold A. Rogow, *Thomas Hobbes. Radical in the Service of Reaction*, p. 9.
5 Thomas Hobbes, *Leviathan*, pt 1, chapter 11, p. 161.
6 Ibid., pt 1, chapter 13, p. 186.
7 Ibid., pt 2, chapter 17, p. 227. Hobbes thought that this is how the State actually is, whatever people may claim.
8 This of course goes back to the feudal arrangements, classically in England after 1066, with the major reassignment of land to Norman lords; with king as supreme (land) lord, from whom all others "hold." What is new is for rulers to claim authority over church "tenancy" and rights and jurisdiction, for example, to appointments, to taxation, to appeals of church and clerical cases etc. The struggle continued in Catholic countries, with various different balances being struck with Rome. England, Sweden, and the Northern German States cut off all ties with Rome. In this respect it is a matter of degree.
9 To anticipate the theme of this chapter, it is worth noting that the theory of absolute state sovereignty had been modified by "rights," for example, in England by John Locke. He asserted political (and legal) rights for property owners (the basis for the vote until the late nineteenth century) and limited religious toleration (it did not extend to Roman Catholics and atheists).
10 This is especially true of certain European countries, for example Germany and Italy. It is less true of the United Kingdom, where geography was more a key, especially after the union with Scotland.
11 David P. Forsythe, *Human Rights in International Relations*, p. 21.
12 It is a commonplace in the literature to distinguish between legal and political sovereignty. Andrew Heywood for example explains that "legal sovereignty is based upon the belief that ultimate and final authority resides in the laws of the state" while "political sovereignty is not in any way based upon legal authority but is concerned simply with the actual distribution of power, that is, *de facto* sovereignty." See Andrew Heywood, *Political Theory*, p. 91. For an attack on this distinction see D.D. Raphael, *Problems of Political Philosophy*, chapter 6.
13 David P. Forsythe, *Human Rights in International Relations*, p. 127
14 See Reinhold Niebuhr, *Moral Man and Immoral Society*.
15 Noam Chomsky, *The New Military Humanism*, p. 16.
16 "The Declaration," in *Daily Telegraph* Friday, 4 February, 2000.
17 See "Haider Loses Libel Battle Over Nazi Language," in *Daily Telegraph* Wednesday, 27 September, 2000.
18 "Haider Defends War Veterans," in *Daily Telegraph* Monday, 2 October, 2000.
19 See http://194.96.203.5/englisch/Program.htm.
20 See http://www.fco.gov.uk/news.
21 See "Victory for Austria as EU Lifts Sanctions," in *Daily Telegraph* Wednesday, 13 September, 2000.

22   The text of the House of Lords Ruling is found at www.parliament.the-stationery-office.co.uk. The judgment is *Regina* v. *Bartle and the Commissioner of Police for the Metropolis and others, ex parte Pinochet (on appeal from Divisional Court of the Queen's Bench Division). Regina* v. *Evans and another and the Commissioner of Police for the Metropolis and others, ex parte Pinochet (on appeal from a Divisional Court of the Queen's Bench Division).*

23   Collins J. is the Lord Chief Justice and his argument has been referred to above.

24   Amnesty International News Release, "Pinochet Case: No Turning Back in the Global Fight Against Impunity," 15 April, 1999.

25   It might be objected that this only applied to matters ecclesiastical. This is true in practice. However, for my purpose, there was at least a theoretical higher authority.

26   Of course, this is not to imply that Cromwell was a Reformer in the Martin Luther sense. He did however provide some of the politics of the English Reformation.

6   Assimilation: The Importance of the Black and Feminist Perspectives

1   See the preface to Anne Primavesi, *Sacred Gaia*.

2   See James H. Cone, *Risks of Faith*, pp. 130ff.

3   A magisterial model of engagement is Martyn Percy's excellent book *Salt of the Earth*. In this book you will find the following explored: other religions, race, advertising, soccer, sex, church, and state. It is a model of the kind of theology I am commending.

4   I am grateful to J'annine Jobling for making this point. In feminist perspective, the assimilation of feminism is too often its cooptation into patriarchal structures and discourses. Discussing the eminent feminist theologian Elisabeth Schüssler Fiorenza, she notes: "Schüssler Fiorenza tells a story. The Greek goddess Athena sprang fully grown and armored from the head of her father, Zeus. She seemed then to be motherless. Yet, in fact, this was not the case. Afraid that his child would surpass him, Zeus changed Metis, the pregnant mother of Athena, into a fly. He then swallowed her, that he might always benefit from her wisdom," J'annine Jobling, *Restless Readings*, p. 54. More broadly, I would like to take this opportunity to thank J'annine Jobling for helping me express my argument with more precision and guiding my reading in this area.

5   "With no immediate cause," in Ntozake Shange, *Nappy Edges*. Cited in Elisabeth Schüssler Fiorenza and Mary Shawn Copeland (eds) *Concilium* 1994/1, *Violence Against Women*, p. vii.

6   For example, domestic violence is the most common cause of death among females between the ages of fourteen and forty-four. Abuse is economically institutionalized with, for example, bride trafficking, sex-tourism, and violently or circumstantially enforced prostitution.

7   The United Nations collected a number of statistics for the 1995 conference on women, held in Beijing. It showed that women account for 70 percent of the world's poor, do two-thirds of the world's work, yet earn between 5 and 10 percent of the world's wages and own 1 percent of the world's property.

8   Miriam Therese Winter has done marvelous work at revisiting the text and making explicit the voice of the women that endlessly must be underpinning the text. See for example Miriam Therese Winter, *The Gospel According to Mary.*

9   Tertullian, *On the Apparel of Woman*, chapter 1.

10   Rosemary Radford Ruether, *Sexism and God-Talk*, pp. 12–13. Feminists stress, in particular, the inclusiveness of Jesus' community and the importance of women in stories about Jesus' life and mission. See, for example, Luise Schottroff's pioneering work on the New Testament., see Luise Schottroff, *Let the Oppressed Go Free*. And it was, again, Elisabeth Schüssler Fiorenza who coined the term "discipleship of equals" which has gained much currency.

11   In I Corinthians 11, Paul develops his theology of headship and with it head-covering.

12   Those who have rejected Christianity altogether probably unleash the most devastating critiques in this respect. Daphne Hampson and Mary Daly are both figures of note here. The hallmark of Christian feminism is the attempt to uncover aspects of Christianity's history and traditions which are more favorable to the interests of gender justice, at the same time as holding up for critique and reconstruction its more damaging components.

13   This remains one of the few attempts to cover all the major themes of systematic theology from a feminist perspective.

14   Rosemary Radford Reuther, *Sexism and God-Talk*, p. 19.

15   Kierkegaard is probably the philosopher who comes closest to disagreeing with this principle. His celebrated affirmation of the story of the sacrifice of Isaac by Abraham illustrates his reason for this. There are two difficulties with this approach. The first is that if we cannot use moral insight to distinguish true revelation from false, then the English murderer, Peter Sutcliffe, who, he claimed, was told by God to kill prostitutes, might then be justified. This is a very unsatisfactory conclusion to reach. Second, there is an inappropriate theological anthropology underpinning this view. It is, for most theologians, part of the image of God that we are able to be morally discriminating. I accept the corollary that Abraham was mistaken in believing that God, even as a test, ordered him to try and sacrifice his son. This stands alongside the

commands to put "entire people to the ban" in Joshua and Judges as a testimony to the human capacity to misunderstand God's injunctions.

16   Rosemary Radford Ruether, *Sexism and God-Talk*, p. 12.

17   See, for example, John Hick, *Faith and Knowledge*.

18   Rosemary Radford Ruether, *Sexism and God-Talk*, p. 13.

19   Ibid., p. 13. Valerie Saiving is often credited with the initial insight in the twentieth century that theology was based, not on inclusive human experience, but on male experience in particular. See "The Human Situation: A Feminine View." Saiving's work focused particularly on the categories of sin and redemption, themes notably picked up subsequently by Judith Plaskow and Ruether herself.

20   The history of feminism is typically divided into three "waves." The first wave gathered momentum in the mid-nineteenth century in Western Europe and North America, and was characterized by such significant events as the Women's Rights Convention (Seneca Falls, New York, 1948), deeply involved with the abolitionist movement, and marked by improvement in legal and economic status. The second wave, from the 1960s, reinvigorated women's sociopolitical struggles and saw feminism spread through academic discourses, including theology. The third wave emerged in the mid-1970s and saw the growth of feminisms and theologies more attentive to differences between women.

21   Audre Lorde, *Sister Outsider*, p. 112. We have now feminist theologies articulated from a range of cultural and ethnic contexts: such as womanist, Latina, African, Asian, and so on. (Womanist theology, originating with black women in the United States, is discussed later in this chapter.)

22   The so-called cultural feminists would stand as an exception to this, rooting their feminism in a rhetoric of female moral superiority.

23   It was this insight which prompted Elisabeth Schüssler Fiorenza to coin the term "kyriarchy" – rule of the master or lord – which refers to a graded male status system of domination and subordination. See *But She Said*, p. 117.

24   Rosemary Radford Ruether, "Feminist Interpretation: A Method of Correlation," p. 113. This process of coming to awareness is understood in terms of Paulo Freire's "conscientization" and underlines another aspect of the complexity of "women's experience": its socialized nature, and the internalization by many women of patriarchal ideological norms and patterns of thought.

25   See Sara Ruddick, *Maternal Thinking*.

26   Sharon Welch, *Communities of Resistance and Solidarity*.

27   Linda Hogan, *From Women's Experience to Feminist Theology*, pp. 176–7.

28   Ibid., p. 22.

29   It might be noted that Schüssler Fiorenza believes the identification between feminist and biblical prophetic principles to be rather too facile. She herself identifies women's struggles for liberation from patriarchy to be the criterion for interpretation and calls, not for correlation, but for critical evaluation. See

"The Will to Choose or to Reject," p. 130. She further suggests "that the canon and norm for evaluating biblical traditions and their subsequent interpretations cannot be derived from the Bible or the biblical process of learning within ideologies. . . . The personally and politically reflected experience of oppression and liberation must become the criterion of 'appropriateness' for biblical interpretation." Elisabeth Schüssler Fiorenza, *Bread Not Stone*, p. 60.

30 See Jobling, who makes a similar point in relation to the division between traditional ("Rankean") biblical scholarship and feminist biblical scholarship. (J'annine Jobling, *Restless Readings*, pp. 24–31.)

31 The "full humanity" of women is a rejection of maleness as normative of authentic humanity and, theologically, a claiming of women's equal place in the community of redemption as *imago dei* and subjects of full human and sacramental potential.

32 It was Sherry Ortner who brought the association of women and nature to widespread attention in her 1974 essay "Is Female to Male as Nature Is to Culture?"; and also in 1974 that Françoise d'Eaubonne published *Le Féminisme ou la mort* and introduced "ecofeminism" as a term.

33 Ecotheology in general was also stimulated by Rachel Carson's *Silent Spring* (1964) and Lynn White's essay, "On the Historical Roots of our Ecological Crisis" (originally published 1967).

34 Rosemary Radford Ruether, *Sexism and God-Talk*, p. xv.

35 Echoing, of course, St. Jerome's famous compliment to women who remained virgin to serve Christ: "she will cease to be a woman, and will be called man."

36 The spirit/matter dualism is, indeed, held to be related to a whole series of dualisms which are often attributed to Hellenistic philosophies: mind/body, culture/nature, active/passive, rational/irrational, men/women. We must note that this frame of analysis works differently in non-Western contexts. The antagonism between nature and culture is not a characteristic feature of many Asian traditions. As Kwok Pui-lan puts it: "While Western feminists must either challenge the uneasy connection between women and nature, or reclaim positive dimensions of women's embodiment and their closeness to nature, Asian feminist theologians are faced with the glorification of nature in their cultures, while their own bodies are denigrated" (Kwok Pui-lan, *Introducing Asian Feminist Theology*, p. 115). Kwok suggests this may be related to the connection between female symbols of nature within a patriarchal symbol-system and stereotypical feminine roles. I expand on this point further on.

37 Anne Clifford, *Introducing Feminist Theology*, p. 225.

38 See, for example Sallie McFague, *Models of God*; Sallie McFague, *The Body of God*.

39 In Ian Markham (ed.), *A World Religions Reader*, I take the "role of women" in each tradition as a case study for the ethical expression of each religion.

It seems clear to me that patriarchy persists regardless of the underpinning metaphysical narrative in a tradition.

40 James Cone, *Risks of Faith*, pp. 131–2. Some might object that Cone has oversimplified matters by pointing out that the rulers of Benin, Congo, and Dahomey (amongst others) were responsible for the sale of many slaves. Although in the tragic ambiguity of human affairs this is true, the brutal truth remains: the purchasers were white Europeans. Just because others also sinned does not relieve us of our crime. For a good history see Hugh Thomas, *The Slave Trade*.

41 Olaudah Equiano, *Equiano's Travels*, as cited in Hugh Thomas, *The Slave Trade*, p. 412. Olaudah Equiano was a slave from Gambia and one of the few who documented the experience in some detail.

42 Charles Marsh, *God's Long Summer*, p. 19.

43 Cornel West, *Race Matters*, p. 21.

44 Ibid., p. 5.

45 James H. Cone, "Introduction" to James H. Cone and Gayraud S. Wilmore *Black Theology*, vol. 2, p. 1. I am deeply in debt to Cone and Gayraud's volumes on black theology for much that follows in this chapter.

46 James H. Cone, *Risks of Faith*, p. 106.

47 Kelly Miller Smith Institute, "What does it Mean to be Black and Christian?" in James H. Cone and Gayraud S. Wilmore, *Black Theology*, vol. 2. p. 165.

48 Gayraud S. Wilmore, "Black Power, Black People, Theological Renewal," in James H. Cone and Gayraud S. Wilmore, *Black Theology*, vol. 1. p. 133.

49 Ibid., p. 134.

50 Ibid., p. 136.

51 Statement by the National Committee of Black Churchmen (June 13, 1969) as reproduced in James Cone and Gayraud S. Wilmore, *Black Theology*, vol. 1, pp. 37–9.

52 Cornel West, *Race Matters*, p. 20.

53 Ibid., p. 29.

54 Albert B. Cleage, Jr., "The Black Messiah," in James H. Cone and Gayraud S. Wilmore, *Black Theology*, vol. 1, p. 101. Cleage went much further in his interpretation of the data than many would consider accurate. He believed that Jesus was a black Messiah, a descendent of the Nation of Israel, which became black while in Babylon and Egypt. Although this oversteps the data, it is true that Jesus was not a white European and that he probably was dark skinned. It is also important not to lose sight of the Jewishness of Jesus in this debate. See Gayraud S. Wilmore, "Black Power, Black People, Theological Renewal," in James H. Cone and Gayraud S. Wilmore, *Black Theology*, vol. 1, pp. 127ff.

55 James H. Cone, "The White Church and Black Power,"' in James H. Cone and Gayraud S. Wilmore, *Black Theology*, vol. 1, pp. 70–1.

56 For Theodore Walker, Jr. see "Theological Resources for a Black Neoclassical Social Ethics' in James H. Cone and Gayraud S. Wilmore, *Black Theology*, vol. 2, pp. 35–52.

57 Joseph Washington as quoted in William R. Jones, "Theodicy and Methodology in Black Theology: A Critique of Washington, Cone and Cleage," in James H. Cone and Gayraud S. Wilmore, *Black Theology*, vol. 1, p. 144.

58 One option is to stop talking about a God active in human history. Shannon Ledbetter, in an imaginative article, has suggested that the sense of call should not be defined as a providential interference in human affairs but, on a more process view, as a recognition of our God-given gifts and talents and the best way they can utilized to realize the ends of love. While sympathetic with much of Ledbetter's argument, I want to retain some sense that God is an active partner in enabling those ends of love to be realized. For Shannon Ledbetter, see "Vocation and Our Understanding of God."

59 Kelly Delaine Brown Douglas, "Womanist Theology: What is its Relationship to Black Theology?" in James H. Cone and Gayraud S. Wilmore, *Black Theology*, vol. 2, p. 290.

60 James H. Cone, "The White Church and Black Power" in James H. Cone and Gayraud S. Wilmore, *Black Theology*, vol. 1, pp. 78–9.

61 Charles Marsh, *God's Long Summer*, p. 49.

62 Sam Bowers as cited in Charles Marsh, *God's Long Summer*, p. 70.

63 Ibid., p. 89.

64 Ibid., p. 93.

65 See for example the classic by Ronald Sider, *Rich Christians in an Age of Hunger*.

66 James H. Cone, "Black Theology and Black Liberation," in James H. Cone and Gayraud S. Wilmore, *Black Theology*, vol. 1, p. 112.

7 Overhearing: Clash of Discourses – Secular in the West Against the Secular in India

1 See Kelton Cobb, "Violent Faith," in Ian Markham and Ibrahim Abu-Rabi' *September 11: Religious Perspectives on the Causes and Consequences*, pp. 136–63. In Cobb's defense, he makes it clear that the Christian tradition has a violent past and states that "Christianity has generated the greatest amount of suffering through its violent strands" (p. 140). Nevertheless, the focus of the rest of the chapter is the violence in Islam and Judaism.

2 The two most substantial studies on the nature of the secular in India reach contrasting conclusions. V.P. Luthera believes that India should not be regarded as a secular state, because the state is clearly an agent of religious reform. D.E. Smith believes that Luthera operates with a too narrow a

definition of secular. For Luthera see *The Concept of the Secular State and India*; for Smith see *India as a Secular State*.

3 It is important to note the "some." I accept entirely that other strands of Hinduism are strongly exclusivist.

4 For a fuller discussion of Locke, especially on toleration, see my *Plurality and Christian Ethics*.

5 This is, of course, the propertied individual. This is made explicit in Locke when he discusses rights, which include a person's property and servants.

6 John Dunn, *The Political Thought of John Dunn*, p. 32.

7 Despite Locke's myth of the origins of civil society, his views on atheism reveals a sense that the relationship between public and private is complex. Locke does not really resolve this problem coherently. The way that the Lockean tradition solves the problem has the advantage of clarity even if it is unsatisfactory and unworkable in many situations.

8 Partha Chatterjee, *A Possible India*, p. 241.

9 *Supreme Court, Everson* v. *Board of Education* (1947).

10 Statistics taken from Gerald James Larson, *India's Agony Over Religion* (Delhi: Oxford University Press 1997) p. 19.

11 Gerald James Larson, *India's Agony Over Religion*, p. 19.

12 Brackets indicate amendments made after the 1949.

13 Robert D. Baird, "Expansion and Construction of Religion: the Paradox of the Indian Secular State," p. 189.

14 Marc Galanter, "The Religious Aspects of Caste: A legal View," in D.E. Smith (ed.), *South Asian Politics and Religion* as cited in Gerald Larson, *India's Agony over Religion*, p. 224.

15 Robert D. Baird, "Expansion and Construction of Religion: the Paradox of the Indian Secular State," p. 191.

16 Ibid., p. 192.

17 Under the heading of the "restriction" of religion in India, Baird goes on to discuss two further illustrations. First, the whole issue of the entitlement to "convert" people from one religion to another. This is very limited. Second, the legal protection entitled to the cow. On this, the state permits certain districts to have limited controls over the cow. It is not necessary for me to explore these issues for my argument to be established.

18 Neera Chandhoke, *Beyond Secularism*. p. 22.

19 Ibid., p. 297.

20 Ibid., p. 227.

21 Upendra Ashk, "The Fodder Cutting Machine" in Ashok Bhalla (ed.), *Stories About the Partition of India*, vol. 3 pp. 29–33, at p. 30 as quoted in Chandhoke, *Beyond Secularism,* p. 209.

22 Neera Chandhoke, *Beyond Secularism*, p. 225.

23 Ibid., p. 225.

24 Ibid., p. 95.

25 Partha Chatterjee, *A Possible India*, p. 248.
26 Ibid., p. 249.
27 Ibid., p. 256
28 Ibid., p. 58.
29 Gerald James Larson, *India's Agony Over Religion*, pp. 292–3.

8   Overhearing: Thinking about Hinduism, Inclusivity, and Toleration

1 Heresy is a Christian category that much of Hinduism would not recognize. I use the term nevertheless to capture a theological development of a tradition that would not be recognized as legitimate.
2 What follows is a brief summary of my discussion of the concept of toleration in *Plurality and Christian Ethics*.
3 Gerald Larson, *India's Agony over Religion*, p. 180.
4 Ibid., p. 200.
5 Ibid., p. 190.
6 Jawaharlal Nehru, *The Discovery of India*, p. 274, as cited in Larson, *India's Agony over Religion*, p. 195.
7 Gerald Larson, *India's Agony over Religion*, p. 199.
8 See "BJP HISTORY: It's (sic) Birth, Growth & Onward March" by K.R. Malkani (Vice-President of BJP) at http://www.bjp.org/history/history.html.
9 Ibid.
10 The person who killed Gandhi was Nathuram Godse. It is clear that Godse was linked with the RSS from 1930 to 1934. The RSS insist that Godse was not a member. The website of the organization writes: "In RSS there is nothing like official membership. Thousands of people come to RSS shakha daily, many may stay for some time, many for a longer period, many for their entire life, and many leave after a few days, after a few months, and so on. There can be many reasons for their quitting RSS shakha. Godse was one of those who came to shakha, saw it, did not like it, and then quit it. Nobody denies this. What is denied is that the heinous crime he committed, had anything to do with RSS. People make this charge since once in his early youth he came to RSS. But they forget or deliberately do not tell the entire story, that he was one of the most outspoken critics of RSS philosophy and used to write against it in his edited paper." http://www.rss.org/admcrit/rss_qa.htm
11 See http://www.bjp.org/history/history.html.
12 S. Gurumurthy, "Semitic Monotheism: The root of intolerance in India," at http://www.bjp.org/philo.htm
13 Ibid.
14 Ibid.

15   Ibid.

16   Ibid.

17   Ibid.

18   Mihir Meghani, "Hindutva: The Great Nationalist Ideology," at http://www.bjp.org/philo.htm.

19   M.V. Kamath, "Give us this day our sense of mission. Religion must be used to unite people and not divide them." Originally in *Free Press Journal*, Mumbai, April 4, 1996. Taken from http://www.bjp.org/philo.htm.

20   Neera Chandhoke, "The limits of tolerance."

21   For a brief summary of some of the contrasting attitudes held by Hindus towards others religions see Harold Coward, *Pluralism*.

22   J.F.T. Jordens, "Gandhi and Religious Pluralism" in H.G. Coward, *Modern Indian Responses to Religious Pluralism*, p. 8.

23   Ibid., p. 8. Quotations from Gandhi taken from *The Collected Works of Mahatma Gandhi*, (Ahmedabad: Navajivan Trust) vol XXVII p. 61 and vol XXVIII p. 194 and vol XXXV p. 166.

24   The difference for Gandhi is that the ocean image implies that ultimately in the future the ocean of Hinduism will be recognized, while the tree image recognizes the legitimacy of each religion in their own right.

25   See Gavin D'Costa's study *Theology and Religious Pluralism* for a good description of Karl Rahner's inclusivist theology.

26   M.K. Gandhi, *An Autobiography*, pp. xii–xiv.

27   Julius Lipner, *Hindus*, p. 186.

28   Keith Ward, *Religion and Revelation*, pp. 339–40.

9   Assimilation: Christianity and the Consensus Around Capitalism

1   This is discussed further in chapter 12.

2   *Quadragesimo Anno*, par. 106.

3   *Mater et Magistra*, par. 54.

4   These themes are picked up again in chapter twelve.

5   *Centesimus Annus*, 35.2 in J. Michael Miller (ed.) *The Encyclicals of John Paul II*.

6   Ibid., 42.1.

7   Ibid., 42.2.

8   Richard Bayer in his helpful discussion of these questions provides a survey of not just Roman Catholic social teaching, but also Protestant. He notes the continuing negative engagement with capitalism in Daniel Maguire, John Cobb, Timothy Gorringe, Prentiss Pemberton, Daniel Rush Finn, and Donal Dorr. See, Richard Bayer, *Capitalism and Christianity*, pp. 4–9.

9   Anthony Giddens, *The Third Way*, pp. 4–5.

10   Will Hutton, *The Stakeholding Society*, p. 1.

11   Anthony Giddens, *The Third Way*, p. 99.

12   Ibid., pp. 101–5.

13   One exception to the economic consensus must be noted. The Green movement is, in its strongest form, opposed to it. Its supporters argue that the planet cannot sustain unlimited economic growth. The environmental costs of endless roads, pollution, eradication of farmland are too high. To survive as a planet we need to substantially modify our economic expectations. Space will not permit a sustained discussion of this view. Suffice to say, it is manifestly true that environmentalism is important. Growth, to use the overworked slogan, needs to be sustainable. However, it has not been established that sustainable growth is necessarily at odds with the environment. Our cities and are rivers are cleaner thanks to technology, the development of which has been made possible by economic growth. To anticipate the rest of my argument, it is interesting how the Greens provide an interesting illustration of the cultural vision. At the most extreme, you can find a vision of society, with a substantially reduced population, working largely in small communities, with a direct connection to the land. How one achieves this vision is often unclear and, especially in respect to population, potentially politically extreme.

14   I am aware of T.C.W. Blanning's argument that modern political culture in Europe was made possible by the challenge to the courts and monarchical authority that took place in the late seventeenth and eighteenth centuries. Blanning argues that "during this period a new cultural space developed, which posed new challenges to regimes and their ruling orders. Alongside the old culture, centered on the courts and the representation of monarchical authority, there emerged a 'public sphere', in which private individuals came together to form a whole greater than the sum of the parts. By exchanging information, ideas, and criticism, these individuals created a cultural actor – the public – which has dominated European culture ever since." (p. 2). As Blanning would concede every age as a "culture", it is simply that modern culture with the public space for the middle classes is a relatively modern phenomenon. My stress on cultural vision is part of this modern emphasis. For T.C.W. Blanning see *The Culture of Power and the Power of Culture*.

15   P.J. O'Rouke, *Eat the Rich*, pp. 236–7.

16   R. Putnam, *Bowling Alone*. I am not persuaded by Putnam's implied argument that one factor in decreasing participation in religious activities is generational change coupled with the damage inflicted by capitalism. Capitalism does not determine behavior; the individuals freed by capitalism are making the decisions. We need to offer a cultural vision to these individuals to opt for a community-orientated vision of the future.

10   Assimilation and Overhearing: Rethinking Globalization – Bediuzzaman Said Nursi's Risale-I Nur, Hardt, and Negri

1   Roland Robertson, "Globalization and the Future of 'Traditional Religion,'" in Max L. Stackhouse with Peter J. Paris, *God and Globalization*, vol. 1, pp. 53–4.

2   As quoted in Max Stackhouse, "General Introduction" in Max L. Stackhouse with Peter J. Paris, *God and Globalization*, vol. 1, p. 5.

3   See http://www.genoa-g8.it/eng/index.html.

4   Taken from the IMF website and a paper on "Globalization: Threat or Opportunity." See http://www.imf.org/external/np/exr/ib/2000/041200.htm#II.

5   Francis Fukuyama, "The End of History?".

6   See Richard John Neuhaus, *Doing Well. Doing Good*.

7   Michael Hardt and Antonio Negri, *Empire*, p. xii.

8   Ibid., pp. xiv–xv.

9   Ibid., pp. 326–32.

10   Ibid., pp. 44f. The latter is the emphasis on the struggle within "place-based" movements or politics.

11   Ibid., p. 393.

12   Ibid., p. 54 (their italics).

13   Ibid., p. 400.

14   Ibid., p. 403.

15   Ibid., p. 407.

16   See Max Weber, *The Protestant Ethic and the Spirit of Capitalism*.

17   V.A. Demant, *Religion and the Decline of Capitalism*, p. 48. Demant was of the view that capitalism was in decline in the twentieth century as the "state principle" (as he called the growth of socialism) took over. His comments, however, about the relationship of the market to the social and ethical substructure are, I suggest, still true, even if capitalism has proved more persistent than he anticipated. For a good discussion of this irony, see Ronald Preston, *Religion and the Persistence of Capitalism*.

18   Bediuzzaman Said Nursi, "The Second Station of the Twentieth Word," in *The Words*. From vol. 1 of the Risale-I Nur Collection, p. 260.

19   Ibid., vol. 3, p. 408.

20   Ibid., vol. 1. p. 272.

21   Sükran Vahide, *Bediuzzaman Said Nursi*, p. 90. The sermon being referred to is the Damascus Sermon.

22   Bediuzzaman Said Nursi, vol. 1 of the Risale-I Nur Collection, pp. 421–2.

23   Ibid., vol. 1, p. 38.

24   Ibid., vol. 3, p. 168.

11 Keith Ward: An Engaged Theologian

1 Keith Ward, *Religion and Revelation*. p. 319.
2 Ibid., p. 320.
3 Keith Ward, *Rational Theology and the Creativity of God*, p. 1.
4 Others who are like Swinburne include Thomas Morris and Alvin Plantinga.
5 Ward has written on most questions in philosophy of religion. He takes issues with Swinburne in several areas. Swinburne has a strongly personalist view of God, while Ward retains a doctrine of God's necessary existence. Swinburne is more critical of the cosmological and ontological arguments, while Ward defends certain versions of these arguments. Swinburne generates a theodicy that makes "heaven" look rather undesirable, while Ward is much more nuanced.
6 Parts of what follows are outlined briefly in my introduction and opening chapter of my *Truth and the Reality of God*.
7 Keith Ward, *Religion and Creation*, p. 135.
8 Ibid., p. 150.
9 Ibid., p. 155.
10 Keith Ward, *Religion and Revelation*. p. 11.
11 Keith Ward, *A Vision to Pursue*, p. 49.
12 Keith Ward, *Divine Action*, p. 252.
13 Keith Ward, *Religion and Revelation*, p. 240fn75.
14 Ibid., p. 272.
15 Ibid., p. 2.
16 Ibid., p. 1.
17 Ibid., p. 1.
18 Ibid., p. 37.
19 Ibid., pp. 339–40.
20 Ibid., p. 340.
21 The Rubicon image is used very effectively in John Hick and Paul Knitter (eds), *The Myth of Christian Uniqueness*.
22 Keith Ward, *Religion and Revelation*, p. 310.
23 Keith Ward, *Religion and Human Nature*, p. 1.
24 Ibid., p. 75.

12 Engaging with the Pope: Engagement yet Not Engagement

1 See my *Plurality and Christian Ethics*, pp. 18–19.
2 See V.A. Demant, *Religion and the Decline of Capitalism*.
3 Grace Davie, *Religion in Britain since 1945*, p. 69.
4 Ibid., p. 1 and p. 79. Martyn Percy has a delightful take on the secularization thesis: his view is that the British were both affectionate and simulta-

neously disinterested; so it is not true that there has been dramatic decline in explicit practice. There is as much commitment as always. For Martyn Percy see *The Salt of the Earth*, pp. 81–101.

5   See Ian Markham, *Truth and the Reality of God*.

6   See Alasdair MacIntyre, *After Virtue*.

7   I discuss these questions in some detail in my *Plurality and Christian Ethics*.

8   For my views on September 11 see '9.11: Contrasting Reactions and the Challenge of Dialogue' in Ian Markham and Ibrahim M. Abu-Rabi', *September 11. Religious Perspectives on the Causes and Consequences*, pp. 206–30.

9   See Carl Bernstein and Marco Politi, *His Holiness. John Paul II and the Hidden History of Our Time*.

10   *Centesimus Annas* 22.1, in Miller (ed.) *The Encyclicals of John Paul II*.

11   Pope John Paul II, *Fides et Ratio*, "Conclusion," pp. 101–5.

12   *Sollicitudo Rei Socialis* 7.2, in Miller (ed.) *The Encyclicals of John Paul II*.

13   Ibid., 3.1.

14   Ibid., 35.2.

15   Ibid., 42.1.

16   Ibid., 42.2.

17   *Veritatis Splendor* 12.1, in Miller (ed.) *The Encyclicals of John Paul II*.

18   Ibid., 76.2.

19   There are a number of ethicists who are engaging with the tradition in creative ways. Jean Porter is one in particular who provides an interesting critique of both virtue ethics and natural law as seen in Aquinas. Her *Moral Action and Christian Ethics* is especially important.

20   *Evangelium Vitae*, 18.4–18.5, in Miller (ed.) *The Encyclicals of John Paul II*.

21   *Vertatis Splendor* 113.2

22   See Kevin Kelly, *New Directions in Moral Theology*.

23   *Ut Unum Sint*, 95.3, in Miller (ed.) *The Encyclicals of John Paul II*.

24   Ibid., 96.

25   Ronald H. Preston, *Confusions in Christian Social Ethics*, p. 49.

26   *Ethics in Advertising*, para 15. See The Pontifical Council for Social Communications, *Ethics in Advertising*, which is widely available by searching on the Internet.

27   The British Codes of Advertising and Sales Promotion, 7.1, see the ASA website www.asa.org.uk.

28   I spent six very enjoyable years serving on the Council of the Advertising Standards Authority. The Authority's current theologian is Martyn Percy. For a different view on some of the broader cultural issues surrounding advertising see Martyn Percy, *The Salt of the Earth*, chapter 6.

29   *Ethics in Advertising*, para 19.

30   Ibid., para 5.

31   Ibid., para 10.

32 For a wider perspective on these shifts of view, I invite the reader to look at the Introduction.

33 See Reinhold Niebuhr, *Moral Man and Immoral Society*.

34 Kevin Kelly, *New Directions in Moral Theology*, p. 69.

35 See V.A. Demant, *Christian Sex Ethics*.

36 For a more developed form of this argument, see J.L. Houlden, *Bible and Belief*, chapter 11.

37 This chapter started life as my professorial inaugural when I became the first holder of the Liverpool Chair of Theology and Public Life. A significantly revised version of the lecture served as the Barry Marshall Memorial Lecture delivered at Trinity College, Melbourne in 1997.

13   The Shape of an Engaged Theology

1   See Wilfred Cantwell Smith, *The Meaning and End of Religion*. He identifies four meanings of the word. The first concentrates on piety; the second and the third concentrates on "religion" as a set of doctrines, rituals, and ethics; and the fourth is a generic summation. He concludes: "I suggest that the term 'religion' is confusing, unnecessary, and distorting" (p. 50). While I concur with Cantwell Smith that the complexity of the religious phenomena is confused by the label "religion," I am less sure about Cantwell Smith's historical claim, namely that the category is an invention of modernity. On this point Roger Johnson is persuasive – a reading of *The Peace of Faith* by Nicholas of Cusa illustrates that the category of "religion' was operational many years before David Hume. For Roger Johnson see "The Beginnings of a Modern Theology of Religions: Nicholas of Cusa," unpublished paper.

2   See Karl Jaspers, *The Origin and Goal of History*.

3   Ramanuja, *The Vedanta-Sutras*, p. 95. As quoted in Keith Ward, *Images of Eternity*, p. 31.

4   Charles Hartshorne, *The Divine Relativity*, p. xv.

5   Charles Hartshorne, *Man's Vision of God*, pp. ix, 346–7.

6   Allama Muhammad Iqbal, *The Reconstruction of Religious Thought in Islam*, p. 44.

7   Ibid., p .48.

8   See James Packer, *God Has Spoken: Revelation and the Bible*.

9   See Norman Lamm, *The Condition of Jewish Belief*.

10 See John Hick, *Faith and Knowledge*.

11 See Abraham Joshua Heschel, *God in Search of Man*.

12 See John Hick (ed.) *The Myth of God Incarnate*. This set of essays argued that the Chalcedonian language of incarnation is problematic on a number of levels. First, it is not justified by historical study of the New Testament texts.

Second, it is but one of many Christologies both in the New Testament and beyond. Therefore it is not obvious why Chalcedon should be so privileged. Third, it is an obstacle to interfaith relations.

13   William Johnson, *Arise my Love; Mysticism for a new Era* gives Abhishiktananda as an illustration of a high Christology. Johnson on page 193 reports that Abhishiktananda, who studied under Ramana Maharshi, explained that "the experience of the Absolute to which India's mysticism points is included in the words of Jesus, 'My Father and I are one', he [i.e., Abhishiktananda] continues: 'All that the Maharshi, and countless others before him, knew and handed on of the inexorable experience of nonduality, Jesus also knew himself, and that in a preeminent manner.'"

14   Sandy Martin, "Jesus Darshan," p. 18.

15   *The Vision of Sri Ramakrishna* (Madras: Sri Ramakrishna Math, undated), pp. 75–7. As quoted in Sandy Martin, "Hindu Perspectives on Jesus: The Ramakrishna Mission and Self-Realization Fellowship," p. 97.

16   In this respect I share Keith Ward's understanding of criteria as opposed to the position of Gavin D'Costa. For Keith Ward see *Religion and Revelation*, pp. 319ff. For Gavin D'Costa see "Whose Objectivity? Which Neutrality?." For an interesting defense of D'Costa see Victoria La'Porte, *An Attempt to Understand the Muslim Reaction to the Satanic Verses*.

17   It is also a point that is made by traditional Christology.

18   For a good study on US Roman Catholics see James D. Davidson, *The Search for Common Ground*.

19   Colin Gunton, *The One, The Three and the Many*, p. 7.

20   Karl Barth, *Church Dogmatics*, vol. 1, pt 2, pp. 299–300.

21   Keith Ward, *Religion and Divine Revelation*, pp. 6–7.

22   See Alasdair MacIntyre, *Whose Justice? Which Rationality?*

23   I am deliberately using the term "Old Testament" instead of Hebrew Bible. I am thinking here of the contribution that these scriptures have made to the Christian revelation as found in the Bible. In this context they operate as an "old testament." They are also, of course, the scriptures of Judaism and in that context I would use the term Hebrew Bible.

24   It is beyond the remit of this book to revisit the many arguments for the critical approach to the Bible. Suffice to say, for a refutation of fundamentalism one can do little better than revisit Bishop Colenso. See John William Colenso, *The Pentateuch and Book of Joshua Critically Examined*. For a more recent discussion of some of the issues see James Barr, *Fundamentalism*.

25   The work of Leslie Houlden is interesting on this point. In his marvelous book *Connections*, he develops the theme that we need a Christology that explains how Jesus fills our "meditorial space" – the space between humanity and God. This is the role of all Christologies and Chalcedon is only one such example that worked for a certain people at a certain time in the church's history. Although this opens up the possibility of a degree of plu-

ralism in Christology, it is my contention that he overstates the extent of that pluralism. The reason for this is that our liturgy has entrenched the sense that our mediator "Jesus" is worthy of worship; Jesus is effective because he brings God to us – Emmanuel. Although we might be able to find a number of ways of expressing these ideas, it seems to me inevitable that almost all of them will involve an incarnational and Trinitarian (or at least Binitarian) element. Finally it is worth noting that Houlden elsewhere in his work clearly thinks it is entirely proper to worship Jesus. See his delightful book of Lectures, *Backward into Light*.

26　See my *Truth and the Reality of God*.

27　This is a modified version of the Dalai Lama's statement that "The Bodhisattva ideal is thus the aspiration to practice infinite compassion with infinite wisdom." This is taken from Tenzin Gyatso, *Freedom in Exile: The Autobiography of the Dalai Lama* as reproduced in Roger Eastman, *The Ways of Religion*, p. 107.

28　It might be objected that Jesus colors and validates all the others in a special way. It is true that the Jesus lens has an impact upon prayer and compassion. However, this should not stop us seeing that these assertions carry both meaning and authority in their own right. And the difference that Christology makes should not be granted a disproportionate significance.

29　I am aware that for some New Testament scholars Luke is guilty of distortion rather than simplification.

30　These are the requirements stipulated in the rabbinic tractate *Sanhedrin*. For a good discussion of the Noahide laws see David Novak, *Jewish – Christian Dialogue*, pp. 26–41.

31　Howard Clark Kee, *To Every Nation Under Heaven*, p. 182.

32　I am grateful for the help of Leslie Houlden on this point. Given the significance of this text in Luke/Acts, it is surprising that there are not more Christian groups committed to observing some version of the food laws. The main exception seems to be the Seven Day Adventists (but of course they have a distinctive take on the observation of the Old Testament food laws more generally). For most Christians the significance of this text disappeared behind 1 Corinthians 8 (where Paul explains that one should abstain from eating food offered to idols for the sake of the weaker brother) and Mark 7:14–23 (where Jesus argues that defilement comes from the inside not from unclean foods going in from the outside).

33　Other illustrations include the Book of Jonah or Ruth, where the vision of God's providence is extended beyond "the people" and "the land."

34　Judy Fentress Williams "The Bible and Dialogue," in Ian Markham and Ibrahim M. Abu-Rabi' (eds) *September 11. Religious Perspectives on the Causes and Consequences*, p. 191.

35　Leslie Houlden, *Bible and Belief*, p. 161.

36 I do recognize that this was always seen. However, the problem of the rela-
    tionship between the Synoptics did become a problem that required expla-
    nation. In this sense it provoked "engagement."

Conclusion

1 Rowan Williams, *On Christian Theology*, p. xii.
2 John Paul II, *Fides et Ratio* 8.73.
3 Ibid., 8.70.

REFERENCES

Abraham, William J., *Divine Revelation and the Limits of Historical Criticism* (Oxford: Oxford University Press, 1982).

Aquinas, Thomas, *Summa Theologicae*, trans. by Fathers of the English Dominican Province, rev. edn, (Westminster, Maryland: Christian Classics, 1948).

Armstrong, A. Hilary. *Plotinian and Christian Studies* (London: Variorum Reprints, 1979).

Armstrong, A. Hilary. "Reason and Faith in the First Millenium AD," *Plotinian and Christian Studies*, pp. 92–112 (London: Variorum Reprints, 1979).

Armstrong, A. Hilary, *St. Augustine and Christian Platonism* (Villanova: Villanova University Press, 1976).

Augustine, St., *Confessions*, trans. by H. Chadwick (Oxford: Oxford University Press, 1991).

Augustine, St., *Confessions*, trans. by R.S. Pine-Coffin, (Harmondsworth: Penguin, 1961).

Augustine, St. *De vera religione, On True Religion*, Introduction by L.O. Mink, trans. by J.H.S. Burleigh (South Bend, Indiana: Regnery/Gateway, 1953).

Augustine, St., *The Fathers of the Church* a series of *The Writings of St. Augustine* (New York: Fathers of the Church Inc, 1947–).

Augustine, St., *The Problem of Free Choice*, trans. by Mark Pontifex, (London: Longman, 1955).

Baird, Robert D., "Expansion and Construction of Religion: the Paradox of the Indian Secular State," in J. McLaren and H. Coward, (eds), *Religious Conscience, the State, and the Law*, pp. 198–205 (New York: SUNY Press, 1999).

Banner, Michael. *Christian Ethics and Contemporary Moral Problems* (Oxford: Oxford University Press, 1999).

Banner, Michael, "Some Comments on Two Critics," *Crucible*, Jan–Mar, 2002.

Barr, James, *Fundamentalism* (Philadelphia: Westminster Press, 1978).

Barth, Karl, *Church Dogmatics*, 2 vols (Edinburgh: T&T Clark, 1956).

Bayer, Richard, *Capitalism and Christianity* (Washington: Georgetown University Press, 1999).

Bentham, Jeremy, *Anarchical Fallacies; Being an Examination of the Declaration of Rights Issued During the French Revolution* in J. Waldron, *Nonsense upon Stilts: Bentham, Burke and Marx on the Rights of Man*, pp. 50–62 (London: Methuen, 1987).

Bernstein, Carl and Marco Politi, *His Holiness. John Paul II and the Hidden History of Our Time* (New York: Doubleday, 1996).

Bhalla, Ashok, (ed.), *Stories About the Partition of India*, vol. 3 (Delhi: Indus, 1994).

Blackburn, Robert, and John Taylor, (eds), *Human Rights for the 1990s* (London: Mansell, 1991).

Blanning, T.C.W., *The Culture of Power and the Power of Culture* (Oxford: Oxford University Press, 2002).

Bodin, Jean, *On Sovereignty*, ed. and trans. by Julian H. Franklin, (Cambridge: Cambridge University Press, 1992).

Brown, Peter, *Augustine of Hippo. A Biography* (London: Faber and Faber, 1967).

Burrell, David B., *Knowing the Unknowable God. Ibn Sina, Maimonides, Aquinas* (Notre Dame, Indiana: University of Notre Dame Press, 1986).

Burrell, David, "Aquinas and Islamic and Jewish Thinkers," in Norman Kretzmann and Eleonore Stump (eds), *The Cambridge Companion to Aquinas*, pp. 60–84 (Cambridge: Cambridge University Press, 1993).

Byrne, Peter and Peter Clarke, *Definition and Explanation in Religion* (Basingstoke: Macmillan, 1993).

Caird, G.B. *The Language and Imagery of the Bible* (Philadelphia: Westminister Press, 1980).

Cantwell Smith, Wilfred, *The Meaning and End of Religion: A New Approach to the Religious Traditions of Mankind* (New York: Macmillan, 1963).

Carson, Rachel, *Silent Spring* (New York: Fawcett Crest, 1964).

Chadwick, Owen, "Introduction of Origen," *Contra Celsum*, trans. by and with an Introduction and Notes by Henry Chadwick (Cambridge: Cambridge University Press, 1953).

Chandhoke, Neera, *Beyond Secularism. The Rights of Religious Minorities* (Oxford: Oxford University Press, 1999).

Chandhoke, Neera, "The limits of tolerance," *The Hindu*, February 22, 1999.

Chatterjee, Partha, *A Possible India. Essays in Political Criticism* (Delhi: Oxford University Press, 1997).

Chomsky, Noam, *The New Military Humanism. Lessons from Kosovo* (Monroe: Common Courage Press, 1999).

Cleage, Jr., Albert B., "The Black Messiah," in James H. Cone and Gayraud S. Wilmore, (eds), *Black Theology. A Documentary History.* vol 1., pp. 101–5 (Maryknoll, New York: Orbis Books, 1993).

Clifford, Anne, *Introducing Feminist Theology* (Maryknoll, New York: Orbis, 2001).

Colenso, John William, *The Pentateuch and Book of Joshua Critically Examined* (London: Longman, Green, Longman, Roberts and Green, 1862–79).

Collins. J., House of Lords, The judgment is *Regina* v. *Bartle and the Commissioner of Police for the Metropolis and others ex parte Pinochet* (on appeal from Divisional Court of the Queen's Bench Division).

Cone, James. H. *Risks of Faith. The Emergence of a Black Theology of Liberation 1968–1998*, (Boston: Beacon Press, 1999).

Cone, James. H., and Gayraud S. Wilmore, (eds), *Black Theology. A Documentary History*, 2 vols, (Maryknoll, New York: Orbis Books, 1993).

Coward, Howard, (ed.), *Modern Indian Responses to Religious Pluralism* (New York: State University of New York, 1987).

Coward, Harold, *Pluralism. Challenge to World Religions* (Maryknoll, New York: Orbis Books, 1985).

D'Costa, Gavin, "Christ, the Trinity, and Religious Plurality," in Gavin D'Costa, (ed.), *Christian Uniqueness Reconsidered. The Myth of a Pluralist Theology of Religions*, pp. 16–29 (Maryknoll, New York: Orbis Books 1990).

D'Costa, Gavin, *Theology and Religious Pluralism* (Oxford: Blackwell, 1986).

D'Costa, Gavin, "Whose Objectivity? Which Neutrality?," *Religious Studies*, 29, March, 1993.

Davidson, James D., Andrea S. Williams, Richard A. Lamanna, Jan Stenftenagel, Kathleen Maas Weigert, William J. Whalen, Patricia Wittberg, *The Search for Common Ground. What Unites and Divides Catholic Americans* (Huntington, Indiana: Our Sunday Visitor Publishing Division, 1997).

Davie, Grace, *Religion in Britain since 1945* (Oxford: Blackwell, 1994).

Demant, V.A., *Christian Sex Ethics* (London: Hodder and Stoughton, 1963).

Demant, V.A., *Religion and the Decline of Capitalism*, (London, Faber and Faber, 1952.)

Douglas, Kelly Delaine Brown, "Womanist Theology: What is its Relationship to Black Theology?" in James H. Cone and Gayraund S. Wilmore, (eds), *Black Theology. A Documentary History*. vol. 2, pp. 290–9 (Maryknoll, New York: Orbis Books, 1993).

Dunn, John, *The Political Thought of John Dunn* (Cambridge: Cambridge University Press, 1969).

Eastman, Roger, *The Ways of Religion*, 2nd edn, (Oxford: Oxford University Press, 1993).

d'Eaubonne, Françoise, *Le Féminisme ou la mort* (Paris: P. Horay, 1974).

Elford, R. John, and Ian Markham, (eds), *The Middle Way. Theology, Politics and Economics in the Later Thought of R.H. Preston* (London: SCM Press, 2000).

Equiano, Olaudah, *Equiano's Travels*, 2 vols, ed. by Paul Edwards (New York: Praeger, 1967).

Fentress Williams, Judy, "The Bible and Dialogue," in Ian Markham and Ibrahim M. Abu-Rabi', (eds), *September 11. Religious Perspectives on the Causes and Consequences* (Oxford: Oneworld, 2002).

Fitzgerald, A.D., (ed.), *Augustine Through the Ages. An Encyclopedia* (Grand Rapids, Michigan: Eerdmans, 1999).

Forsythe, David P., *Human Rights in International Relations* (Cambridge: Cambridge University Press, 2000).

France, R.T. and Alister McGrath, (eds), *Evangelical Anglicans: Their Role and Influence in the Church Today* (London: SPCK, 1993).

Fukuyama, Francis, "The End of History?," *The National Interest*, 16, pp. 3–18, 1989.

Gandhi, M.K., *An Autobiography: The Story of My Experiments with Truth*, trans. by Mahadev Desai (Boston: Beacon Press, 1957).

Giddens, Anthony, *The Third Way* (Cambridge: Polity Press, 1998).

Gilson, Etienne, *The Christian Philosophy of St. Augustine* (New York: Random House, 1960).

Gunton, Colin, *The One, The Three and the Many. God, Creation and Culture of Modernity* (Cambridge: Cambridge University Press, 1993).

Gurumurthy, S., "Semitic Monotheism: The Root of Intolerance in India," at http://www.bjp.org/philo.htm

Gustafson, James, "The Sectarian Temptation: Reflections of Theology, the Church, and the University," in *Proceeding of the Catholic Theology Society*, 40, pp. 83–94, 1985.

Hankey, Wayne, "Ratio, reason, rationalism," in A.D. Fitzgerald, (ed.), *Augustine through the Ages. An Encyclopedia*, pp. 698–702 (Grand Rapids, Michigan: Eerdmans, 1999).

Harakas, Stanley S., "Human Rights: An Eastern Orthodox Perspective," in Arlene Swidler, (ed.), *Human Rights in Religious Traditions*, pp. 215–24 (New York: The Pilgrim Press, 1982).

Harakas, Stanley S. "The Natural Law Teaching of the Eastern Orthodox Church," *Greek Orthodox Theological Review*, vol. 9, no. 2, pp. 14–24, 1963–4.

Hardt, Michael, and Antonio Negri, *Empire* (Cambridge, Massachusetts: Harvard University Press, 2000).

Hartshorne, Charles, *Man's Vision of God; And the Logic of Theism* (Chicago and New York: Willett, Clark and Company, 1941).

Hartshorne, Charles, *The Divine Relativity. A Social Conception of God* (New Haven: Yale University Press, 1948).

Harvey, A.E., *Jesus and the Constraints of History* (Philadelphia: Westminster Press, 1982).

Hauerwas, Stanley, *After Christendom?* (Nashville: Abingdon Press, 1991).

Hauerwas, Stanley, *Christian Existence Today: Essays on Church, World, and Living In-Between* (Durham, North Carolina: Labyrinth Press, 1988).

Heschel, Abraham Joshua, *God in Search of Man; a Philosophy of Judaism* (New York: Farrar, Straus and Cudahy, 1955).

Heywood, Andrew, *Political Theory. An Introduction*, 2nd edn (Basingstoke: Macmillan, 1999).

Hick, John, *Faith and Knowledge*, 2nd edn (Collins: Fount, 1978).

Hick, John and Paul Knitter, (eds), *The Myth of Christian Uniqueness* (Maryknoll, New York: Orbis Books, 1987).

Hick, John, (ed.), *The Myth of God Incarnate* (London: SCM Press, 1977).

Hobbes, Thomas, *Leviathan* edited with an introduction by C.B. Macpherson, (Harmondsworth: Penguin, 1985).

Hogan, Linda, *From Women's Experience to Feminist Theology* (Sheffield: Sheffield Academic Press, 1995).

Houlden, J.L., *Backward into Light* (London: SCM Press, 1987).

Houlden, J.L., *Bible and Belief* (London: SPCK, 1991).

Houlden, J.L., *Connections: the Integration of Theology and Faith* (London: SCM Press, 1986).

Hurtado, Larry, *At the Origins of Christian Worship* (Carlisle: Paternoster Press, 1999).

Hutton, Will, *The Stakeholding Society* (Cambridge: Polity Press, 1999).

Iqbal, Allah Muhammad, *The Reconstruction of Religious Thought in Islam* (Lahore: Institute of Islamic Culture, 1999).

Jaspers, Karl, *The Origin and Goal of History* (London: Routledge & Kegan Paul, 1953).

Jawaharlal Crane, Robert I., (ed.), *The Discovery of India* (New York: Doubleday Anchor Books, 1960).

Jobling, J'annine, *Restless Readings* (Aldershot: Ashgate, 2002).

John XXIII, Pope, *Mater et Magistra* (Boston: St Paul Editions, 1961).

John Paul II, Pope, *Fides et Ratio* (Dublin: Veritas Publications, 1998).

Johnson, William, *Arise my Love; Mysticism for a New Era* (Maryknoll, New York: Orbis Books 2001).

Jordens, J.F.T., "Gandhi and Religious Pluralism," in H.G. Coward (ed.), *Modern Indian Responses to Religious Pluralism* pp. 8–16 (New York: State University of New York, 1987).

Kee, Howard Clark, *To Every Nation Under Heaven. The Acts of the Apostles* (Harrisburg, Pennsylvania: Trinity Press International, 1997).

Kelly, Kevin, *New Directions in Moral Theology* (London: Geoffrey Chapman, 1992).

Kelly Miller Smith Institute, "What does it Mean to be Black and Christian?," in James H. Cone and Gayraud S. Wilmore, (eds), *Black Theology. A Documentary History*, vol. 2., pp. 160–74 (Maryknoll, New York: Orbis Books, 1993).

Küng, Hans, *Global Responsibility. In Search of a New World Ethic* (London: SCM Press, 1991).

Lamm, Norman, *The Condition of Jewish Belief* (London: Macmillan 1988).

La'Porte, Victoria, *An Attempt to Understand the Muslim Reaction to the Satanic Verses* (Lewiston, New York: Edwin Mellen Press, 1999).

Larson, Gerald James, *India's Agony Over Religion* (Delhi: Oxford University Press, 1997).

Lawless, G., "Augustine of Hippo and his critics," in J.T. Wenhard, E.C. Muller, and R.J. Teske, (eds), *Collectanea Augustiniana. Augustine Presbyter Fachs Sum*, pp. 12–22 (New York: Peter Lang, 1993).

Ledbetter, Shannon, "Vocation and Our Understanding of God," *Modern Believing*, 2(4), pp. 38–49, October 2001.

Lipner, Julius, *Hindus. Their Religious Beliefs and Practices* (London, Routledge, 1994).

Lochhead, David, *The Dialogical Imperative* (Maryknoll, New York: Orbis Books, 1988).

Lorde, Audre, *Sister Outsider* (Trumansburg: Crossing Press, 1984).

Luthera, V.P. *The Concept of the Secular State and India* (Calcutta: Oxford University Press, 1964).

MacCormack, Sabine, *The Shadows of Poetry. Vergil in the Mind of Augustine*, (Berkeley: University of California Press, 1998).

MacIntyre, Alasdair, *After Virtue* (London, Duckworth, 1985).

MacIntyre, Alasdair, *Whose Justice? Which Rationality?* (London: Duckworth, 1988).

Macquarrie, John, *Principles of Christian Theology*, rev. edn (London: SCM Press, 1977).

Markham, Ian S., (ed.), *A World Religious Reader*, 2nd edn (Oxford: Blackwell, 2000).

Markham, Ian S. and Abu-Rabi' Ibrahim, *September 11: Religious Perspectives on the Causes and the Consequences* (Oxford: Oneworld, 2002).

Markham, Ian S., *Plurality and Christian Ethics* (Cambridge: Cambridge University Press, 1994).

Markham, Ian S., "Ronald Preston and the Contemporary Ethical Scene," in R. John Elford and Ian Markham, (eds), *The Middle Way. Theology, Politics and Economics in the Later Thought of R.H. Preston*, pp. 257–65 (London: SCM Press, 2000).

Markham, Ian S., *Truth and the Reality of God* (Edinburgh: T&T Clark, 1999).

Marsh, Charles, *God's Long Summer. Stories of Faith and Civil Rights* (Princeton: Princeton University Press, 1997).

Marshall, Bruce D., *Trinity and Truth* (Cambridge: Cambridge University Press, 2000).

Martin, Sandy, "Hindu Perspectives on Jesus: The Ramakrishna Mission and Self-Realization Fellowship," in *Dialogue and Alliance*, 12(2), pp. 94–101, Fall 1998.

Martin, Sandy, "Jesus Darshan," in *World Faiths Encounter*, No. 6, pp. 7–22, November 1993.

Marx, Karl, "On the Jewish Question," in J. Waldron, *Nonsense upon Stilts: Bentham, Burke and Marx on the Rights of Man*, pp. 139–52 (London: Methuen, 1987).

Matthews, Alfred Warren, *The Development of St. Augustine from Neoplatonism to Christianity 386–391 AD* (Washington: University Press of America, 1980).

McFague, Sallie, *Models of God* (Augsberg: Fortress, 1987).

McFague, Sallie, *The Body of God* (Augsberg: Fortress, 1993).

McGrath, Alister, *A Passion for Truth. The Intellectual Coherence of Evangelicalism* (Downers Grove, Illinois: InterVarsity Press, 1996).

McGrath, Alister and John Wenham, "Evangelicalism and Biblical Authority," in R.T. France and Alister McGrath, (eds), *Evangelical Anglicans: Their Role and Influence in the Church Today* (London: SPCK, 1993).

McGrath, Alister, *Evangelicalism and the Future of Christianity* (London: Hodder and Stoughton, 1993).

McGrath, Alister, *The Genesis of Doctrine* (Oxford: Blackwell, 1990).

McLaren, J. and H. Coward, (eds), *Religious Conscience, the State, and the Law* (New York: SUNY Press, 1999).

Mihir Meghani, "Hindutva: The Great Nationalist Ideology," at http://www.bjp.org/philo.htm.

Milbank, John, *Theology and Social Theory* (Oxford: Blackwell Publishers, 1990).

Miller, J. Michael, (ed.), *The Encyclicals of John Paul II* (Huntington, Indiana: Our Sunday Visitor Publishing Division, 1996).

Moltmann, Jürgen, *On Human Dignity. Political Theology and Ethics* (London: SCM PRESS, 1984).

Nehru, Jawaharlal, *The Discovery of India*, ed. by Robert I. Crane (New York: Doubleday Anchor Books, 1960).

Nelson, J. Robert, "Human Rights in Creation and Redemption: A Protestant View," in Arlene Swidler, (ed.), *Human Rights in Religious Traditions*, pp. 3–12 (New York: The Pilgrim Press, 1982.)

Neuhaus, Richard John, *Doing Well. Doing Good. The Challenge to the Christian Capitalist* (New York: Doubleday, 1992).

Newlands, George, *Generosity and the Christian Future* (London: SPCK, 1997).

Niebuhr, Reinhold, *Moral Man and Immoral Society* (London: SCM PRESS, 1963).

Novak, David, *Jewish–Christian Dialogue. A Jewish Justification* (Oxford: Oxford University Press, 1989).

Nursi, Bediuzzaman Said, Vols 1 to 4 of the *Risale-I Nur Collection* (Istanbul: Sözler Nesriyat, Ticaret ve Sanayi, A.S., 1992).

O'Meara, John J., *Understanding Augustine* (Dublin, Four Courts Press, 1997).

Origen, *Contra Celsum*, trans. by with an Introduction and Notes by Henry Chadwick, (Cambridge, Cambridge University Press, 1953).

O'Rouke, P.J., *Eat the Rich* (New York: Atlantic Monthly Press, 1998).

Ortner, Sherry, "Is Female to Male as Nature Is to Culture?," in Wendy Kolman and Frances Bartokowski, (eds), *Feminist Theory: A Reader* (Mountain View, California: Mayfield, 1974).

Packer, James, *God has Spoken: Revelation and the Bible* (London: Hodder & Stoughton, 1993).

Percy, Martyn, *Salt of the Earth. Resilience in a Secular Age* (London: Sheffield Academic Press, 2002).

Pius XI, Pope, *Quadragesimo Anno* (New York: American Press, 1938).

Plant, Raymond, *Politics, Theology and History* (Cambridge: Cambridge University Press, 2001).

Porter, Jean, *Moral Action and Christian Ethics* (Cambridge: Cambridge University Press, 1995).

Preston, Ronald H., *Confusions in Christian Social Ethics. Problems for Geneva and Rome* (London: SCM Press, 1994).

Preston, Ronald H., *Religion and the Persistence of Capitalism* (London: SCM Press, 1979).

Primavesi, Anne, *From Apocalypse to Genesis: Ecology, Feminism and Christianity* (Minneapolis: Fortress Press, 1991).

Primavesi, Anne, *Sacred Gaia* (London: Routledge, 2000).

Pui-lan, Kwok, *Introducing Asian Feminist Theology* (Sheffield: Sheffield Academic Press, 2000).

Putnam, R., *Bowling Alone: The Collapse and Revival of American Community* (New York: Simon & Schuster, 2000).

Race, Alan, *Christians and Religious Pluralism* (London: SCM Press, 1983).

Radford Ruether, Rosemary, "Feminist Interpretation: A Method of Correlation," in Letty Russell, (ed.), *Feminist Interpretation of the Bible*, pp. 111–24, (Westminster: John Knox, 1985).

Radford Ruether, Rosemary, *Sexism and God-Talk. Towards a Feminist Theology with a new introduction* (Boston: Beacon Press, 1993).

Ramanuja, *The Vedanta-Sutras*, trans. by George Thibaut (Delhi: Motilal Banarsidass, 1962).

Raphael, D.D., *Problems of Political Philosophy*, 2nd edn (Basingstoke: Macmillan, 1990).

Rist, John, *Augustine* (Cambridge: Cambridge University Press, 1994).

Robertson, Roland, "Globalization and the Future of 'Traditional Religion,'" in Max L. Stackhouse with Peter J. Paris, (eds), *God and Globalization. vol. 1. Religion and the Powers of the Common Life*, pp. 53–68 (Harrisburg, Pennsylvania: Trinity Press International, 2000).

Rogow, Arnold A. and Hobbes, Thomas, *Radical in the Service of Reaction* (New York: W.W. Norton, 1986).

Ruddick, Sara, *Maternal Thinking* (London: The Women's Press, 1990).

Russell, Letty, (ed.), *Feminist Interpretation of the Bible* (Westminster: John Knox, 1985).

Saiving, Valerie, "The Human Situation: A Feminine View," *Journal of Religion*, 40, pp. 100–12, 1960.

Schottroff, Luise, *Let the Oppressed Go Free: Feminist Perspectives on the New Testament*, (Louiseville, Kentucky: John Knox Press, 1993).

Schüssler Fiorenza, Elisabeth, *Bread Not Stone* (Boston: Beacon Press, 1986).

Schüssler Fiorenza, Elisabeth, *But She Said* (Boston: Beacon Press, 1992).

Schüssler Fiorenza, Elsabeth, *Violence Against Women*, in Elisabeth Schüssler Fiorenza and Mary Shawn Copeland, (eds), *Concilium* 1994/1 (London: SCM Press; Maryknoll, New York: Orbis Books, c1994).

Schüssler Fiorenza, Elisabeth, "'The Will to Choose or Reject,' Continuing our Critical Work," in Letty M. Russell (ed.), *Feminist Interpretation of the Bible* (Louisville, KT: John Knox Press, 1991).

Shange, Ntozake, *Nappy Edges*, (New York: Publisher, 1972).

Sider, Ronald, *Rich Christians in an Age of Hunger* (London: Hodder and Stoughton, 1977).

Smith, D.E., *India as a Secular State*, (Princeton: Princeton University Press, 1963).

Smith, D.E., (ed.), *South Asian Politics and Religion* (Princeton, Princeton University Press 1966).

Spong, John Selby, *Why Christianity must Change or Die* (London: Harper Collins, 1999).

Stackhouse, Max L., with Peter J. Paris, (eds), *God and Globalization. vol. 1. Religion and the Powers of the Common Life* (Harrisburg, Pennsylvania: Trinity Press International, 2000).

Stead, Christopher, *Philosophy in Christian Antiquity* (Cambridge: Cambridge University Press, 1994).

Supreme Court, *Everson v Board of Education*, 1947.

Swidler, Arlene, (ed.), *Human Rights in Religious Traditions* (New York: The Pilgrim Press, 1982).

Swidler, Leonard, *After the Absolute. The Dialogical Future of Religious Reflections* (Minneapolis: Fortress Press, 1990).

Swinburne, Richard, *The Coherence of Theism* (Oxford: Oxford University Press, 1977).

Tertullian, *On the Apparel of Woman*, in Alexander Roberts and James Donaldson, (eds), *Ante-Nicene Fatehrs, vol. IV* (New York: C. Scribner's Sons, 1899–1900).

Thomas, Hugh, *The Slave Trade. The History of the Atlantic Slave Trade 1440–1870* (London: Picador, 1997).

Tracy, David, *Plurality and Ambiguity* (London: SCM Press, 1987).

Vahide, Sükran, *Bediuzzaman Said Nursi* (Istanbul: Sözler Publications, 1992).

Waldron, J. *Nonsense upon Stilts: Bentham, Burke and Marx on the Rights of Man* (London: Methuen, 1987).

Walker, Jr., Theodore, "Theological Resources for a Black Neoclassical Social Ethics," in James H. Cone and Gayraud S. Wilmore, (eds), *Black Theology. vol. 2. A Documentary History* pp. 35–52 (Maryknoll, New York: Orbis Books, 1993).

Ward, Keith, *Images of Eternity. Concepts of God in Five Religious Traditions* (London: Darton, Longman and Todd, 1987).

Ward, Keith, *A Vision to Pursue* (London: SCM Press, 1991).

Ward, Keith, *Divine Action* (London: Collins, 1990).

Ward, Keith, *Rational Theology and the Creativity of God* (Oxford: Blackwell, 1982).

Ward, Keith, *Religion and Creation* (Oxford: Oxford University Press, 1996).

Ward, Keith, *Religion and Community* (Oxford: Oxford University Press, 2000).

Ward, Keith, *Religion and Human Nature* (Oxford: Oxford University Press, 1998).

Ward, Keith, *Religion and Revelation* (Oxford: Oxford University Press, 1994).

Weber, Max, *The Protestant Ethic and the Spirit of Capitalism* (London: Unwin University Books, 1930).

Welch, Sharon, *Communities of Resistance and Solidarity* (Maryknoll, New York: Orbis Books, 1985).

Wenhard, J.T., E.C. Muller, and R.J. Teske, (eds), *Collectanea Augustiniana. Augustine Presbyter Fachs Sum* (New York: Peter Lang, 1993).

West, Cornel, *Race Matters* (New York: Vintage Books, 1994).

White, Lynn, "On the Historical Roots of our Ecological Crisis," in R. Gottileb, (ed.), *This Sacred Earth*, pp. 184–93 (London: Routledge, 1995).

Williams, Rowan, *On Christian Theology* (Oxford: Blackwell, 2000).

Williams, Rowan, "The Paradoxes of Self-Knowledge in the *De trinitate*" in J.T. Wenhard, E.C. Muller, and R.J. Teske, (eds), *Collectanea Augustiniana*, pp. 121–34 (New York: Peter Lang, 1993).

Wilmore, Gayraud S., "Black Power, Black People, Theological Renewal," in James H. Cone and Gayraud S. Wilmore, (eds), *Black Theology. vol. 1., A Documentary History*, pp. 125–40 (Maryknoll, New York: Orbis Books, 1993).

Winter, Miriam Therese, *The Gospel According to Mary* (New York: Crossroad, 1993).

INDEX